Free Appropriate Public Education | Law and Implementation

H. Rutherford Turnbull III and Ann P. Turnbull,
University of North Carolina
at Chapel Hill

LOVE PUBLISHING COMPANY
Denver · London

Second printing 1979. Relevant information that
has been updated is presented as a *1978 Supplement*
at the end of appropriate chapters.

Copyright © 1978 Love Publishing Company
Printed in the U.S.A.
ISBN 0-89108-080-5
Library of Congress Catalog Card Number 78-50504
10   9   8   7   6   5   4   3   2

CONTENTS

SECTION II: THE SIX MAJOR PRINCIPLES

SECTION III: TECHNIQUES FOR IMPLEMENTING THE SIX PRINCIPLES

SECTION IV: FREE APPROPRIATE PUBLIC EDUCATION
                AND THE AMERICAN VALUE SYSTEM

APPENDIXES

DEDICATION

To Jay, who has these rights,
and
Amy and Kate, who deserve them.

"The goal of American education is to value each child as equally an individual and entitled to equal opportunity of development of his own capacities, be they large or small in range . . . Each has needs of his own as significant to him as those of others are to them. The very fact of natural and psychological inequality is all the more reason for establishment by law of equality of opportunity, since otherwise the former becomes a means of oppression of the less gifted."

– Thomas Dewey

Dewey's sentiments have a familiar ring to those of us who have been involved in establishing the rights of handicapped children to a free appropriate education: value the individual, whoever and whatever he is; recognize his needs and satisfy them; establish by law equal educational opportunity; change a system that oppresses some because of their inequalities. How surprised Dewey would be to learn that his views have become so widely accepted, but how sad he would be that they are still rejected by so many.

It is the story of rejection and acceptance that we tell here, a story that shows the initial rejection and eventual acceptance of an idea (equal educational opportunities for the handicapped) as well as a special group of children. The public schools—the governmental system that casts the widest net and exercises the greatest influence over us (next to the tax and revenue departments)—have finally begun to come to terms with educating all the children. How the nation's public schools have dealt with the challenge and opportunity of educating handicapped children in the past and how they must do so under recent law, and what it all means for the handicapped, for higher education, and for "consumers" is our story.

We begin our discussion by introducing the American legal system, particularly as it affects the educational rights of handicapped children. We then describe the major underpinnings of the current legal status of the handicapped child's right to an education: the exclusionary and discriminatory practices followed by schools in the past, the reasons used to justify those practices, and the characteristics of court decisions and federal and state legislation that attempt to correct those practices. We also provide a brief comparison of the most recent significant federal laws establishing equal educational opportunities for handicapped children.

We analyze in detail the six principles of the cases and federal legislation that speak most directly to the rights of the handicapped child: (1) zero reject, or the right to be included in a free appropriate publicly supported educational system; (2) nondiscriminatory classification, or the right to be fairly evaluated so that correct educational programs and placement can be achieved; (3) individualized and appropriate education, so that an education can be meaningful; (4) "least restrictive" educational placement, or the right to normalization; (5) procedural due process, or the right to protest; and (6) participatory democracy, or the right to participate in the educational process.

We have been rigorous in analyzing the cases and legislation in exactly this order because the sequence is the logical process the parent or guardian and the schools will follow in seeking an appropriate education for a child: (1) put the child in the school; (2) assess his strengths and weaknesses; (3) tailor his education to maximize his strengths and remediate his weaknesses; (4) surround him with nonhandicapped students to the maximum extent appropriate to his needs; (5) give him and his advocates an opportunity to challenge any aspect of his education; and (6) provide him with ways to be involved in what happens to him in school. We then describe the major techniques of judicial decisions and federal legislation for assuring that the six principles are carried out.

Recognizing that the six principles are generating widespread resistance, we present the most common objections to them and attempt to answer those objections on two major grounds: (1) the beliefs that support the principles; and (2) the system of values that undergird the principles.

Even the most casual reader will recognize our bias: as a lawyer and special education professor active in advocating for the handicapped, as parents of a handicapped child, as trainers of future professionals, and as professionals who have tried to help educators, professionals, and consumers learn how to carry out their responsibilities to handicapped children, we frankly acknowledge that we favor laws requiring a free appropriate public education for handicapped children. We are heartened that the law is responding favorably to the claims made by the handicapped to an equal educational opportunity, and we believe that this book can be useful to all who are affected by the right-to-education movement. We want our readers to understand the origins of the present laws and the implications of those laws. The past is indeed prologue, and we hope that all who are involved in the movement will be able to profit by learning where special education and the law have been, where they are, and where they are headed.

H.R.T.III
A.P.T.

Chapel Hill, North Carolina
January, 1978

SECTION I:

INTRODUCTION TO THE LAW

1

Introduction to the American Legal System

The law serves many purposes, among them ordering the public affairs of individuals and their governments and resolving disputes between them. These seemingly simple purposes are accomplished through an intricate network. In order to explain the workings of that network, we will use some familiar images.

FEDERALISM

It helps to think of public law in terms of three parallel ladders—descending rungs of parallel authority affecting the relationships between individuals and their governments and between various levels of government. At the top of the federal ladder is the United States Constitution; in the middle are laws enacted by Congress pursuant to Constitutional authority; and on the bottom are regulations issued by federal agencies pursuant to Congressional authority. Next to this ladder stands one representing the state governments, and it has similar rungs of parallel authority: state constitutions, state statutes, and state agency regulations. Finally, next to the state ladder is the local ladder, with its three rungs: the charters of local governments, local ordinances, and local regulations. The whole picture shows that the highest source of law in each system (or ladder) is the fundamental governing document: the federal constitution, the state constitution and the local

9

charter. Federal, state, and local statutes are next in line, followed by federal, state, and local agency regulations:

Federal	*State*	*Local*
Constitution	Constitution	Charter
Statutes	Statutes	Ordinances
Regulations	Regulations	Regulations

This system of parallel governments (federal, state, and local) is known as the "federal system;" as a form of government, it is known as "federalism."

LAWMAKERS: WHO MAKES THE LAW?

For each source of law, there is a lawmaker; a group of persons who make the law. For the federal constitution and its amendments, the initial lawmakers were the delegates to the constitutional convention and subsequently the legislatures of the various states that acted to ratify constitutional amendments (other than the first ten, the so-called Bill of Rights, which were drafted by delegates themselves). The delegates were representatives of the franchised citizens of the states; thus, the source of the federal constitution was the citizenry of the United States. This is generally true, too, with respect to the constitutions of the states and the charters of local governments.

This is not true, however, of statutory law. In that case the lawmaker is not the citizenry, but their elected representatives serving in Congress or in the state legislatures. The Congress and the legislatures may not enact laws that violate the provisions of the federal constitution or the constitution of the state in whose legislature they serve. All federal and state laws are subject to "testing" to determine if they are "constitutional" under the federal constitution and the applicable state constitution because the federal constitution provides that the constitution shall be the supreme law of the land, protecting all citizens of the United States and regulating all state and local governments. Also, the fundamental law of each state is the state constitution, and no state law or state agency regulation has the effect of law unless authority for it can be found in the state constitution. There is, then, a lawmaker for each source of law, a fundamental law that has greater authority than any other, and a hierarchy of law in each of the three governments.

Although it may appear that all lawmakers are alike, that is, that there are no basic differences between legislatures and legislators and regulations and regulators, there is a fundamental difference. Statutes are enacted by legislatures whose members are elected by the franchised citizens. Regulations are made by regulatory agencies whose staffs are not elected but are rather appointed by the legislatures. Agency regulations must be based on authority given to them by the legislatures; the regulators are both executives — persons who execute or carry out the legislature's statutes — and legislators — in the limited sense that they write regulations designed to carry out legislation.

We obviously have a complex system for enacting and carrying out law, and this is especially true in the area of education for handicapped children. The system can be illustrated as follows:

✻ 1. *Constitutional law*
   Federal constitution (especially Fifth and Fourteenth Amendments)
   State constitution (especially provisions about education)
   Local charter (especially provisions creating schools or school boards)
2. *Legislature (legislative body)*
   Congress (e.g., P.L. 94–142, The Education of All Handicapped Children Act)
   State (e.g., "equal educational opportunities" legislation)
   Local (e.g., school board policies establishing programs for handicapped children)
3. *Regulations (executive agency)*
   Federal (Bureau for Education of the Handicapped, Office of Education, Department of Health, Education, and Welfare)
   State (e.g., Illinois Office of Education, Division for Exceptional Children, or North Carolina State Board of Education, Department of Public Instruction, Division of Exceptional Children)
   Local (e.g., director of pupil services or coordinator of special education)

CASE LAW AND THE COURTS

One important type of law and lawmaker has not yet been identified: "case" law (judicial decisions) and the courts. When the delegates to the federal and state constitutional conventions wrote those constitutions, they created three branches of government—legislative, executive, and judicial. The function of the legislature is to make law and the executive is to carry it out, but it is the function of the judiciary to resolve disputes between citizens or between a citizen and his government. Courts do this by applying law to a given set of facts and interpreting the meaning of the law in that factual context. It is their unique function to say what the constitution or a federal statute or regulation means in a given case, to issue a decision setting forth the facts that underlie their interpretation, and to enter an order commanding the parties in the case (or other courts, if the case is on appeal) to take certain action.

Within the overall federal system, there are three parallel systems: the federal court system consists of trial courts; United States Courts of Appeals; and a court of last resort, the United States Supreme Court. The state and local system also consists of trial and appellate courts and a court of last resort. It is a matter of great complexity why a case is tried in one court, appealed or reviewed by another, and finally disposed of by yet another. We do not need to enter that thicket; a brief outline of court jurisdictions will serve our purposes.

The U.S. Supreme Court is the court of last resort, and its decisions are binding throughout the United States. The U.S. Courts of Appeals (in each of the ten circuits or appellate districts) have appellate power over cases decided in the trial courts in their circuits. Their decisions are binding throughout the circuit but may only be persuasive (not binding) in other circuits and in all district courts. The United States District Courts are the trial courts in their respective districts, and their decisions are generally binding in the district only (not throughout the appellate circuit in which they are located) and may only be persuasive (but not binding) on circuit courts and other district courts.

The state court systems are parallel to the United States court system. Each state has a court of last resort (Court of Appeals or Supreme Court) whose decisions are binding throughout the State. Diagram 1.1 illustrates the relationships between the courts in a federal system.

U.S. Supreme Court

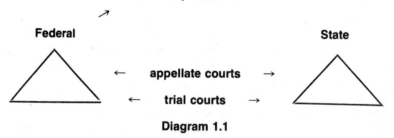

Diagram 1.1

BROWN v. BOARD OF EDUCATION

In the field of education law, the diagram is well reflected by the original school desegregation case, *Brown v. Board of Education*, 347 U.S. 483 (1954). (Typically, cases are given a shorthand name, usually the name of the appealing party, for easy reference in discussions. The name—in this case, *Brown*—is italicized to indicate the case, not the person being discussed.) *Brown* was not one case, but four that were consolidated and heard as one by the United States Supreme Court. Three of the cases were on appeal from federal district courts (the appeals went directly to the Supreme Court and bypassed the Circuit Courts of Appeals because, under the Federal Rules of Civil Procedure, a federal constitutional issue was an indispensable element of the case). One was on appeal from a state appellate court after having been heard first in a state trial court. Thus, *Brown* can be illustrated as follows:

U.S. Supreme Court

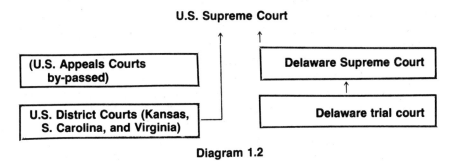

(U.S. Appeals Courts by-passed)

Delaware Supreme Court

U.S. District Courts (Kansas, S. Carolina, and Virginia)

Delaware trial court

Diagram 1.2

Aside from the structural (functional) aspects of the case, *Brown* was a landmark because it had impact on so many issues of educational law and procedure:

1. *Brown* illustrates the principle that the federal constitution, as interpreted by the U.S. Supreme Court, is the supreme law of the land, is binding on all federal, state, and local governments, and is the precedent that must be followed by all federal and state courts in subsequent similar cases.

2. *Brown* is a nearly perfect example of one of the major lessons of this book: all educational issues (such as the educational rights of handicapped students) are essentially political policy and social issues cast in the guise of constitutional litigation (should handicapped students be educated, and, if so, how and by whom?) and, because they are presented in the garments of the law, ultimately they are resolved by the courts.

3. *Brown* also demonstrates that the truly difficult educational issues are fought on various civil rights battlefields. Just as *Brown* was the first case on the battlefield of racial desegregation of the schools, it was the seed that gave birth to other civil rights battles and to grounds for successful challenges to governmental discrimination against certain persons because of their unalterable personal characteristics (such as race and sex). *Brown* gave rise to the ''right-to-education'' cases, and they in turn helped establish other rights for handicapped persons. The point—so obvious, but so important—is that judicial resolution of educational issues on constitutional grounds becomes precedent for judicial resolution of related civil rights issues on similar constitutional grounds.

4. *Brown* gave immense comfort and support to civil rights activists, legitimizing their legal arguments and furnishing them with a powerful tool for persuading legislatures, particularly Congress, to enact antidiscrimination legislation. Case law frequently is the underpinning of legislation, and federal cases and legislation frequently precede state case law and legislation. Nowhere has this

been more true than in establishing the rights of handicapped pupils to an education.

   5. *Brown* caused a fundamental change in the federal system. As precedent for other federal school desegregation cases and as the legal foundation for federal school and other civil rights legislation, *Brown* heralded the entry of the federal government into public education in the United States and thus it made significant inroads into an area that had been reserved almost wholly by states and local governments as their province. Over the long run, its effect has been to shift the balance of the federal system heavily toward the side of the federal government. Right-to-education cases and legislation have also shown us that the areas of state and local autonomy in education are quickly diminishing. According to current interpretation, it is questionable if there is any such thing as a "purely local" concern in education. Are all educational concerns truly national and thus require national leadership in the form of case law precedents and legislation enacted at the federal level? This surely is the conclusion that has been reached in the right-to-education movement.

   6. In *Brown* it was proven that although the United States Constitution never once refers to a public education, its principles of equal protection and due process under the Fifth and Fourteenth Amendments have a significant effect on public education. Nowhere is this fact clearer than in the right-to-education cases.

   7. *Brown* illustrates one kind of law suit—the "civil action"—that is typical of litigation between citizens and their governments. This type of suit is brought by a citizen who alleges that a government or a governmental official denied him rights or benefits to which he is entitled under the law (constitution, statutes, or regulations). In this case, the plaintiff, Brown, sued the defendant, the Topeka Board of Education. In two of the consolidated cases, other citizens sued governmental officials representing school agencies. A civil action is typical of the right-to-education cases. Criminal actions—the state prosecuting a person accused of a crime—are alien to education law.

   8. *Brown* is almost ideal for teaching someone how to read a case and how cases are decided, particularly in the right-to-education area. If "handicapped" is substituted for "Negro" and "nonhandicapped" for "white" wherever those words appear in *Brown*, it is fairly easy to understand why *Brown* is important to the education of the handicapped and how the Fourteenth Amendment became the constitutional basis for the rights of the handicapped to be educated (Appendix A).

   a) *What are the "controlling" (or dispositive) facts of the case?* Blacks are denied admission to schools attended by whites under laws requiring or permitting segregation according to race, and racial segregation in public education is inherently damaging to the educational opportunities of black children.

   b) *What are the allegations?* The facts constitute a denial of equal protection of law as guaranteed by the Fourteenth Amendment because segregated public schools are not and cannot be made equal, and the "separate but equal" doctrine should be set aside.

c) *What are the "issues of law" the Court must resolve?* Whether the "separate but equal" doctrine applies to public education and whether segregation, under that doctrine, violates the equal protection clause.

d) *What is the Court's "holding" (answer to the issue)?* Segregation solely on the basis of race in the public schools violates equal protection and denies minority (black) children an equal educational opportunity.

e) *What is the Court's reasoning?* Equal educational opportunities are denied when, in light of (1) the importance of education, (2) the stigmatizing effects of racial segregation, and (3) the detrimental consequences of racial segregation on the education of those against whom segregation is practiced, a state segregates by race.

f) *What is the Court's "order"?* The cases are to be argued again before the Court and the argument should focus on the nature of the remedy that the Court should order.

g) *What is the "principle" of the case?* State action in segregating the races in public education violates equal protection, and, by extension, any state-required or state-sanctioned racial segregation is unconstitutional. Ultimately, any state-required or state-sanctioned segregation solely because of a person's unalterable characteristic (race or handicap) is usually unconstitutional.

h) *What are the "implications" of the case?* They are massive, and will be discussed throughout this book.

i) *What is the "public policy" in the case?* State-created stigma or badges of inferiority based on race (or other characteristics, such as handicaps) are constitutionally intolerable because they mean that the state acts invidiously (i.e., discriminatorily, by denying equal opportunities) with respect to persons who have certain traits. In brief, invidious (discriminatory) action is unconstitutional.

j) *Whose "interests" are at issue?* The interests or "claims" of blacks to an equal educational opportunity.

k) *Finally, what "functions" of government are at issue?* The functions of education; namely, cultural assimilation, preparation for participation in the political process, and training so that economic opportunities might become available. Given the interests, the functions could not be parcelled out or denied solely according to race.

Brown is worth an extended discussion here because it speaks directly to public schools, special education, and handicapped children. There are undeniable similarities between the *Brown* plaintiffs and handicapped children: both can prove they have been denied equal educational opportunities; both allege an unconstitutional denial and base their arguments on equal protection principles; both challenge separateness in education; both find comfort in the holding of *Brown* and the right-to-education cases concerning denials of equality; both are strengthened by the reasoning which relies on concepts of stigma and detrimental educational consequences; both successfully advance a public policy against invidious state action; both have similar interests in obtaining an education; and both lay claim to the functions of the schools to meaningfully educate all students.

2

Introduction to Law and Free
Appropriate Public Education

EGALITARIANISM

A major legal development in this decade has been the extension of the principle of egalitarianism to handicapped persons. This principle—that all persons, however unequal they may be in terms of their abilities, should be treated equally by being granted equal opportunities—has been expressed in two different ways.

Many professionals, including educators, have argued for egalitarianism in the treatment of handicapped citizens. Their arguments are couched in terms of "normalization." Normalization stands for the proposition that handicapped persons should live and be treated as nonhandicapped persons as much as possible and that their differences from nonhandicapped people can be reduced by minimizing the degree to which they are treated differently than the nonhandicapped. One step in minimizing those differences is to acknowledge that the handicapped do, in fact, have an equal right to an education.

EQUAL PROTECTION: JUDICIAL PRECEDENTS

In the eyes of the law, egalitarianism invokes the concept of equal protection and gives rise to the argument that limiting the civil liberties of handicapped students violates their constitutional rights to equal protection under the Fourteenth Amendment because there is no rational reason for imposing special burdens or limitations on them. This argument also asserts that the educational opportunities granted to nonhandicapped pupils are constitutionally required to be granted to handicapped pupils.

"Equal protection of the laws" is such a simple phrase, but it is by no means as simple to understand and apply as one might think. As Chapter 3 will show, simplicity in interpretation and application is hardly the case when the educational rights of handicapped students are involved. Long before those rights were affirmed under the doctrine of equal protection, however, other disadvantaged persons were successfully arguing that their rights had been infringed unconstitutionally. The establishment of their rights was the indispensable foundation for establishing educational rights of handicapped students.

The high-water marks made by the equal protection doctrine on the shore where the disadvantaged waited can be delineated by looking first to *Brown* and its progeny—the many cases that held that equal educational opportunities may not be predicated (granted or limited) upon race.[1] Under the equal protection doctrine, a person's financial status also cannot be used as a basis for denying him benefits. For example, the Supreme Court has held that the right to vote,[2] ensured access to court in order to settle disputes with others,[3] and entitlement to financial assistance from a state a person has the right to move into[4] are rights that may not be denied to those who cannot afford them. Equal protection, the Court said, requires that the poor be treated as though they were not poor—they must have free access to the franchise, to courts, and to interstate movement.

Other "disadvantaging" characteristics have been added to those of race and poverty. The fact that a person is illegitimate,[5] an alcoholic,[6] a narcotics user,[7] a convict,[8] or a female[9] has been held by the Court to be improper grounds upon which to base legislation if the result of the legislation is to discriminate against such persons but not against others in similar circumstances.

The point, here, is to highlight a series of cases that indicates a strong egalitarian movement; a movement that, despite recent cases, furnished a solid foundation for extending concepts of egalitarianism and equal protection to the handicapped. This line of cases did more than provide precedents that were adapted and tailored to remedy unhappy conditions the public schools were imposing on handicapped children; it also, and perhaps just as significantly, made law-reformers realize that they should—and could successfully—move from other civil rights battlefields to the school grounds and work to extend the equal protection doctrine to handicapped children.

THE HISTORY OF FEDERAL LEGISLATION: STATUTORY PRELUDES TO P.L. 94–142

It takes more than a cursory review of constitutional developments to explain how the handicapped child's right to an education was established. To be sure, the case precedents were indispensable (as we will demonstrate in later chapters), but a slowly evolving federal role that turned into a massive involvement in the education of handicapped children was an equally indispensable ingredient.

The earliest federal role—creating special schools for the mentally ill, blind, and deaf between the 1820s and the 1870s—paralleled a similar movement at the state level, in which state schools for the handicapped were established as early as 1823. No further significant federal activity occurred until World Wars I and II spurred the government into vocational rehabilitation programs and aid for disabled veterans and other disabled persons. Public assistance programs were evidence of increasing federal concern for the handicapped. The application of the Social Security Act to the blind, disabled, aged, and dependent; the grant of benefits under Medicare and Medicaid programs; the payment of Supplementary Security Income; and a host of programs under Title XX of the Social Security Act all give testimony to the federal government's concerns.[10]

The "parent movement," typified by the formation of the National Association for Retarded Citizens in the 1950s and its increasing clout on the federal and state scene in the 1960s, was enhanced in the early 1960s when President Kennedy and Vice President Humphrey used their influence to advance the interests of the mentally retarded by establishing the President's Committee on Mental Retardation.

The strands of federal legislation that included the Elementary and Secondary Education Act,[11] the Vocational Education Amendments of 1968,[12] the Economic Opportunities Act of 1972 (Headstart),[13] and the Education of the Handicapped Act,[14] came together and P.L. 93–380 (which provided funds for the education of handicapped students under Title VI–B) and P.L. 94–142 were the logical results in the 1970s. The Rehabilitation Act of 1973,[15] the Higher Education Amendments of 1972,[16] and the Developmental Disabilities Assistance and Bill of Rights Act of 1974[17] also contributed to the political feasibility of P.L. 94–142. By small increments, and then by ever widening strides, the federal government became involved in and concerned with the education of handicapped children and the treatment of handicapped adults. The streams of constitutional litigation and federal legislation flowed into each other and created a river whose current carried forward the education of handicapped students.

SCHOOL PRACTICES

As a general rule, the nation's public schools were highly ingenious and very successful in denying educational opportunities, equal or otherwise, to handicapped children. Their success was evidenced by data showing how many children were excluded: as reported in Sec. 602 (b) of P.L. 94–142, Congress found that approximately one-half of the nation's eight million handicapped children were not receiving an appropriate education and about one million received no education at all. The multitude of exclusionary practices the courts found violating the educational rights of the handicapped were also proof of the problem. Among those practices, two dominated: exclusion and classification.

Exclusion

Exclusion occurs when a child is denied education (denied access to all public educational programs or provided with an inadequate education for his needs). Total exclusion may involve the school's refusing to admit the child or placing him on a long waiting list. Exclusion also occurs when programs are inadequate or unresponsive to the student's needs, as when Spanish-speaking children are given an English curriculum and no special provision is made to accommodate the fact that they do not understand English, or when moderately retarded children are put in large regular classes and given little or no training or education. Such practices constitute "functional exclusion"; although the child has access to a program, the program is of such a nature that he cannot substantially profit from it and therefore receives few or none of the intended benefits of education.

The schools have excluded school-aged handicapped persons individually and as a class.[18] They admitted some but not all students with the same disability.[19] They inadequately funded tuition-subsidy programs that would have enabled families to purchase appropriate education from alternative sources (such as private schools) when appropriate education was not available in the schools.[20] When appropriate programs were not available, the schools placed handicapped pupils in special education programs that were inappropriate for them.[21] When faced with a shortage of special education programs, they created waiting lists for admission to the few available programs, thus excluding many eligible pupils.[22]

The schools also created different admission policies for the handicapped.[23] They placed handicapped pupils in situations with virtually no program of instruction available.[24] They excluded retarded children on the grounds that they created behavioral or disciplinary problems.[25] And finally, they limited the number of students that could be enrolled in special education programs by using incidence projections that bore little relation to the actual number of the handicapped in the school district[26] or by restricting state-level funding for hiring of special education teachers by establishing artificial quotas such as one state-paid teacher for every twelve pupils in each special education class.[27]

Classification

Classification is at issue when children are misplaced or wrongly tracked.[28] Misclassification denies a child his right to an equal educational opportunity because it results in his being denied schooling that will benefit him.

Challenges to school placement criteria are often accusations of racial discrimination as much as they are complaints about denial of an education. The objection is that the tests used to classify children are biased toward knowledge of the English language and familiarity with white middle-class culture. Accordingly, test scores cause minority children to be placed in special education programs in far greater numbers than other children; the result is dual systems of education based on race or cultural background.

A host of other practices, not easily categorized, have also denied education to handicapped students. State and local appropriations for special education have been shamefully sparse. Institutionalized children have often been denied even the barest programs of care and habilitation. The responsibility of state and local governments for educating handicapped children has been fragmented, and competitive bureaucratic structures within the school or institutional agencies have rarely undertaken any cooperative efforts, with the result that meager resources (money and personnel) were diluted, gaps existed in service, services often overlapped and accountability was nearly impossible. Architectural barriers to the physically handicapped; the lack of adaptive equipment and materials for the sight, speech, or hearing impaired; and the inability or unwillingness of school personnel to teach some handicapped children (the emotionally disturbed, learning disabled, or mentally retarded) likewise contributed to their exclusion. It has not been unusual for teachers of the handicapped to be uncertified to teach them or to be the least skilled teachers in a school system. The teachers have often been required to use the oldest, least adequate facilities located far away from the classrooms of the nonhandicapped. The separateness and devaluation of handicapped children has been underscored by separate financing, administration, and organization of special education services.[29]

Once a child was placed in a special education program, his placement often became permanent. For him it was a terminal assignment, and reconsideration or reevaluation was out of the ordinary. The assignment usually was carried out without parental participation and without opportunities for due process. Frequently, schools failed to identify the handicapped children in their districts: child census procedures have been rare, and the school's target population was neither known, planned for, or served. Early intervention programs for handicapped children were the exception, not the rule. Placement in private programs has been encouraged, because it relieved the school of any responsibility for serving children whose families were able or desperate enough to pay for private school opportunities. Local noncompliance with state law requiring education of handicapped children has rarely been punished. Preschool, elementary, and secondary school programs—when they existed at all—have been unequally available. Finally, the long-standing discouragement of parents by the school ("we'll call you, don't call us") made many weary of trying to rectify wrongs, kept them in ignorance of their children's rights, and reinforced the unbalanced power relationships between the powerful schools and the less powerful parents.

Many readers may object to these generalized characterizations, and they may be able to point to specific circumstances where some or all of these practices did not exist. But the generalizations have been more often true than not, and the practices have been the rule more than the exception. Some of the better studies of school practices substantiate the generalizations;[30] court decisions have set forth facts that support the generalizations;[31] and Congress itself has filed a broadbased indictment of the public schools, based on findings of many of these practices.[32]

REASONS FOR THE PRACTICES

There are many reasons why schools have followed these practices. Not only is the cost of educating or training a handicapped child normally higher than the cost of educating the nonhandicapped child, but manpower, money, and political clout for handicapped children are limited when compared with the same resources for nonhandicapped children. For many educators, handicapped pupils, particularly mentally retarded ones, do not appear to be educable in the traditional sense; the time-honored ''reading-writing-arithmetic'' philosophy has been a reason for exclusion. The fact that special education is separated from the mainstream of education and the desire of both special educators and educators in programs for nonhandicapped students to stay separate from each other also tends to diminish educational opportunities for handicapped individuals. As pointed out before, once placed in a special education program, a handicapped child often has had little chance to return to a normal program. Placement in special education tended to be permanent. This was so because there were no requirements for periodic reevaluation and the schools were understandably reluctant to question their own decisions. Special education served as an important escape hatch, permitting schools to classify as handicapped those children they considered undesirable— the racial minorities, the disruptive, and the different. Behind this practice (indeed, underlying all of the discrimination) is the widely held attitude that governmental benefits, including education, should be parcelled out to the most meritorious. It is a belief that equates merit with average intelligence or nonhandicapping conditions and asserts that the less able are less worthy.

CHARACTERISTICS OF COURT ORDERS AND LEGISLATION

None of the exclusionary or discriminatory practices has entirely escaped the long arm of the law, and each reason for the practices has been challenged in court or in state or federal legislation. As we will show in greater detail in Chapters 3 through 8, judicial remedies and recent legislation at the federal level have mounted a successful attack on the practices. For present introductory purposes, it will be sufficient to set out the major characteristics of state legislation:[33]

—zero reject (no handicapped child to be excluded) under so-called "mandatory" legislation (requiring education of all handicapped children).

—census of and planning for educating handicapped students,

—enumeration of the ages during which handicapped children *must* be educated and, sometimes, of the ages during which they may obtain an education (early intervention or compensatory education),

—requirements that either a single agency be principally responsible for carrying out court or legislative requirements, or that each agency responsible for some portion of a state's overall special education program cooperate in specified ways with each other,

—nondiscriminatory evaluation,

—individualization of programs,

—placement in the "least restrictive" (most "normal" or most "facilitating") educational program,

—procedural due process (opportunity to protest),

—general confidentiality of records subject to parent access to records,

—assignment of advocates (usually called "agent surrogates") to represent handicapped children who have no known parents or guardians,

—provision of technical assistance and preservice and inservice training and retraining, and requirements of teacher certification or other competency criteria,

—appropriations earmarked for special education programs, and

—sanctions for noncompliance.

It would be premature to discuss how federal statutes respond directly to the manifold exclusionary and discriminatory practices and thus mirror some aspects of judicial remedies and state legislation, but it is important to state that the acts do speak to each practice. At this point it is convenient for us to introduce P.L. 94–142 and Sec. 504 of the Rehabilitation Act.

P.L. 94–142 and SEC. 504: ONCE OVER LIGHTLY

The Relationship of the Two Laws

P.L. 94–142, the Education of All Handicapped Children Act, was enacted in 1975, amending the Education of the Handicapped Act (20 U.S.C. Sec. 1401, 1402, and 1411 through 1420), and Sec. 504, the Rehabilitation Act of 1973, was enacted in 1973 with implementing regulations effective June, 1977 (29 U.S.C. Sec. 794). These two federal laws so significantly affect the education of handicapped children that they overshadow other related federal legislation.

A state, acting through its state educational agency (SEA), and each of its local educational agencies (LEAs) or intermediate educational units (IEUs) (hereafter collectively referred to as an LEA) may receive federal funds under Part B of the Education of the Handicapped Act, as amended by P.L. 94–142. Part B provides formula grants to SEAs and LEAs to assist them in educating handicapped children. As a condition of receiving funds each SEA and LEA must comply with the provision of P.L. 94–142 and the applicable regulations implementing it.

The State Plan

Any state desiring to receive Part B funds must apply for them by submitting an application from its SEA to the U.S. Commissioner of Education. Sections 121a.110–.151 of the regulations deal with the application, which is called the Annual Program Plan. The Annual Program Plan for fiscal year 1977–78, the first such plan to be submitted, must be a "complete, intact document" including all provisions previously required under P.L. 93–380 (a predecessor to P.L. 94–142 that also amended the Education of the Handicapped Act) and any new provisions required by P.L. 94–142 itself. If there are no changes in the application under P.L. 94–142 from the application under P.L. 93–380, the earlier application may be incorporated by reference into the first-year application under P.L. 94–142.

For the fiscal years beginning 1978–79, the SEA may incorporate by reference the basic procedural sections that do not require change, including assurances of due process safeguards, least restrictive placements, nondiscriminatory testing, confidentiality of records, coverage of handicapped children in private schools, and child-identification procedures (*Fed. Reg.*, Dec. 30, 1976, pp. 56967–8.).

Whether or not an SEA or LEA receives Part B funds, it must comply with Sec. 504 and its regulations. That law prohibits any recipient of *any* federal financial assistance from discriminating against a handicapped person solely because of his handicap. Since Sec. 504 is intended to prohibit the same discrimination in the education of handicapped children that P.L. 94–142 prohibits, its regulations are consistent in concept and policy with the regulations under P.L. 94–142. They apply to any SEA, LEA, or any state or local agency that receives funds from the Department of Health, Education, and Welfare. Thus, an SEA or LEA that does not receive Part B funds but receives other federal funds from HEW must comply with essentially the same regulations (under Sec. 504) as for Part B funds under P.L. 94–142.

P.L. 94–142 applies to more than SEAs or LEAs receiving Part B funds. Assume that an LEA chooses not to receive Part B funds, but that the SEA does. Is the LEA exempt from P.L. 94–142? No, not entirely. If an LEA elects not to receive Part B funds, it does not have to comply with the requirements of P.L. 94–142; however, the SEA, as a recipient of Part B funds, is required to insure that the handicapped children residing in the LEA's jurisdiction are granted all of the rights and protections of P.L. 94–142. Moreover, if the LEA receives any other federal funds, it must of course comply with Sec. 504.

The SEAs and LEAs are not the only state and local agencies affected by P.L. 94–142. All state and local agencies (including LEAs) that furnish "special education" and "related services" to handicapped children, such as state departments of mental health, welfare, or corrections (hereafter called "public agencies") are treated by P.L. 94–142 as though they were SEAs or LEAs. There are two reasons for this. First, Sec. 612(6) of P.L. 94–142 requires the SEA to assure the federal government that the act is carried out statewide; it assigns the SEA the responsibility for general supervision of all educational programs for handicapped children in the state. Thus, the requirements of the act are binding on the state itself, not just on an agency or a department of the state. Second, since the basic rights granted handicapped pupils under P.L. 94–142 are also included in the regulations for Sec 504, *any* recipient of HEW funds has to comply with these provisions [Sec. 504 and Sec. 84.3(f)].* Accordingly Sec. 121a.2 of the regulations under P.L. 94–142 provides that the regulations apply to each *state* (not just to an agency or department thereof) that receives Part B funds. The SEA submits an application for Part B funds on behalf of the state as a whole; as a consequence, the act and the regulations apply to all agencies and political subdivisions of the state involved in educating handicapped children.

The effect of P.L. 94–142 and Sec. 504, then, is to assure that handicapped children receive a free appropriate education and are not discriminated against in or by any public agencies furnishing special education services. Together, the two laws cover all handicapped children without regard to where they live in the state (whether in the community or in an institution, for example) or which state or local agency serves them (whether a department of public education or a department of human resources, for example). There is no real "escape" from these acts for state and local agencies dealing with handicapped children. The two acts seal all the cracks in services and carry out a policy of zero reject and nondiscrimination.

Handicapped Children

For the purposes of P.L. 94–142, handicapped children are those who are mentally retarded, hard of hearing, deaf, speech impaired, visually handicapped,

---

*References to sections of P.L. 94–142 cited in brackets, as, for example [Sec. 601(b)13], are distinguishable from references to other statutory material or regulations because all sections of P.L. 94–142 begin with a "6." References to the regulations implementing P.L. 94–142 also cited in brackets, as, for example [Sec. 121a.1], are distinguishable from references to other statutory material or regulations because all sections of the regulations begin with the number "121." References to Section 504 are to "Sec. 504" without brackets, but references to the regulations implementing Sec. 504 are cited in brackets, as, for example [Sec. 84.31], and are distinguishable from references to other statutory material or regulations because all sections of the regulations are numbered in the "80s."

seriously emotionally disturbed, orthopedically or otherwise health impaired, or who have specific learning disabilities. (See Appendix B.) The term "specific learning disability" is further defined by other regulations (*Fed. Reg.*, December 29, 1977, pp. 65082-5). These regulations key in on diagnostic procedures and criteria for determining whether a particular condition in the child meets the statutory definition. They emphasize a proper evaluation of the child by a team of professionals. In order to qualify as learning disabled, the child must suffer from a severe discrepancy between achievement and intellectual ability in one or more of the following areas: oral expression, written expression, listening or reading comprehension, basic reading skills, or mathematical calculations or reasoning.

Under Sec. 504, which prohibits discrimination against an otherwise qualified handicapped individual, the term "handicapped person" means any person who has a physical or mental impairment that substantially limits one or more major life activities, has a record of such an impairment, or is regarded as having such an impairment [Sec. 84.3(j)]. "Physical or mental impairment" means (1) any physiological disorder or condition, cosmetic disfigurement, or anatomical loss affecting one or more of the following body systems: neurological; musculoskeletal; special sense organs; respiratory (including speech organs); cardiovascular; reproductive; digestive; genito-urinary; hemic and lymphatic; skin; and endocrine; or (2) any mental or physiological disorder, such as mental retardation, organic brain syndrome, emotional or mental illness (including addiction to alcohol or drugs), and specific learning disabilities.

"Major life activities" means functions such as caring for one's self, performing manual tasks, walking, seeing, hearing, speaking, breathing, learning, and working.

"Has a record of such an impairment" means the person has a history of or has been misclassified as having a mental or physical impairment that substantially limits one or more major life activities.

"Is regarded as having an impairment" means the person (1) has a physical or mental impairment that does not substantially limit major life activities but is treated by a recipient of federal funds as constituting such a limitation, (2) has a physical or mental impairment that substantially limits major life activities only as a result of the attitudes of others toward such impairment, or (3) has none of the impairments listed above but is treated by a recipient of federal funds as having such an impairment.

With respect to public preschool, elementary, secondary, or adult educational services conducted by public schools other than universities, a "qualified handicapped person" is someone who is (1) of an age at which nonhandicapped persons are provided such services, (2) of any age at which it is mandatory under state law to provide such services to handicapped persons, or (3) guaranteed a free appropriate public education under the terms of Sec. 612 of P.L. 94–142 [Sec. 84.3(j) and (k)]. Notice that Sec. 84.3(k) defines "qualified handicapped persons'' without using the qualifying word ''otherwise,'' which is used in the statute. HEW believes that the omission of ''otherwise'' is necessary to preserve the intent of the statute. If, for example, the statute is read literally, ''otherwise'' handicapped persons would include those who are qualified except for their handicap, rather than in spite of their handicap. Under this reading, a student who is confined to a wheelchair but has all the other qualifications for attending school could be said to be ''otherwise qualified'' for attending school. Since HEW believes that such exclusion was not the intent of Congress, it omits ''otherwise'' from the regulation's language although in all other respects ''qualified'' and ''otherwise qualified'' are used interchangeably.

Differences Between PL. 94—142 and Sec. 504

The language of Sec. 504 provides that no recipient of federal funds shall discriminate against an otherwise qualified handicapped person solely on account of his handicap, and the regulations for implementing this law make it clear that Sec. 504 applies to preschool, elementary, and secondary public education programs that receive *any* federal assistance from HEW [Subpart D, Regulations, *Fed. Reg.*, May 4, 1977, pp. 22676–94]. They also make it clear that the schools must adopt a zero-reject policy; provide a free, suitable education to each handicapped person who is a legal resident of the recipient's jurisdiction, regardless of the nature or severity of his handicap; conduct nondiscriminatory testing; place handicapped children in the least restrictive environment; and guarantee due process for handicapped children. Thus, Sec. 504 and its implementing regulations accomplish largely the same results as P.L. 94–142 with respect to prohibiting exclusion and discrimination against handicapped children.

Despite a similarity to P.L. 94–142, Sec. 504 and its regulations differ from P.L. 94–142 in several important respects:

1. Sec. 504 was effective upon enactment (1975) and required immediate full compliance; P.L. 94–142 permits schools to comply over an extended period of time.

2. Sec. 504 includes as handicapped those persons who are so defined by P.L. 94–142, but it also includes many others, such as persons addicted to the use of drugs and alcohol. The two laws take different approaches to the issue of who is handicapped. P.L. 94–142 basically relies on a categorical approach and anticipates the continuation of categorical labelling of children: a child is ''MR'' or ''LD'' or ''ED.'' Sec. 504, however, relies on both a categorical approach and an entirely different approach, best described as ''functional.'' Under that approach, a child is handicapped if he functions as though he were handicapped, or if a state or local government receiving HEW funds acts as if the child were handicapped: there is an impairment in his major life activities, he has a record of an impairment,

or he is treated as having an impairment. Although Sec. 504 generally applies to handicapped persons without respect to their age, age *is* at issue when the person is a handicapped student because the regulations define a handicapped student as one who, under state law or P.L. 94–142, is entitled to a public education (ages 3–21 under P.L. 94–142).

Since the term "handicapped" is more broadly defined by Sec. 504, P.L. 94–142 will most likely apply to a smaller portion of a state's or LEA's school-aged population. Some persons may want to classify a child as handicapped under the regulations of Sec 504 so as to entitle him to the benefits of that act and thus to many of the benefits of P.L. 94–142.

3. Sec. 504 prohibits discrimination not only in preschool, elementary, secondary, and adult public education, but also in the employment of the handicapped and in social and health services. By contrast, P.L. 94–142 prohibits discrimination only with respect to preschool, elementary, secondary, and adult education. Both laws, however, speak to the problems of architectural barriers and access to facilities and, in a limited sense, to the employment of the handicapped by the public schools (see Chapter 3).

4. Sec. 504 does not require individualized educational programs for handicapped children; P.L. 94–142 does. Both require appropriate education.

5. Sec. 504 does not by its terms create a private right of action (that is, the right of an individual to sue under the provisions of Sec. 504); P.L. 94–142 grants such a right, after administrative due process appeals have been exhausted. Although Sec. 504 does not grant the right of private action, it does not prohibit it, and cases brought under Sec. 504 have successfully challenged discrimination in public education. The real difference, then, is that under Sec. 504 an aggrieved handicapped person may be entitled to file his lawsuit before exhausting any administrative remedies he might have available. Under P.L. 94–142 he must first exhaust the administrative remedies available—only then may he file his lawsuit. This difference may mean that Sec. 504 will become the preferred route for redress.

NOTES

1. Brown v. Board of Educ., 347 U.S. 483 (1954).
2. Harper v. Va. Bd. of Elections, 383 U.S. 663 (1966).
3. Boddie v. Connecticut, 401 U.S. 371 (1971).
4. Shapiro v. Thompson, 394 U.S. 618 (1969).
5. Weber v. Aetna Cas. & Sur. Co., 406 U.S. 164 (1972), and Levy v. Louisiana, 391 U.S. 68 (1968).
6. Wisconsin v. Constantineau, 400 U.S. 433 (1971).
7. Robinson v. California, 370 U.S. 660 (1962).

8. Martarella v. Kelley, 349 F. Supp. 575 (S.D.N.Y. 1972).

9. Reed v. Reed, 404 U.S. 71 (1971).

10. LaVor, M.L. Federal Legislation for Exceptional Persons: A History. In F. Weintraub et al. (Eds.), *Public Policy and the Education of Exceptional Children*. Reston, Va.: Council for Exceptional Children, 1976; and Boggs, E.M. Federal Legislation affecting the mentally retarded. In J. Wortis (Ed.), *Mental Retardation* (Vol. III). Grune and Stratton, New York, 1971.

11. P.L. 89–10

12. P.L. 90–576

13. P.L. 92–424

14. P.L. 91–230

15. P.L. 93–122

16. P.L. 92–328

17. P.L. 91–517

18. *See, e.g., Children Out of School in America: A Report of The Children's Defense Fund, Washington Research Project, Inc*. Ch. 4, The Exclusion of Children with Special Needs. Washington, D.C.: The Fund, 1974; Mills v. Board of Educ. of Dist. of Columbia, 348 F. Supp. 866,868,875 (D.D.C. 1972); PARC v. Commonwealth, 334 F. Supp. 1257 (E.D. Pa. 1971) and 343 F. Supp. 279, 282, 296 (E.D. Pa. 1972); Wolf v. Legislature of Utah, Civ. No. 182464 (3d Dist., Salt Lake Cty., Jan. 8, 1969); Maryland Ass'n for Retarded Children v. Maryland, Equity No. 100/182/77676 (Cir. Ct., Baltimore Cty., May 3, 1974); North Carolina Ass'n for Retarded Children v. North Carolina, Civ. No. 3050 (E.D.N.C., filed May 18, 1972); and Tidewater Ass'n of Autistic Children v. Tidewater Bd. of Educ., Civ. No. 426–72–N (E.D. Va., Dec. 26, 1972).

19. Mills v. Board of Educ. of Dist of Columbia, 348 F. Supp. 866, 871, 875 (D.D.C. 1972); PARC v. Commonwealth, 334 F. Supp. 1257 (E.D. Pa. 1971) and 343 F. Supp. 279, 282 (E.D. Pa. 1972); Tidewater Ass'n of Autistic Children v. Tidewater Bd. of Educ., Civ. No. 426–72–N (E.D. Va., Dec. 26, 1972).

20. PARC v. Commonwealth, 334 F. Supp. 1257 (E.D. Pa. 1971) and 343 F. Supp. 279, 286 (E.D. Pa. 1972); Maryland Ass'n for Retarded Children v. Maryland, Equity No. 100/182/77676 (Cir. Ct., Baltimore Cty., May 3, 1974).

21. Maryland Ass'n for Retarded Children v. Maryland, Equity No. 100/182/77676 (Cir. Ct., Baltimore Cty., May 3, 1974).

22. Mills v. Board of Educ. of Dist of Columbia, 348 F. Supp. 866, 868 (D.D.C. 1972); LeBanks v. Spears, 60 F.R.D. 135 (E.D. La. 1973); Reid v. Board of Educ., 453 F. 2d 238 (2d Cir. 1971); David P. v. State Dep't of Educ., Civ. No. 858–826 (S. F. Super. Ct., filed April 9, 1973).

23. PARC v. Commonwealth, 334 F. Supp. 1257 (E.D. Pa. 1971) and 343 F. Supp. 279, 282 (E.D. Pa. 1972) and Mills v. Board of Educ. of Dist. of Columbia, 348 F. Supp. 866, 874 (D.D.C. 1972).

24. PARC v. Commonwealth, 343 F. Supp. 279, 296 (E.D. Pa. 1972);

Maryland Ass'n for Retarded Children v. Maryland, Equity No. 100/182/77676 (Cir. Ct., Baltimore Cty., May 3, 1974).

25. Mills v. Board of Educ. of Dist. of Columbia, 348 F. Supp. 866, 878, 880, 882 (D.D.C. 1972) and Flaherty v. Connors, 319 F. Supp. 1284 (D. Mass. 1970).

26. David P. v. State Dep't of Educ., Civ. No. 658–826 (S.F. Super Ct., filed April 9, 1973).

27. North Carolina's Department of Public Instruction allocated funds to local units, for use in hiring special education teachers, on the basis of 12 TMR handicapped children per classroom.

28. Hobson v. Hansen, 269 F. Supp. 401 (D.D.C. 1967), *aff'd sub nom.* Smuck v. Hobson, 408 F.2d 175 (D.C. Cir. 1969) and Larry P. v. Riles, 343 F. Supp. 1306, 1315 (N.D. Cal. 1972).

29. Milofsky, C. Why Special Education Isn't Special. *Harvard Educational Review*, 1974, *44*, 437–58.

30. *Supra*, n. 19

31. See *infra*, Chs. 3, 4, 5, 6, and 7.

32. P.L. 94–142, Sec. 602(b).

33. Bolick, N. State Statutory Law. In *Public Policy and the Education of Exceptional Children*. Reston, Va.: Council for Exceptional Children, 1976.

1978 Supplement

n. 15. Amended by P.L. 95–602.
n. 17. Amended by P.L. 95–602.

Authors' Notes

The Office for Civil Rights, Department of Health, Education, and Welfare, has issued six "policy interpretations" of Sec. 504, published in the *Federal Register*, May 1, 1978, Part II, pages 18630-2, and August 14, 1978, Part II, pages 36034-6. Policy Interpretations 3 and 4 deal with program accessibility; Interpretation 5 with handicapped students' participation in contact sports (parental and physician consent required); and Interpretation 6 with school board members as hearing officers (not permitted).

Final Regulations for Title I (education of institutionalized handicapped children under P.L. 99–313) are contained in the *Federal Register*, April 13, 1978, pages 16262-73.

BEH and the Office for Child Health have announced a national policy agreement, dated June 22, 1978, that allows Medicaid payment for some medical services that are "related services" required by a handicapped child.

Also, the Office of Education and Rehabilitation Services Administration have entered into a memorandum of understanding, dated December, 1977, concerning the responsibilities of vocational rehabilitation agencies in dealing with handicapped people who are in V.R. programs but also in LEA programs governed by P.L. 94–142. SEA directors have been furnished copies of the memorandum.

For an analysis of the prospects for special education law, see Turnbull, H., "Litigation's Impact on Special Education," *The Kappan*, April 1978, pp. 523-6.

SECTION II:

THE SIX MAJOR PRINCIPLES

3
Zero Reject

CONSTITUTIONAL FOUNDATIONS

The Fourteenth Amendment provides that no state may deny to any person within its jurisdiction the equal protection of the laws. As interpreted by the courts, the amendment has produced a remarkable series of judicial results which effectively prevent government from denying governmental benefits to persons because of their unalterable and uncontrollable characteristics (such as age, sex, race, or handicap) and in many cases require affirmative action to redress the unequal treatment those people have experienced at the government's hand.[1] Inequalities have existed in the opportunity to be educated and handicapped children have been among the victims of educational discrimination. The Fourteenth Amendment has recently become the vehicle for redressing that inequality.

Brown as Precedent in Right-to-Education Cases

The recent judicial attacks on the many exclusionary practices of the schools focus on the importance of education, its protected status under *Brown*, and its claim to favored treatment under the Fourteenth Amendment. In holding that racial segregation in public education violated the Fourteenth Amendment, *Brown* stressed the importance of education in terms that have been quoted or cited with approval in nearly every subsequent related case. "The importance of education to our democratic society" and the relationship of education to "the performance of our most basic public responsibilities" were the grounds on which the Court reached the conclusion that the opportunity of an education, "where the state has undertaken to provide it, is a right which must be made available to all on equal terms."[2]

Representatives of handicapped students, relying on *Brown*, have claimed that handicapped children have the same rights to education as nonhandicapped children. Their complaint has two major elements. First, they complain that there is a differential treatment among and within the class of handicapped children—that is, some handicapped children are furnished education while others are not. They seek the remedy that all excluded handicapped children be given an education. Second, they complain that some handicapped children are not furnished an education while nonhandicapped children are. They seek the remedy that all children, including the handicapped, be included in the public education systems.

The basic argument of *Brown* was that the equal protection doctrine protected a "class" of persons—in this instance, a racial minority. In applying the equal protection doctrine, the courts have asked whether a state's action in distributing benefits and burdens (such as educating some but not others) was based on a "classification" of persons with apparently equal characteristics, and whether that classification resulted in some "members" of the "class" being treated less equally than others. For example, in the school desegregation cases the "class" to be protected was all students, whether white or black. When a state treated black students differently by requiring them to attend segregated schools, the courts found that black students had been denied equal protection of the school laws on the basis of an unalterable and uncontrollable trait—their race.

In the right-to-education cases, the "class" is all students, whether handicapped or not. A state undertakes to provide a free public education system for its school-age citizens; when the state treats handicapped students differently by denying them an opportunity to attend school or by inappropriately assigning them to special education programs, the courts found that the handicapped had been denied equal protection of the school laws on the basis of their unalterable and unchosen trait—their handicap.

The Evolution of Equal Protection Analysis

Until the advent of the Warren era of the Supreme Court, the Court generally held that governmental action, alleged to be discriminatory and in violation of the equal protection doctrine, was not unconstitutional. When the "traditional" equal-protection analysis applied in these cases failed to correct abuses of individual rights, the Warren Court applied a "new" equal protection analysis. The application the Court used depended principally on who the complaining party was, what the nature of his interest was or what right was being infringed upon, and the ability of the government to justify its action.

Under the new equal protection concept, if the case involved a "suspect classification" (such as a person being classified by race) or a "fundamental interest" (such as the right to vote), the Court subjected the classification to "strict scrutiny" and required the state to show a "compelling interest."[3] The Court also required the state to prove that the distinction drawn by the law was necessary, not merely convenient, in order to achieve the government's purpose.

If no fundamental interest or suspect classification was involved, the Court resorted to the "rational basis" standard, asking only whether the ends or purposes sought were legitimate state purposes and whether there was a rational relationship between the ends or purposes and the particular classification. A state practice was much more likely to survive an equal-protection attack under the rational-basis test than under the strict scrutiny test. The present Court is relying far more on the traditional analysis and far less on the new analysis.

Understanding the basic equal-protection analyses is necessary to appreciate how a claim of equal protection is generally made and resolved in the right-to-education cases, despite the fact that the recent right-to-education cases generally lack a clear or formal equal-protection analysis. Until very recently, the courts deciding those cases have typically cited the equal-protection clause and added an accompanying reference to *Brown*. However, they have failed to state whether education is a "fundamental interest" or whether the handicapped plaintiffs are a "suspect class," and they usually have not specified which equal-protection tests finally apply.[4] *Pennsylvania Association for Retarded Children (PARC)* v. *Pennsylvania*[5] was resolved by consent decree (a final order entered by consent of all parties and approved by the court) and *Mills* v. *D.C. Board of Education*[6] fell under the Fifth Amendment due-process principles. Moreover, when *PARC* and *Mills* were decided, approximately a year before *Rodriguez*,[7] it apparently was not necessary to decide whether education was a fundamental interest in the usual constitutional sense.[8] Perhaps it seemed unimportant then because the courts had frequently attested to the importance of education.

PARC, Mills, and MARC. Although *Brown* established the right to an equal educational opportunity based upon Fourteenth Amendment grounds, it was not until *PARC, Mills,* and *Maryland Association for Retarded Children (MARC)* v. *Maryland*[9] that *Brown* became meaningful for the handicapped.

In both *PARC* and *Mills* the courts relied on legal and educational authorities to support their finding that education was essential to enable a child to function in society and that *all* children can benefit from education, and they applied the equal-protection and due-process guarantees of the Fifth and Fourteenth Amendments to furnish this important right to handicapped students. Neither court engaged in careful legal analysis; each was content to make the assertion of fundamental interest and strike down school policies denying education to handicapped children. *Mills*, citing *Brown* and *Hobson* v. *Hansen*, concluded:

> In *Hobson* v. *Hansen*, *supra*, Judge Wright found that denying poor public school children educational opportunities equal to that available to more affluent public school children was violating the Due Process Clause of the Fifth Amendment. *A fortiori*, defendants' conduct here, denying plaintiffs and their class not just an equal publicly supported education but all publicly supported education while providing such education to other children is violative of the Due Process Clause.[11]

Subsequent cases have closely followed the arguments made in *PARC* and *Mills*, and the form of the decision and the relief granted have been similar. *PARC* relied on the following findings:

> — 1. Expert testimony in this action indicates that . . . all mentally retarded persons are capable of benefiting from a program of education and training; that the greatest number of retarded persons, given such education and training, are capable of achieving self-sufficiency and the remaining few, with such education and training, are capable of achieving some degree of self-care; that the earlier such education and training begins, the more thoroughly and the more efficiently a mentally retarded person will benefit from it; and, whether begun early or not, that a mentally retarded person can benefit at any point in his life and development from a program of education and training.
> — 2. The Commonwealth of Pennsylvania has undertaken to provide a free public education to all of its children between the ages of six and twenty-one years, and further, has undertaken to provide education and training for all of its mentally retarded children.
> — 3. Having undertaken to provide a free public education to all of its children, including its mentally retarded children, the Commonwealth of Pennsylvania may not deny any mentally retarded child access to a free public program of education and training.
> — 4. It is the Commonwealth's obligation to place each mentally retarded child in a free, public program of education and training appropriate to the child's capacity, within the context of the general educational policy that, among the alternative programs of education and training required by statute to be available, placement in a regular public school class is preferable to placement in a special public school class and placement in a special public school class is preferable to placement of any other type of program of education and training.

One important premise is absent from the court's findings: it is generally true that educators have the ability to educate and train the handicapped. Without both the ability of handicapped children to learn and the ability of educators to help them learn, it would be a futile expenditure of public money to attempt to teach the handicapped in the public schools. It would instead be rational and arguably constitutional for the state to exclude them from school if they could not benefit from it and if there were no educators competent to teach them. It was significant that the defendants in *PARC* and *Mills* did not deny that they were under a duty to educate *all* children or that mentally retarded or other handicapped children could be educated.

From the point of view of the principle of zero reject, the changes ordered in *PARC* were comprehensive. The state was required to locate and identify all school-aged persons excluded from public schools. State and local school districts were required to place all retarded children in a "free public program of education and training appropriate to the child's capacity.'' In addition, the state's Department of Public Welfare, insofar as it was charged with arranging for the care, training, and supervision of a child committed to it, was also required to provide a program of education and training appropriate to the child's capacity. Parents of retarded children were excused from liability under the compulsory school-attendance statutes if, with the approval of the local school board and the secretary of education and upon a finding by an approved school psychologist, they chose to withdraw their child from school. School districts were enjoined from using the withdrawal provisions as a means of excluding retarded children against the parents' wishes. The compulsory school-attendance statutes were construed to mean that when a child is between eight and seventeen years of age his parents must make sure that he attends an educational or training program.

Any school district that provided free preschooling to nonhandicapped children under the age of six was prohibited from denying such schooling to retarded children of the same age. A similar result was reached in *Denver Association for Retarded Children* v. *School District No. 1 in City and County of Denver*.[12] The court decided that kindergarten education for the nonhandicapped is a "regular school program" and the school district accordingly must pay for the kindergarten education of children who, but for their being handicapped, would be eligible to attend the program.

The state's tuition-maintenance statute (granting funds for payment of tuition at private schools) was interpreted by *PARC* to mean that a mentally retarded child is entitled to its benefits if he attends a private school. Previously, the statute had been interpreted to apply only to children that were blind, deaf, cerebral palsied, brain damaged, or afflicted by muscular dystrophy. Statutory provisions for at-home instruction were construed to mean that such instruction must be made available to retarded children even though they may not be physically handicapped or suffering from a short-term disability as well.

Unlike *PARC*, *Mills* was not resolved by a consent decree but, rather, by judgment against the defendant school board. Also unlike *PARC*, the suit was brought on behalf of children who had disabilities other than mental retardation. Like *PARC*, however, *Mills* resulted in a court order that before any handicapped child eligible for a publicly supported education may be excluded from a regular school assignment, he must be furnished adequate alternative educational services suited to his needs, including (if appropriate) special education or tuition grants. The District of Columbia school board was required to provide each handicapped school-aged child a free and suitable publicly supported education, regardless of the degree of his mental, physical, or emotional disability. It was also enjoined from making disciplinary suspensions for any reason for longer than two days unless school authorities gave the child a hearing before his suspension and continued his education while he was suspended.

School authorities were ordered to provide suitable education to all handicapped children then known to them within thirty days after the date of the order. Handicapped children who might later come to their attention were to be provided for within fifty days. The authorities were also required to advertise the availability of free public education for handicapped children, to identify previously excluded handicapped children and advise them of their rights under the court order, and to evaluate the educational needs of all identified handicapped children. Finally, they were required to file a proposal with the court for placing each handicapped child in a suitable educational program. The proposal was to include compensatory educational services where required; a plan for identifying, notifying, evaluating, and placing the handicapped children; a report showing the expunction from or the correction of all official records of the plaintiffs' former expulsions, suspensions, or exclusions made in violation of the due-process requirements contained in the court order; and a plan for allowing the children's parents to attach to their records any clarifying or explanatory information.

In *MARC*, the Circuit Court for Baltimore County interpreted the state laws as requiring local and state school authorities to provide a free appropriate public education to children with handicaps, particularly mentally retarded children, regardless of how severely and profoundly retarded they might be. The court ordered that local boards of education must provide an appropriate education for a handicapped child, and that placement in a nonpublic day facility, a public or private residential facility, or a home and hospital instruction program may (but does not necessarily) constitute an appropriate program. The court said that the local boards were failing to discharge their responsibilities when they referred a child to a private or public agency that had a waiting list, when the child was already on a waiting list for admission to the agency's program. At-home instruction was found not to be justified simply because of a child's mental retardation; it is justified only when the child's physical condition prevents him from attending school. Private placements by public schools must be fully paid for by the schools—there may be no cost to the parents—and local boards must provide daily transportation for handicapped children to and from their educational programs.

At roughly the same time a series of cases that paralleled *PARC* and *Mills* established the right of institutionalized mentally handicapped persons to receive treatment.[13] The right-to-treatment cases also relied on the Fourteenth Amendment. The timing of the right-to-education and right-to-treatment cases was fortunate, for each judicial development fueled the other.

It came as no surprise to those who followed the right-to-education and right-to-treatment movements that *PARC* and *Mills* gave rise to numerous related law suits. What did come as a shock, however, was one court's *failure* to find that it was a denial of equal protection for a state to exclude some mentally handicapped students from the public school system. That jarring note was sounded by a three-judge federal district court in *The Cuyohoga County Association for Retarded Children and Adults* v. *Essex*.[14] At issue was the Ohio system of educating and training the mentally retarded.

As the court interpreted the Ohio statutes, the effect of the state laws was to classify mentally retarded people into two categories: those who could and those who could not "profit substantially from further instruction" under a broadly based public education system. Those who could profit were required to attend public schools; those who could not, were not. In determining whether this interpretation of the Ohio statutes was constitutional, the court asked first if the classification was "rational" and found that it was. It is not arbitrary, the court held, for the state to determine that only those children who can derive actual benefit from a broadly based system of public education should be included while the others are excluded. The court further construed the Ohio statutes and state school board regulations to mean that the establishment of special education classes is not discretionary; programs for educable mentally retarded students—and only for them—must be provided by each local school agency. In short, the court held that free public education must be provided under state law, as analyzed through the traditional equal protection approach, to *educable* mentally retarded students, not to the more disabled retarded (the "trainable," severely retarded, or profoundly retarded children).

What makes the Ohio case so surprising, at least on the surface, is its limited application: education for educable retarded persons, and nothing for other retarded persons. In this respect, it flies in the face of the all-encompassing scope of the orders in *PARC* and *Mills* and the cases that followed them. But the Ohio case is open to serious question on several grounds.

First, the case was decided on a motion for summary judgment and without testimony; the parties agreed that there was no real dispute as to any material facts and that the only dispute was one of law; namely, the proper interpretation of the Ohio statutes. As the court was careful to point out, it decided merely that Ohio statutes were constitutional as construed by the court, not that they were unconstitutional as applied. Hence, with sufficient proper evidence, it might later be shown that the statutes were applied in such a way as to exclude even educable mentally retarded children, thus violating their equal protection rights. If there was a failure on the plaintiffs' part, it was in not having put forward evidence (if any was to be found) that even educable mentally retarded children were denied a right to attend school.

Second, the case involved Ohio's unique system of training the mentally retarded, a system apparently not followed in other states. In Ohio, the public school system was responsible for furnishing an education to the educable mentally retarded; the mental health system was responsible for the more disabled mentally retarded persons. Thus the court was able to hold that the compulsory school-attendance laws required the educable mentally retarded to attend and thus did not discriminate against them. More to the point, the court was also able to treat the second system—the mental health system—as a social services system with "social problems" such as the training and education of the moderately, severely, and profoundly retarded of all ages, not just of school age. Citing the Supreme Court's decision on the power of a state to make classifications for the purpose of providing welfare benefits to the poor, the court found that the Ohio system did not violate the equal protection clause by singling out some of the retarded for school benefits and others for exclusion from school. The court said that a state is allowed great latitude in deciding whether and how to attack a social problem, and its decision has to be tested, for constitutional (equal protection) purposes, only by whether its action is rationally based and free from invidious classification. Inasmuch as Ohio had undertaken "only to train the mentally retarded on a potentially limited basis commensurate with the funds allotted by the legislature for that purpose," the court declined to substitute its judgment for the legislature's in determining how best to administer the "social welfare program." The distinction between *PARC, Mills, MARC,* and the other right-to-education cases, and *Cuyohoga* is easy to make and rests upon the unique, dual system in effect in Ohio. In light of this crucial factual distinction, *Cuyohoga* is not as shocking as it may have appeared.

In *Taylor* v. *Maryland School for the Blind*,[15] a federal district court held that a state-aided private school was not violating a student's right to due proccess by terminating her enrollment. The dismissal was based on the judgment of the school's staff that the plaintiff—a multiply handicapped, legally blind girl—did not appear to be benefitting from the [school's] educational program and showed a lack of progress. The plaintiff claimed she had been denied substantive due process (a right to education) because there was *no* evidence that she had not sufficiently progressed in relation to her ability. She claimed, in effect, that since her ability could not be measured, the defendant had no basis for saying she had not progressed in relation to her ability. The defendant admitted the plaintiff's ability could not be measured but said that the real issue was whether its action was arbitrary and capricious and the court agreed. The court, noting it could not substitute its judgement for the defendant's, said that the key to the case was whether the defendant's decision was supported by some evidence, not whether it was supported by substantial evidence. Making its decision depend on the scope of judicial review and the burden of proof, the court held that, although the student's ability was not measurable, it was clear from the evidence that the plaintiff had made no progress during the time she was enrolled. Moreover, the fact that her ability could not be measured was a special circumstance that authorized the school to deviate from its own policy of discharging students only if they are not making progress in relation to their abilities.

Taylor is clearly distinguishable from *Cuyohoga*. It involves only one person, not a class of people. It rests not on an interpretation of state law but on an interpretation of a private school's policies. The case turns on the scope of judicial review when there is a conflict of testimony; in *Cuyohoga*, there was *no* evidence from either side, and the decision was made on a motion for summary judgment.

There was no dual system of education and training in Maryland to justify the court's reliance on the "rational basis" test, instead, there was the "special circumstance" that the plaintiff's ability could not be measured. Nevertheless, the *Maryland* case is instructive in that it reveals that the courts may be unwilling to substitute their judgment for educators' and that they may apply a limited scope of judicial review, asking only whether the educators' decision is arbitrary and capricious, not whether it is supported by the substantial weight of the evidence, which would clearly place a heavier burden on educators.

The Uses of Equal Protection for Zero Reject

The equal protection doctrine can be put to many uses in the context of zero-reject policy. It can be used to prevent (1) the total exclusion of all or some handicapped children in the schools, (2) the total exclusion of some handicapped children when others with the same handicap are included, and (3) the total exclusion of all persons with one kind of handicap (such as autism) when persons with different types of handicaps (such as physical disabilities) are included. In each of these instances, the "class" of persons entitled to equal protection is "students," not just some students.[16]

A fourth use of equal protection comes into play when handicapped children are included in school programs on a different basis than nonhandicapped students. For example, it applies when handicapped children's parents are required to pay tuition for attending public schools but the parents of nonhandicapped children are not.[17] It also applies to handicapped children who are ruled medically ineligible to attend school (because they are nonambulatory or not toilet trained) when nonhandicapped children are not screened out because of their medically related characteristics.[18] And it also operates for handicapped children who are denied free transportion to school when nonhandicapped students are given such service.[19]

Equal Access Doctrine. The fifth way the equal protection doctrine has been applied in the right-to-education cases is in establishing a new doctrine of equality; namely, the equal access doctrine. *Brown* and other school desegregation cases interpreted the equal protection doctrine as requiring that black students be given *equal access to the same resources* as whites. Typically, the courts ruled that when a school system provides facilities to white children, exactly the same facilities (not an equivalent separate set of facilities) must be made available on the same terms to black children.

In the recent right-to-education cases, the theory of equal protection is quite different and can be best understood in terms of claims for the handicapped to *differing* resources for *differing* objectives.[20] Under this approach, the right to education for handicapped students means that the schools must furnish *all* handicapped children equal opportunities to develop their own capabilities. Thus, they are required to provide different programs and facilities for pupils with different needs, according to those needs. This "new access" doctrine was originally developed in *Mills, PARC,* and *LeBanks* v. *Spears,*[21] all of which required not only that the handicapped plaintiffs be provided with public education, but also that the education be "appropriate" to their capacities or "suited to their needs."

Although the courts have developed the new access theory, they have been unwilling to abandon the earlier *Brown* theory of equal protection. For example they have responded favorably to cases challenging the placement of disproportionate numbers of minority students in classes for the mentally retarded.[22] In a sense, the cases assert the traditional *Brown* doctrine that the minority students be given "equal access to the same resources." In those cases, equal protection is being used in a sixth way to expand educational opportunity on the basis of discrimination because of race rather than handicap.

Whenever this sixth use of the *Brown* theory might be applied so that school systems would be able to restrict appropriate educational opportunity to the handicapped on the theory that they were furnishing equal access to the same resources, it tends not to be followed. For example, the plaintiffs in *Lau* v. *Nichols*[23] argued that equal educational opportunities had been effectively denied to Chinese-speaking children because public school programs were taught only in English. They claimed that equal protection required that school programs take into account the children's inability to understand English. The Ninth Circuit Court of Appeals responded with a *Brown*-type "equal access" theory of equal protection, saying that equal protection is not denied because all children are given equal access to the standard, English-taught curriculum available to other students. The United States Supreme Court reversed the decision. The Court's opinion closely paralleled the equal-protection arguments made in the recent right-to-education cases, stating that some school practices deny a meaningful opportunity for education. However, the Court decided the case solely on the basis of Sec. 601 of the 1964 Civil Rights Act (prohibiting racial discrimination in any federally assisted educational program) and did not touch on the equal-protection issue.

The fact that the Supreme Court disposed of *Lau* on the nonconstitutional grounds may give a clue to the nature of forthcoming litigation; it suggests that state or federal statutory grounds for a claim to appropriate education are more likely to be favorably received that a "new access" claim. But *Lau* by no means undercuts the new access theory; if anything, it strengthens it by acknowledging that students have a strong claim to appropriate and meaningful educational opportunities.

Appropriate Education. Recent case-law developments seek to litigate what the *Lau* decision avoided—the issues of "functional exclusion" and "appropriate'' education. In *Lau*, the question was whether the plaintiffs were excluded from an equal educational opportunity because they could not learn in the regular school program because of their language handicap. One can cast *Lau* in different terms without changing the nature of the case and say that there were two legal issues. Does the equal protection doctrine come into play when functional exclusion is practiced (as when a seriously emotionally disturbed child who can, hear is placed in a class with hearing-impaired children and receives no additional attention)? And does the equal protection doctrine operate when determining what is an ''appropriate'' education? The answer to both questions is ''yes,'' since both raise the issue of exclusion of a handicapped child from a *meaningful* equal educational opportunity because of his handicap, whereas nonhandicapped children are not excluded from such an opportunity.

To date, the cases have opened the schoolhouse doors for the handicapped. They are just beginning, however, to adequately address the issue of ''appropriate'' education (other than in the ''bi-lingual'' cases, discussed below). In *Allen* v. *McDonough*,[24] a consent decree was entered in a case brought under Massachusetts law that challenged the failure of the school officials to complete the required evaluation process of more than 1000 handicapped students and raised the issue of consequent denial of placement in an adequate program. The case resulted in an order requiring that the children be provided with an ''educational plan'' and a periodic review of that plan, both to be furnished on an accelerated time schedule.

In *Crowder* v. *Riles*,[25] the plaintiffs claimed that their right to an appropriate education as guaranteed by the California constitution was denied when they were assigned to inappropriate public education programs because their parents could not afford to pay the tuition for private programs and because the state's tuition-grant funds were inadequate to cover the needs of all the handicapped children who did not have appropriate public programs available to them. The court has not yet entered an order.

In *Fialkowski* v. *Shapp*,[26] the handicapped plaintiffs, relying on the equal protection and due process clauses of the Fourteenth Amendment, claimed they had been denied their right to an ''appropriate'' education because they had no chance to benefit from the programs offered them in the Philadelphia schools. The federal district court, holding that there is ''a constitutional right to a certain minimum level of education,'' transferred the case to the three-judge federal district court that has jurisdiction in *PARC*, where the decision on ''appropriate'' education apparently will be made.

In *Frederick L.* v. *Thomas*,[27] the federal district court held that the failure of the Philadelphia schools to provide special programs and classes for learning disabled children (who were not physically excluded from attending school) violated the children's rights under state law. The court found that the children were ''effectively excluded,'' since they were unable to learn unless they were given educational services appropriate to their needs.

In *Rhode Island Society for Autistic Children, Inc.* v. *Board of Regents*,[28] the plaintiffs alleged that although they were not actually excluded from an educational opportunity, they were *de facto* excluded (in fact, excluded) because the programs they had been assigned to were lacking in meaningful educational opportunities. In a settlement of the case before trial, the court approved the parties' stipulations designed to prevent misclassification, and hence, functional exclusion.

In *Rockafellow* v. *Brouillet*,[29] the institutionalized plaintiffs alleged that they were not receiving an adequate and appropriate educational program. They defined an adequate program as one (a) equal in quality and duration to that provided for intellectually normal students of the same chronological age in the same school district and (b) directed to the needs, abilities, and limitations of each of the handicapped plaintiffs. The case was dismissed as a result of a settlement that called for the drafting of administrative regulations to assure the plaintiffs of an adequate and appropriate education. Before the dismissal, the court had found that the plaintiffs had established a cause of action.

In *McWilliams* v. *New York City Board of Education*,[30] the handicapped plaintiffs alleged that they were being denied an equal educational opportunity (equal to that given to nonhandicapped students) because the special classes they had been assigned to were being understaffed with teachers and paraprofessionals, and ancillary services such as speech or hearing therapy and psychotherapy were all but nonexistent. They also claimed a denial of equal educational opportunity because their classes had been granted a variance to have a larger pupil to teacher ratio than set by state regulation. These issues have not yet been decided, as a preliminary order concerning venue (place of trial) and exhaustion of administrative remedies is being appealed.

Finally, in *Davis* v. *Wynne*[31] a student suing under Sec. 504 and Fourteenth Amendment equal protection grounds alleged that he had been put out of the public schools because he was learning disabled, had been inappropriately placed, and had experienced behavioral problems as a result of the inappropriate placement. He claimed that he was placed in an educational program that required competencies far beyond his mental abilities and that the placement caused him to continually fail thus denying him an opportunity to learn, frustrating him, and thwarting his efforts to learn. In the settlement agreement (which was neither a consent order nor a court order), the defendant school officials agreed to refer the plaintiff to a technical school, pay for the tuition fees and costs of transportation to the school, and help find psychological counseling for him.

According to the pending cases, then, appropriate education consists of timely and sufficient evaluations, individual programs, and review of the programs (*Allen* v. *McDonough*). It also includes claims for tuition subsidies for private or technical institute schooling when appropriate public programs do not exist (*Crowder* v. *Riles* and *Davis* v. *Wynne*). "Appropriate education" is a justiciable claim (one that can be resolved by a court) under the equal protection clause (*Fialkowski*); includes more than admission to programs, requiring in addition programs that are likely to benefit the handicapped child (*Frederick L.* v. *Thomas* and *R.I.S.A.C.*); and raises issues of whether programs for handicapped children must be equal in quality (not a defined term in the cases) to those for nonhandicapped students (*Rockafellow* v. *Brouillet* and *McWilliams* v. *N.Y.C. Bd. of Ed.*). All of these cases have a "new access" flavor and rely on the use of equal protection for meaningful education.

There is yet another set of "appropriate education" cases. These cases were brought on behalf of Spanish-speaking students allegedly misclassified as handicapped because they were tested in English rather than in Spanish, or who were arguably denied an appropriate (meaningful) education because their classes were not taught bilingually or in Spanish. Some of these cases challenge placing Spanish-speaking students in special education programs, while others seek bilingual education in "regular" or mainstream programs along with enforcement of the Bilingual Education Act.[32]

Free Education. There is, of course, more to zero-reject and equal protection than functional exclusion and appropriate education. Zero-reject and equal protection include the right to compensatory education when a handicapped student has been denied an equal educational opportunity during his school-age years.[33] At-home or other nonschool programs for children who are unable to attend school are also included.[34] The cases extend the right to education to handicapped children whose parents are forced to seek private-school training because appropriate public programs are unavailable.[35]

The recent cases raise the issues of a "free" and "appropriate" education. Although *PARC, Mills,* and *MARC* held that handicapped children are entitled to a free appropriate education regardless of the nature or severity of the child's handicap, it remained for a Virginia court and various New York courts to refine the zero-reject issue as it related to a free education.

In *Kruse* v. *Campbell*,[36] learning disabled students in Fairfax County, Virginia, brought a class action suit that challenged the state's tuition-payment program on equal protection grounds and under Sec. 504. The Virginia program consisted of two basic components. First, when a handicapped child had to be enrolled in a private special education program because there were no appropriate public school programs, the state paid 75 percent of the cost of the private program (up to a maximum of $1250.00 a year for nonresidential care or $5000 a year for residential care), but the parents had to make up the difference between the state tuition subsidy and the actual cost. Although local school boards had the option of paying the difference, they usually did not. Second, the state's welfare department would pay the full cost of residential care only if the child's parents gave the department custody of the child, in which case the local board had no responsibility. Partly because the state's program discriminated against the poor and partly

because of the enforced-custody requirement, a federal district court struck down
the program and ordered the plaintiffs to file a new plan for tuition reimbursement.
The grounds on which the court made its decision were the familiar Fourteenth
Amendment ones (nondiscrimination against the poor), and its finding that
"something is wrong" with the existing system clearly affirmed the plaintiffs'
right to a free and appropriate education.

In subsequent action in the case, the district court ruled that the state must
furnish appropriate education to all poor handicapped students commensurate with
the education available to more affluent handicapped children until the appropriate
public education was made available to them. The decision turned on wealth-
discrimination grounds and treated the poor handicapped students' rights to an
education as equal to those of the more affluent. The court ordered the state to
devise a plan for educating *all* of the handicapped children; also, handicapped
children who had been placed in the state's custody were to be returned to their
parents or guardians within sixty days of the order. The U.S. Supreme Court has
reversed the federal district court and ordered the case to be retried on statutory
grounds (P.L. 94–142 and Sec. 504), rather than on constitutional ones.

Halderman v. *Pittinger*[37] was another case that raised a similar constitutional
claim: denial of an equal educational opportunity under the Fourteenth Amendment due to a state tuition-reimbursement program that had a ceiling that effectively discriminated against the poor, denying their children free and appropriate
programs in the public schools. The initial holding of the court was that the
plaintiffs have raised a constitutional claim and are entitled to have a three-judge
district court hear their case on its merits. A decision on the merits has not yet been
rendered.

The decision in *Doe* v. *Laconia*,[38] a federal-court case decided under New
Hampshire law, may provide some clues for the outcome of *Kruse* and *Halderman*. *In Doe*, the court held that the state board of education's policy of spending
funds allocated for supplemental tuition payments for *all* handicapped children on
a priority basis (geared to the severity of the handicap and discriminatory to
emotionally disturbed children) did not violate the equal protection doctrine.
According to the court, the board's program had a "rational basis for giving those
children with the severest handicap preferential treatment" and it was held that
equal protection does not require the decision to be based on the parents' ability to
pay. Thus, a plan that excludes family wealth as a criterion for determining who is
entitled to a tuition payment but which funds the cost of educating the most
severely handicapped children could be the plan the Virginia and Pennsylvania
courts will adopt.

A series of tuition-payment cases in New York seemed at first to establish that
the parents of handicapped children are entitled to full reimbursement for educational expenses incurred for private education when appropriate public programs
were unavailable. They also seemed to say that the family's ability to pay was

irrelevant to the state's duty to pay.[39] Later cases, however, have held that the family's ability to pay is indeed relevant and, when possible, a family may be ordered to pay a portion of their child's educational expenses.[40] They have also held that it is not a violation of equal protection if the state pays the full cost for maintaining deaf or blind children in an institution, but not for institutionalized mentally retarded children.[41] On the other hand, the courts have been willing to require the state to pay part of the cost for maintaining a mentally retarded child in an institution not approved by the state as an educational institution if it in fact furnishes an education to the child. In some cases, they have ordered the state to pay for summer programs of special education if a child needs them and would regress if he did not receive them.[42] It is difficult to reconcile these discordant results, to find any principle that harmonizes them.

None of the "tuition" cases are based on P.L. 94–142, which guarantees a free appropriate education to all handicapped children. They are instead based on the equal protection doctrine of the Fourteenth Amendment and could well be decided differently if brought under P.L. 94–142. No "free education" cases based on P.L. 94–142 have been filed as yet.

Transportation. The zero-reject issue also extends to transportation to and from an appropriate program. In the only reported case on the issue other than *MARC*, a county school system was ordered to pay the full round-trip costs for transporting a physically handicapped child from home to an appropriate program outside his community despite the fact that the cost was $56.78 daily (or a total of $10,221 for a school year).[43] A related concern has not been litigated: is it a denial of equal protection to require handicapped children to take longer rides than nonhandicapped children, thereby depriving them of more in-class time than the nonhandicapped children?

Rodriguez

San Antonio Independent School District v. *Rodriguez*[44] apparently stands in the way of applying equal protection principles to exclusionary or discriminatory practices with respect to handicapped children. Yet the appearance is greater than the reality; on careful examination *Rodriguez* poses few major barriers to equal-protection claims by handicapped students. *Rodriguez* dealt with intrastate financing of local school districts. The plaintiffs made two allegations: First, since they were residents of relatively "poorer" school districts, they were being unconstitutionally discriminated against because of their relative absence of wealth (a "suspect classification") in a state-financing scheme that made local school district financing depend largely on the tax base of the district. Second, the state-financing scheme should be subject to the new equal-protection "strict-scrutiny" standard since education qualifies as a "fundamental interest." The court rejected the contention of wealth discrimination, and, after defining a fundamental right as one explicitly or implicitly guaranteed by the Constitution, found that education did not qualify as one of those rights. However, the Court did not decide whether "some identifiable quantum of education is a constitutionally protected requisite to the meaningful exercise of either right [freedom of speech or the right to vote]." It suggested that although a Fourteenth Amendment attack on the relative inequalities of educational opportunities probably would be rejected, a similar attack on "an absolute denial of educational opportunities to any of [a state's] children" on the basis that "the [financing] system fails to provide each child with an opportunity to acquire the basic minimal skills necessary for the enjoyment of the rights of speech and of full participation in the political process" would be received favorably.

Rodriguez distinguished between (1) facts showing a poorer quality of education caused by noninvidious (nondiscriminatory) classification based on the relative wealth of the school districts and (2) facts showing a total denial of education. This distinction is crucial for the handicapped under equal-protection principles. Although *Rodriguez* plainly states that a relatively lower-quality education will not be grounds for a successful equal-protection attack, it implies that the total exclusion of handicapped persons from any schooling may be successfully challenged because total exclusion represents an absolute—not relative—denial.

Rodriguez required proof that the school system "fails to provide each child with an opportunity to acquire the basic minimal skills necessary for the enjoyment of the rights of speech and of full participation in the political process." This left open the possibility of an equal-protection attack on school classification and tracking practices. Many of these practices cannot be justified, because they tend to segregate students from an opportunity to acquire the "basic minimal skills" necessary for effectively exercising speech and voting rights.

Rodriguez also may not stand in the way of a successful challenge to the quality of the educational opportunity provided in a special education program. Such a challenge could be constructed on the grounds that neither the original classification nor the special program have produced mastery of the "basic minimal skills" for a particular child. Under this approach, the student would have to be capable of developing such skills. The challenge would be related to the requirement of "appropriate" education. (It would be of no value to the student who was incapable of developing the skills in question. Since his innate incapacity can only be ameliorated, not changed, by educational intervention, intervention can hardly be responsible for failure to meet the constitutional standard.) A major distinction between the plight of the *Rodriguez* plaintiffs and that of handicapped students is the difference in the harm done to them by the state. It is one thing to provide someone with a less well-financed education, and quite another to relegate them to stigmatization and self-limiting education by wrongly classifying them as handicapped and assigning them to special programs.

It is possible that the "suspect classification" argument ("the class is . . . saddled with such disabilities, or subjected to such a history of purposeful unequal treatment, or relegated to such a position of political powerlessness as to command extraordinary protection from the majoritarian political process") may well apply to the handicapped. If so, it might redress exclusionary or discriminatory school practices. This possibility is all the more likely if the practices are such that they totally exclude a pupil or fail to live up to the "qualitative" or "basic minimum skills" tests set out above.

In one post-*Rodriguez* right-to-education case, *Wilson* v. *Redmond*,[45] a federal district court dismissed a complaint by handicapped students, ruling that the claim that they received a "different quality of education" than nonhandicapped children did not meet the *Rodriguez* test of a "complete deprivation." The court said that they were not subject to a "suspect classification" where their handicap is used as the basis of the schools' actions in allocating limited resources among programs for nonhandicapped and handicapped students.

The opposite conclusion was reached by another federal district court. In *Fialkowski* v. *Shapp*,[46] the court refused to dismiss a case brought on the grounds that there is a constitutional right to an appropriate education under the equal protection clause and that the right was violated when the plaintiffs were assigned to school programs they could not benefit from. The defendants relied on the *Rodriguez* holding that there is no "fundamental" right to an education and they contended that the plaintiffs' claim to an appropriate education could not therefore present a constitutional question. The district court rejected the defense, however, holding that there is a constitutional right to "a certain minimum level of education." It distinguished *Rodriguez* from the plaintiff's case on the ground that *Rodriguez* was an attack on the method of financing public education, not on a system that allegedly resulted in a *complete* denial of an educational opportunity because the program was of no benefit (that is, inappropriate) to the plaintiffs. In another *Rodriguez*-related holding, the court held that the *Fialkowski* plaintiffs were a "suspect class" entitled to have the court apply the "strict scrutiny" test to the state's actions.

The plaintiffs of *Wilson* v. *Redmond* seemed doomed to fail in their assertion that they had a right to an appropriate education because they failed to bring out facts that were essential to the disposition of *Fialkowski*, such as the failure of the state to offer even a minimum education. *Wilson* is not so much an affirmation of *Rodriguez* in the right-to-education movement as an ill-conceived and ill-pleaded case that, on its facts, did not bring *Rodriguez* into sharp and distinguishable focus. In short, its value as precedent is questionable, while *Fialkowski's* is undoubtedly great.

Except as otherwise noted, none of the cases described in the preceding discussion of zero reject and equal protection were disposed of under federal statutes granting handicapped persons protection against discrimination by public school authorities. They all raised constitutional claims based on the equal protection clause of the Fourteenth Amendment of the due process clause of the Fifth Amendment (*Mills*). This is significant for several reasons: (1) the remedies ordered in many of the cases tend to be reflected in the applicable federal laws (P.L. 94–142 and Sec. 504) dealing with zero reject, free education, and appropriate education; (2) the remedies which were available under litigation brought on constitutional grounds should also be available under litigation that may (and undoubtedly will) be brought under the federal statutes; (3) plaintiffs in right-to-education cases can thus take a ''shotgun'' approach to litigation, using both constitutional and statutory grounds in alleging that their rights have been violated; and (4) when it is not clear that statutory rights have been violated, a claim may still succeed on the basis of the violation of constitutional rights, and vice versa.

FEDERAL LEGISLATION

P.L. 94–142

Nothing is clearer in P.L. 94–142 than the intent of Congress that no handicapped child be excluded from school by recipients of federal funds for the education of the handicapped, and that all involved agencies follow a policy of zero-reject. Finding (as the courts did) that both total and functional exclusion existed [Sec. 601 (b) (3) and (4)] and, concluding that it was in the national interest to provide programs to meet the needs of handicapped children and thereby assure them equal protection of the law [Sec. 601 (b) (9)], Congress declared the purpose of P.L. 94–142 to provide a free appropriate education to the handicapped [Sec. 601 (c)] and acted in numerous ways to implement the zero-reject policy.

Free Appropriate Public Education (FAPE). In order to make LEAs and SEAs implement zero-reject, Congress has required them to establish ''full-service goals '' [Sec. 612(2)(A) and 614(a)(1)(C), (D) and (E)]. These goals are to be adopted for planning purposes only; if an SEA or LEA does not comply with them, no sanctions will be imposed. As the regulation discussion [Sec. 121 a. 304 and .123] of this language makes clear,

> It is an all-encompassing term, which (1) covers all handicapped children aged birth through twenty-one, (2) includes a basic planning dimension (including making projections of the estimated numbers of handicapped children), (3) permits each agency to establish its own timetable for meeting the goal, and (4) calls for the provision of additional facilities, personnel, services to further enrich a handicapped child's educational opportunity beyond that mandated under the ''FAPE'' requirement. The term ''goal'' means an end to be sought. However, while an agency may never achieve its goal in the absolute sense, it must be committed to implementing this provision, and must be in compliance with the policies and procedures in the Annual Program Plan under this provision. Further, the agency is not relieved from its obligations under the ''FAPE'' requirement. [*Fed. Reg.*, Aug. 23, 1977, p. 42506].

Thus, each state must adopt a policy assuring *all* handicapped children of a free appropriate public education [Sec. 612(1)] and must formulate a plan for achieving that goal [Sec. 121a.110–.151]. Congress also required the states to provide a full educational opportunity to all handicapped children between the ages of three and eighteen (''ages-certain'' requirements) by September 1, 1978 (''dates-certain'' requirements) and to all handicapped children between the ages of three and twenty-one by September 1, 1980. Sec. 121a.300(b) of the regulations provides that:

(1) If State law or a court order requires the State to provide education for handicapped children in any disability category in any of these age groups, the State must make a free appropriate public education available to all handicapped children of the same age who have that disability.

(2) If a public agency provides education to non-handicapped children in any of these age groups, it must make a free appropriate public education available to at least a proportionate number of handicapped children of the same age.

(3) If a public agency provides education to 50 percent or more of its handicapped children in any disability category in any of these age groups, it must make a free appropriate public education available to all of its handicapped children of the same age who have that disability.

(4) If a public agency provides education to a handicapped child in any of these age groups, it must make a free appropriate public education available to that child and provide that child and his or her parents all of the rights under Part B of the Act and [the regulations].

The effect of this regulation is that before September 1, 1978, all children previously referred or waiting for evaluation must be evaluated and, if found to be handicapped, given an individualized educational program and appropriately placed.

There is, however, an exception to the regulations. If a state law or practice or court order is inconsistent with the requirements of P.L. 94–142 for children ages three through five and eighteen through twenty-one, the state does not have to follow the requirement [Sec. 612 (2) (B) and Sec. 121a.300]. There is also a special provision for states that either do not have a mandatory special education law or whose laws do not include all handicapped children covered by Part B. The wording of the act requires all states to make a free appropriate education available to all handicapped children (as defined in the act) ages six through seventeen even if the state does not have a mandatory law for children in this age range.

Coverage: LEAs, IEUs, Residential Facilities, and Private Schools. Congress applied the full-service goal—including the dates-certain and ages-certain provisions—to public elementary and secondary LEAs and IEUs [Secs. 612 (2) (A), 614(a) (1) (C) and (D)], certain private schools [Sec. 613 (a) (4) (A) and (B)], and publicly operated residential facilities for the handicapped that provide elementary or secondary education [Secs. 612 (1), 602 (9) and 602 (10)]. By providing for such extensive coverage, Congress obviously intended to prevent ''service gaps'' or ''cracks''; it attempted to reach all handicapped children without regard to the nature of the educational system by which they are, might, or should be served. As noted in Chapter 2, Congress was able to affect the LEAs, IEUs, and state residential facilities by requiring compliance with the requirements of P.L. 94–142 as a condition for receiving Part B funds and by applying Sec. 504 to them.

Congress distinguished between two types of private school placement. One type concerns those children not referred or placed in private schools by public agencies. Each state's Annual Program Plan contains policies and procedures to assure that, to the extent consistent with the number and location of handicapped children in the state who are in private elementary and secondary schools, the plan will provide for their participation in the state program by furnishing them special education and related services [Sec. 613 (a) (4) (A) and Secs. 121a.451].

To implement this policy, the LEA must grant handicapped children residing in the agency's jurisdiction and enrolled in private schools genuine opportunities to participate in special education and related services as their needs dictate [Sec. 121a.452]. To plan for the number of such children and the nature of their participation in the LEA program, the LEA must consult with persons knowledgeable about their needs [Sec. 121a.453]. Services that differ from those typically offered to public school children are to be provided only when dictated by the special needs of the private school children. These services must be comparable in quality with the public school programs [Sec. 121a.455]. Arrangements for providing services may be made through dual enrollment, educational radio and TV, or mobile educational services [Sec. 121a.454]. Public school personnel may be assigned outside public school facilities when necessary to meet the private school children's needs in the absence of comparable private school services. Administrative control over SEA or LEA services will remain with the agencies providing those services (the SEA or LEA).

The public agencies may not spend Part B money to pay salaries of private school employees unless they perform services outside their regular working hours, nor may the funds be used to construct private school facilities [Sec. 121a.456]. However, Part B funds may be used to buy equipment for use in private schools on a limited time basis, with the agencies maintaining administrative control over the equipment [Sec. 121a.457]. It is unlawful to put children in programs that segregate them by whether they are enrolled in public or private school or by their religion [Sec. 121a.458]. Part B funds may not benefit any private school [Sec. 121a.459]. Nor may Part B funds be used to finance the existing level of instruction in private schools [Sec. 121a.460].

There are additional requirements for children placed in private schools by public agencies. They must (1) be provided with special education and related services (2) in conformance with an individualized educational program (3) at no cost to their parents if the public agency refers them to such schools or facilities as a means of carrying out requirements of P.L. 94–142 [Sec. 613 (a) (4) (B) (i) and Sec. 121a.401]. Moreover, when the agency makes such a placement or referral, the State must previously have determined that the private school or facility meets the standards set by the State and that the child retains all of his rights under P.L. 94–142 [Sec. 613 (a) (4) (B) (ii) and Sec. 121a.401]. The SEA must monitor private schools' compliance with P.L. 94–142, make copies of its standards available to them, and give them opportunities to develop and revise those standards [Sec. 121a.402].

If a free appropriate public education is available to a child in a public agency but the parent chooses to place him in a private school, the agency is not required to pay for his education. The agency must, however, make services available to him if he attends the private schools, as described above. If the agency and the parents disagree about whether an appropriate program for the child is available or whether the agency is financially responsible for the private school fees, either may initiate a due process hearing [Sec. 121a.403]. Clearly, Congress intended for zero reject to apply to handicapped children placed in private schools by their parents or by school authorities. Congress keeps pressure on the public sector to remain responsible for them, thus attempting to answer its findings that, "because of the lack of adequate services within the public school system, families are often forced to find services outside the public school system, often at great distance from their residence and at their own expense" [Sec. 601 (b) (6)].

The reasons for applying the act to private schools are easy to understand. If an LEA places a child in a private school as its way of discharging its duties to him under P.L. 94–142, the child's rights to a free appropriate education should follow him to the private placement because he is a citizen of the State and entitled to benefit from P.L. 94–142 in the same manner as any other citizen of the state; the place of his education is irrelevant to his rights. Moreover, the LEA is not allowed to divest itself of its duties to the child by making a private-school placement when it cannot discharge those duties by educating him itself. Finally, because LEAs are not always able to provide an appropriate education to every handicapped child and enter into contracts with private schools to educate some of the children, the children in the private schools become the beneficiaries of the contract between the LEA and the private school. In that capacity, the children retain the rights they have with the LEA, and the LEA should not be able to deprive them of their rights by contract.

Child Census. Each SEA and LEA must conduct an annual program to identify, locate, and evaluate all handicapped children residing in their respective jurisdictions, regardless of the severity of their handicaps [Sec. 612 (2) (C) and 614 (a) (1) (A) and Sec. 121a.128, .220, and .750-.754]. Congress recognized that a zero-reject policy would be meaningless without a child-identification program. It also realized that identification of handicapped children was a necessary prerequisite to planning, programming, and appropriating for them to attend school. In light of past school practices that excluded the most severely handicapped children, it is significant that Congress specified that the programs must identify *all* children, *"regardless of the severity of their handicap"* (emphasis added). The requirement of a child census is consistent with Congress' findings that many handicapped children are totally excluded from schools and are denied "a successful educational experience because their handicaps are undetected" [Sec. 601 (b) (4) and (5)].

Service Priorities. Realizing that many excluded handicapped children are the most seriously handicapped and that they usually do not receive an appropriate education, Congress required recipients to use federal aid for two "service priorities" [Sec. 612 (3) and Sec. 121a.320-.324]. First in line are those handicapped children receiving no education ("first priority" children) and, next are the children with the most severe handicaps within each disability who are not receiving an adequate education ("second priority" children). The policy was designed to overcome the total exclusion of some children [Sec. 601 (b) (4)] and the inadequate education or the functional exclusion of others [Sec. 601 (b) (3) and (5)] as a method of implementing a zero-reject policy [Sec. 601 (c)]. Apparently Congress intended to make sure that funds would be distributed across the whole spectrum of handicapping conditions, and prevent them from being spent wholly on one class of severely impaired children (e.g., the seriously emotionally disturbed). There is a strong equal protection flavor in this approach. Sections 121a.320–121a.324 of the regulations interpret the statute with respect to implementing these priority requirements.

A number of questions have been raised concerning the scope and extent of the requirement for first-priority children. If a State is educating children aged three to eighteen, must all of the Part B funds be spent for the first-priority children in these age ranges before funds may be spent on second priority children? And are there any age priorities with respect to implementing the requirements? The regulations answer these questions by requiring Part B funds to be used to provide special education and related services to all first-priority children aged three to twenty-one to the extent that the state educates children in this age range. For example, if a state educates children aged four to seventeen, the funds must be spent to provide a free appropriate public education to all first-priority children in that age range, and may not be used for second-priority children until this requirement is met [Sec. 121a.323 and .324]. The regulations themselves do not set priorities as to the ages of the children. Thus, if a state's mandate is three to eighteen, the state may spend its funds to provide special education and related services to any first-priority child in that age range [Sec. 121a.321 and .323].

When may an LEA use its Part B funds for the second priority? The regulations make it clear that before Part B funds can be used for any other purpose, the LEA must provide the SEA with satisfactory assurances that all first-priority children have a free appropriate public education available to them; that there is a system for identifying, locating, and evaluating the handicapped children; and that whenever a first-priority child is identified, located, and evaluated, the LEA will make a free appropriate public education available to that child in accordance with an individualized education program [Sec. 121a.321 through .324]. If an SEA or LEA has met the first-priority requirement, as according to the ages set by state law, must it move directly to the second priority, or may it target Part B funds on first-priority children younger than the age range set by state law? Under the regulations, the agency has the option of spending its Part B funds on other unserved handicapped children (from birth to two years old) not covered in the age range set by state law, or meeting the second priority, or doing both. [Sec. 121a.323].

May an SEA use its portion of the Part B funds for inservice training if the training is related to the priorities? In accordance with the act and with Congressional intent, the first priority must be met before Part B funds could be used for any other purpose. Sec. 121a.322 provides that in the 1977–78 school year, Part B funds may not be spent on inservice training until all first-priority children are furnished an interim program of services. An individualized educational program must be developed for each of these children for full implementation no later than September 1, 1978. Part B money may be used for inservice training only after these requirements have been met [Sec. 121a.322].

After the 1977–78 school year, if there are known first-priority children in the state, the SEA must make sure that a free appropriate public education is available to them within the age ranges set by state law. Having met that priority, however, the state may spend its funds for direct services to second-priority children, inservice training to meet staff needs under either priority, or other services under either priority as authorized under Sec. 121a.360 (use of SEA funds for direct and support services).

What does "inadequate education" mean in the second priority (e.g., handicapped children within each disability, with the most severe handicaps, who are receiving an inadequate education)? The regulations do not define the term. The comments on Sec. 121a.320 explain that, after September 1, 1978, there should be no second-priority children because the SEA must, as a condition of receiving Part B funds for 1979, assure that *all* handicapped children will have a free appropriate public education by September 1, 1978. However, there will always be first-priority children discovered each year through the child census and evaluations.

Appropriate Education and Functional Exclusion. Congress answered the problem of functional exclusion by requiring SEAs and LEAs to provide an "appropriate" education to handicapped children [Secs. 601 (c) and 612 (1). It defines "appropriateness" in two ways.

First "appropriate" is defined in terms of the procedure the schools must use in dealing with handicapped children: the child must be furnished an individualized education program; he must be evaluated on a nondiscriminatory basis;

he is entitled to a due process hearing if the appropriateness of his education is in doubt; his parents are entitled to be included in the development of his individualized education program; he is entitled to appropriately and adequately trained teachers; he has the right of access to his school records; he is entitled to a barrier-free school environment; he may be included in preschool programs; and his representatives (parents or others) are entitled to participate in and be given notice of school actions affecting special education programs and his own education. Although separately provided for by P.L. 94–142, as a whole these requirements are intended to answer the problem of functional exclusion and to assure an appropriate education.

Second, Sec. 121a.4 defines "free appropriate education" to mean special education and related services that: (1) are provided at public expense, under public supervision and direction, and without charge; (2) meet the standards of the SEA, including the requirements of P.L. 94–142; (3) include preschool, elementary, or secondary school education in the state involved; and (4) are provided in conformity with the child's individualized educational program.

Chapter 5 will discuss the details of "appropriate" education. The point here is that P.L. 94–142 and Sec. 504 both attempt to prevent functional exclusion by requiring that the handicapped child be given an education appropriate to his conditions and needs.

Hiring the Handicapped. Congress pushed the zero-reject principle a step farther than the courts by requiring that a child's education be meaningful to him after he leaves school. SEAs and LEAs were charged with making positive efforts to hire and promote qualified handicapped persons in programs receiving Part B funds [Sec. 606 and Sec. 121a.150]. Thus, an SEA or LEA must take affirmative action on employment of the handicapped in P.L. 94–142 programs (like hiring a blind teacher to teach handicapped children or promoting an orthopedically impaired person to supervise special education programs funded under Part B).

All the education and training the schools provide is meaningless to students unless they have a realistic opportunity to make later use of it. Zero-reject in special education should not be an empty promise—equal protection should be meaningful to its intended beneficiaries. And, of course, economic benefits will accrue to the public if handicapped individuals are hired. The employment provisions in Sec. 606 dovetail with Sec. 503 and Sec. 504 of the Rehabilitation Act to prohibit discrimination in employment.

Single-agency Responsibility. Congress sought to make the zero-reject principle effective by providing for one, and *only one*, point of responsibility and accountability. It required a *single* state agency, the SEA, to be responsible for assuring HEW that the requirements of P.L. 94–142 are carried out. In addition, all educational programs for handicapped children within the state, including programs administered by *another* state or local agency (such as departments of social services, mental health, mental retardation, human resources, public health, corrections, or juvenile services), were placed under the *general* supervision of the persons responsible for educational programs for handicapped in the SEA, must be monitored by the SEA, and must meet the SEA's educational standards [Sec. 612 (6), and Sec. 121a.134 and .600–.602]. To buttress the single-agency device for zero reject. Congress enabled the SEA to preempt LEA programs [Sec. 614 (d)] and to require LEAs to consolidate their services [Sec. 614 (c)]. Sec. 121a.602 provides for a complaint procedure for local and state agencies. There is no doubt that these provisions were designed to close the service gaps and prevent the buck-passing and responsibility-shuffling that resulted in some handicapped children not being included in educational programs in the past.

Other zero-reject provisions. Some of the provisions dealing primarily with functional exclusion authorize grants for the elimination of architectural barriers [Sec. 607], incentive grants for early childhood programs [Secs. 619 and 624, and Sec. 121m.1–.10 and *Fed. Reg.*, Aug. 10, 1976, p. 33558], and ensure that student records will be available to parents [Sec. 615 (b) (1) (A) and Sec. 121a.560–.576]. Finally, Congress granted handicapped children the right to sue, in either federal or state courts, to enforce their rights under P.L. 94–142 after they had exhausted their administrative remedies under the procedural safeguards of Sec. 615 [Sec. 615 (e) (2) and Sec. 121a.511].

Sec. 504

Regulations implementing Sec. 504 make it clear that Sec. 504 applies to preschool, elementary, and secondary public education programs receiving *any* federal assistance [Sec. 84.31 and Subpart D, Regulations, *Fed. Reg.*, May 4, 1977, pp. 22676–94]. They also make it clear, especially in Sec. 84.33 (a), that a zero-reject policy is required by the schools. Sec. 84.32 requires the schools to undertake a child-identification program. Sec. 84.33 (b) requires them to provide an appropriate education to each handicapped person who is a legal resident of the recipient's jurisdiction, regardless of the nature or severity of the person's handicap. Sec. 84.33 (c) insures that the program will be without cost to the child's family.

As pointed out in Chapter 2, Sec. 504 and its implementing regulations differ in important respects from P.L. 94–142. There are other differences related to the principle of zero reject.

Sec. 504 applies to public schools not only as providers of educational services [Subpart D of the regulations] but also as providers of health, welfare, and social services [Subpart E], and as employers [Subpart B]. It applies to school facilities as well, requiring them to be accessible to the handicapped [Subpart C]; P.L. 94–142 authorizes grants of federal funds to SEAs and LEAs to enable them to comply with federal architectural barriers legislation [Sec. 607]. Under the

Sec. 504 regulations, all new school construction must be barrier free [Sec. 84.23], and all other programs must be made accessible within three years [Sec. 84.22].

Schools do not have to make each existing school accessible to handicapped students if programs "as a whole" are accessible. Schools can, instead, redesign equipment, reassign classes or other services to accessible buildings, and make aids available to students. Each building in a school district need not be completely accessible, but the district may not make only one facility or part of a facility accessible if the result is to segregate handicapped students. All nonstructural changes were to be completed within 60 days after the "504" regulations went into effect.

If a school district finds there is no possible way to make its education program accessible without structural changes, those changes must be made "as expeditiously as possible . . . and not later than three years" after June 1, 1977. Outside ramps, however, must be built immediately after June 1, 1977, since they can be constructed quickly and at relatively low cost.

The schools have six months to develop a transition plan outlining the necessary steps for making the structural changes. The plan is to be developed in consultation with "interested persons," including handicapped persons or organizations representing them, and a copy of the transition plan must be made available for public inspection. The plan must, at a minimum, identify physical obstacles, describe the methods to make facilities accessible, and set out the schedule for removing the obstacles. Schools must make available to citizens, including the hearing and visually impaired, information about the location of accessible services and facilities.

Subpart D also sets forth requirements for nondiscrimination in preschool, elementary, secondary, and adult education programs, including secondary vocational education programs. "Adult education" refers only to those educational programs and activities for adults operated by elementary and secondary schools. The provisions of Subpart D apply to both public and private state and local educational agencies that are federally assisted. Secs. 84.32 and 84.33 apply only to public programs; Sec. 84.39 applies only to private programs; and Secs. 84.35 and 84.36 apply to both public programs and to private programs that include special services for handicapped students.

The basic requirements of Sec. 504's regulations, which parallel the cases and P.L. 94–142, are that handicapped persons, regardless of the nature or severity of their handicap, must be furnished a free appropriate public education, and educational agencies must undertake to identify and locate all unserved handicapped children. These requirements are designed to insure that no handicapped child is excluded from school on the basis of a handicap. Thus, a funding recipient that operates a public school system must either educate handicapped children in its regular program or provide them with an appropriate alternative education at public expense.

HEW does not, except in extraordinary circumstances, review the result of individual placement or other educational decisions as long as the school district complies with the "process" requirements of Subpart D concerning identification and location, evaluation, and due process procedures. However, HEW places a high priority on investigating cases that involve exclusion of a child from the education system or patterns or practices of discriminatory placements or education.

Under Sec. 84.34(a), a school (or an SEA, LEA, or private school receiving federal aid) is responsible for providing a free appropriate public education to each qualified handicapped person in the recipient's jurisdiction. The word "in" means where the person is at present and where he resides, if that is a different place. If a school places a child in a program other than its own, it remains financially responsible for the child, whether or not the other program is operated by another recipient or educational agency. Moreover, a school may not place a child in a program that is inappropriate to him or that otherwise violates the requirements of Subpart D. And in no case may a school refuse to provide services to a handicapped child in its jurisdiction because of another person's or entity's failure to assume financial responsibility.

If a school does not itself provide handicapped persons with the necessary services, it must assume the cost of any alternate placement [Sec. 84.33(c)]. If, however, it offers adequate services and alternate placement is chosen by a student's parent or guardian, it need not assume the cost of the outside services. If the parent or guardian believes that his or her child cannot be suitably educated in the school's program, he may make use of the due process procedures to seek private placement at public expense.

A school's obligation extends beyond the provision of tuition payments when a child is placed outside the regular program. Schools must provide adequate transportation and pay for psychological services and those medical services necessary for diagnostic and evaluative purposes. If , because of his handicap, a student is placed in a program that requires him to be away from home, the payments must also cover room and board and nonmedical care (including custodial and supervisory care). If residential care is required not by the student's handicap but by factors such as the student's home conditions, the school need not pay the cost of room and board. A school's financial obligations need not be met solely through its own funds. It may rely on funds from any public or private source, including insurers and similar third parties.

P.L. 94–142 requires a free appropriate education to be provided to handicapped children no later than September 1, 1978, but Sec. 504 contains no provisions for enforcing a specific compliance date. To resolve this problem, Sec. 84.33 (d) requires recipients to achieve full compliance with the free appropriate public education requirements of Sec. 84.33 as early as possible, but no later than September 1, 1978. The provision also makes clear that, as of June 1, 1977, no school may exclude a qualified handicapped child from its educational program. This protection from exclusion is consistent with the "first priority" requirement of Sec. 612 (3) of P.L. 94–142, which places the highest priority on providing services to handicapped children who are not receiving an education.

Sec. 84.38 prohibits discrimination on the basis of handicap in preschool and adult education programs.

Sec. 84.39 sets forth the requirements that apply to recipients that operate private programs and activities. Private schools receiving HEW funds are subject to the evaluation and due process provisions of Subpart D only if they operate special education programs. Under Sec. 84.39 (b), they may charge more for providing services to handicapped students than to nonhandicapped students to the extent that additional charges can be justified by increased costs.

Sec. 84.39 (a) makes it clear that recipients of HEW funds operating private education programs and activities do not have to provide an appropriate education to handicapped students with special educational needs if they do not offer programs designed to meet those needs. A private school that has no program for mentally retarded persons does not have to admit such a person into its program nor must it arrange or pay for the person's education in another program. A private school that lacked a special program for blind students, however, would not be permitted to exclude, on the basis of blindness, a blind applicant who could participate in the regular program with minor adjustments in the way the program is offered.

Sec. 84.3(k) (2) defines a "qualified handicapped person," with respect to preschool, elementary, and secondary programs, in terms of age. It states that a person is qualified for those programs if (1) he is of an age during which nonhandicapped persons are provided services in those programs, (2) he is at an age during which state law requires educational services to be provided to handicapped persons, or (3) he is in the age ranges of handicapped children for whom an SEA or LEA must provide services under P.L. 94–142 (ages three through twenty-one, with exceptions). Under the "remedial action" provisions of Sec. 84.6 (a) (3), persons beyond the age limits prescribed in Sec. 84.3 (k) (2) may, in appropriate cases, be provided services that they were formerly denied because of a recipient's violation of Sec. 504.

In addition to the provisions of Subpart D, schools must also comply with the general provisions against discrimination, set forth in Subpart A. Sec. 84.4 (b) (1) (c) of that Subpart prohibits the exclusion of qualified handicapped persons from aids, benefits, or services. Paragraph (ii) requires that equal opportunity to participate or benefit be provided. Paragraph (iii) requires that services provided to handicapped persons be as effective as those provided to the nonhandicapped. In paragraph (iv), different or separate services are prohibited except when necessary to provide equally effective benefits.

The term "equally effective," defined in paragraph (b) (2), is intended to encompass the concept of equivalent, as opposed to identical, services. It acknowledges the fact that, in order to meet the individual needs of handicapped persons to the same extent that the corresponding needs of nonhandicapped persons are met, adjustments to regular programs or the provision of different programs may sometimes be necessary. This requirement parallels the one established under Title IV of Civil Rights Act of 1964 with respect to the provision of educational services to students whose primary language is not English. (See *Lau* v. *Nichols*, discussed earlier in this chapter.) To be equally effective, however, an aid, benefit, or service need not produce equal results; it merely must afford an equal opportunity to achieve equal results. As Chapter 5 will explain, the requirements of Sec. 84.4 (b) (2), coupled with those of Sec. 84.33, should help define "appropriate education."

HEW emphasizes that although separate services must be required in some instances the provision of unnecessarily separate or different services is discriminatory. The addition of the phrase "in the most integrated setting appropriate to the person's needs" to paragraph (b) (2), is intended to reinforce this general concept. Paragraph (b) (3) of Sec. 84.4 requires schools to give qualified handicapped persons the option of participating in regular programs despite the existence of permissibly separate or different programs. The requirement has been reiterated in Sec. 84.37 in connection with physical education and athletics programs.

Sec. 84.37 (c) prohibits discrimination in physical education courses, athletics, and similar programs and requires a school to offer qualified handicapped students an equal opportunity to participate in those activities. It permits a school to offer separate programs to handicapped students only if separation or differentiation is consistent with the "mainstream" requirements of Sec. 84.34 and only if no qualified handicapped student is denied an opportunity to compete for teams or to participate in courses that are not separate. One case, brought under Sec. 504—not under Subpart D ("public school" regulations), but under comparable Subpart E ("post secondary" regulations)—held that Sec. 504 had been violated when a student who was blind in one eye was denied the opportunity to compete for a university's basketball team because of his blindness. In another case, a student who was totally deaf in one ear and partially deaf in the other was denied the opportunity to compete in contact sports because of his deafness. The court did not rule a violation, but the case was not brought under Sec. 504. In light of conflicting medical testimony as to whether the student would be put in jeopardy by playing contact sports and whether other participants might be endangered by him, the court held that it was not arbitrary for the school to exclude him (the "rational basis" test of the "traditional" equal protection analysis seems to be at work here). On the basis of these two cases, it is not clear what "qualified" means, or could mean, in the regulations.

Sec. 84.4 (b) (1) (v) prohibits a school from supporting another entity or person that subjects program participants or employees to discrimination on the basis of their handicaps. For example, this section prohibits financial support from a school to a community recreational group or to a professional or social organization that discriminates against handicapped persons. Among the criteria to be considered in each case are the substantiality of the relationship between the school and the other entity (including financial support from the school), and whether the other entity's activities relate so closely to the school's program or activity that they fairly should be considered activities of the school itself.

Several advocates for the handicapped had urged HEW to incorporate a provision granting the handicapped a private right of action against schools under Sec. 504. The Department declined, arguing that to confer such a right was beyond the authority of the executive branch of government. There is, however, case law holding that such a right exists, *Hairston* v. *Drostick*.[47] In that case, a person with spina bifida who was of normal intelligence and otherwise qualified to enter first grade was denied admission, sued under Sec. 504, and was successful. The federal district ordered the plaintiff to be admitted and found that her admission should be into the regular program and that she had been denied due process in her exclusion.

In *Mattie T.* v. *Holladay*,[48] handicapped students are relying on Sec. 504 and P.L. 94–142, alleging that their rights under those statutes have been violated on several grounds: (1) total exclusion of some handicapped children from any educational program and no child identification; (2) functional exclusion of handicapped children in both regular and special programs; (3) discriminatory classification procedures; (4) placement in other than the least restrictive or most "normal" school programs; and (5) noncompliance with procedural safeguards in identification, evaluation, and placement matters. The case has not yet been decided on its merits.

Sec. 84.10 (a) states that compliance with the regulation is not excused by state or local laws limiting the eligibility of qualified handicapped persons to receive services or to practice an occupation. The provision applies only with respect to state or local laws that unjustifiably differentiate on the basis of handicap. Paragraph (b) provides that the presence of limited employment opportunities in a particular profession does not excuse a recipient from complying with the regulation. Thus, a law school could not deny admission to a blind applicant because blind lawyers might find it more difficult to find a job than a nonhandicapped person.

In *Davis* v. *Southeastern Community College*,[49] however, a federal court found that a severely hearing impaired person does not have abilities adequate to the needs of patients and that she was not discriminated against when she was denied admission to a community college "Associate in Nursing" program. A contrary result was reached in *Gurmankin* v. *Costanzo*,[50] in which the Philadelphia school district was held to have violated the equal protection rights of a blind teacher by refusing to consider her application to teach sighted students. Although the case was brought on both equal protection and Sec. 504 grounds, the court did not decide it on the basis of Sec. 504 because the school district's discrimination predated the effective date of Sec. 504. It did say that the district's practice was the type of discrimination that Sec. 504 was meant to prohibit.

In a related case, *Kampmeier* v. *Nyquist*,[51] students who were wholly or partially blind in only one eye were denied the right to participate in school contact sports. When their motion for a preliminary injunction (to forbid the schools from excluding them) was denied by a United States District Court, they appealed and alleged a violation of Sec. 504. In ruling on the narrow issue—whether to reverse the District Court and order the temporary injunction to be issued—the Court of Appeals said that the plaintiffs had not satisfied the criteria by which the Court must judge whether to reverse the district court. They had not made a sufficient factual showing of likely success in a trial on the merits, and they had not shown that they would be denied irreparable harm by not being able to participate in contact sports, since there were a host of non-contact sports available to them.

In addressing the issue of the burden of proof in the context of a preliminary injunction, the Court of Appeals construed Sec. 504 as *not* prohibiting exclusion of a handicapped child from a school activity (in this case, contact sports, not an appropriate educational program) when there is substantial justification for the school's policy. Sec. 504, the court said, only prohibits the exclusion of otherwise qualified persons. Here, the plaintiffs presented little evidence, medical, statistical, or otherwise, to cast doubt on the defendants' evidence that students with sight in only one eye are not qualified to play contact sports because of the high risk of injury to their sighted eye. As in *Taylor* v. *Maryland School for the Blind*, the court was reluctant to overturn educators' decisions in the absence of proof the school had inadequate grounds on which to act.

In yet another "504" case tried before a state court, *Columbo* v. *Sewanhaka Central High School District No. 2*,[52] a similar result was reached, also based on conflicting views on the danger a hearing-impaired student represented to himself and others as a participant in contact sports, and also involving the court's reluctance to overturn an administrative determination made on a rational basis.

STATE LEGISLATION

The case law on the right to an education is not based solely upon federal constitutional or statutory grounds. Nearly all state constitutions provide for educating the children in the state. Many states have enacted statutes guaranteeing education to all children or to all exceptional children. In applying these provisions to a claim that handicapped children have been illegally excluded from education, the courts generally have interpreted these provisions as guaranteeing education to *all* handicapped children.

Compulsory attendance laws are another reflection of the state's desire to provide education to all children. After noting that failure to comply with the District of Columbia compulsory attendance law constitutes a criminal offense, the Court in *Mills* said: ''The Court need not belabor the fact that requiring parents to see that their children attend school under pain of criminal penalties presupposes that an educational opportunity will be made available to the children.''

Many of the recently enacted statutes guaranteeing education to all children or to all handicapped children seem to respond to litigation brought against the state or a school district within the state. Legislation enacted in Michigan in 1971 rendered moot the complaint in *Harrison* v. *State of Michigan*.[53] The court stayed the proceedings in *Panitch* v. *Wisconsin*[54] while awaiting implementation of recent legislation. And the federal court abstained in *Florida Association for Retarded Children* v. *State Board of Education*,[55] pending a determination by a state court as to whether remedies were available to the plaintiffs under new state law.

State legislation requiring inclusion of all exceptional children in education could have a more positive effect than court-ordered inclusion, but implementation of state legislation has been slow and irregular. For example, suit was brought in Tennessee to force initiation of the programs called for by legislation enacted in 1972, and other states also seem to be lagging well behind their intended implementation deadlines. (See Chapter 9 on court-ordered implementation and associated problems of mootness and abstention.)

IMPLICATIONS FOR PUBLIC SCHOOLS

The implications of zero-reject policies and requirements for public schools are pervasive. As mentioned earlier, Congress has found that more than half of the eight million handicapped children in the United States have not received an appropriate education—an education designed to help them capitalize on their strengths, minimize their weaknesses, and reach their maximum capacities. Congress has also determined that there are one million handicapped children totally excluded from free public education. There are, as well, another 125,000 mentally retarded, emotionally disturbed, and physically handicapped children who reside in state institutions. Typically, the educational programs for students in state institutions have been inferior to those in public schools and in many cases have been nonexistent. The mandate to include all children in public schools and to provide an appropriate education for them represents a new responsibility for public school systems.

The major implications for each of the legislative requirements previously discussed in this chapter will be analyzed in this section. These eight requirements include: (1) full-service goals; (2) free appropriate public education; (3) coverage; (4) child census; (5) service priorities; (6) appropriate education and functional exclusion; (7) hiring the handicapped; (8) single-agency responsibility; (9) elimination of architectual barriers; and (10) right to sue.

Full-Service Goals

The requirement of full-service goals exists for the purpose of planning only. SEAs and LEAs must write plans that include all handicapped children (birth through twenty-one), but they have the freedom to specify their own timelines. The full-service goals serve as a vehicle for enabling the public agencies to specify long-term goals. Congress and HEW realize that the SEAs and LEAs may never achieve these goals, and thus planning need not be constrained by financial realities, personnel shortages, staff development needs, or other such factors. On the basis of these goals, the public agencies must develop the specific plan discussed in the next section.

Free Appropriate Public Education: Deadlines and Exceptions

LEAs are required to provide a free appropriate public education to all handicapped children between the ages of three and eighteen by no later than September 1, 1978 and to all handicapped children between the ages of three and twenty-one by no later than September 1, 1980. As stated previously in this chapter, the exception to this requirement is that it does not have to be followed in regard to the age groups three through five and eighteen through twenty-one if a state law or practice or a court order is inconsistent with the requirement pertaining to these specified age groups. In order to implement these dates-certain and ages-certain regulations, it is necessary for LEAs to develop plans including information such as: child census procedures (discussed later in the chapter), the *projected* number of students who are totally or functionally excluded, the types of projected educational alternatives (regular class, special class, or home-bound instruction) needed by these students, the type of classification procedures that will be used to evaluate the students, the range of related services (e.g. physical or occupational therapy) needed, the instructional materials that should be available (e.g., auditory trainers, braille materials, or typewriters), the areas of expertise to be covered by personnel, transportation considerations, and financial requirements and sources. This plan should be developed in accordance with the service priorities: handicapped children who are receiving no education are to be provided for first, and then the most severely handicapped children within each disability category who are not receiving an adequate education. Further, the plan must comply with the other five principles of P.L 94–142 and Sec. 504: (1) classification, (2) individualized educational programs, (3) placement in the least restrictive alternative, (4) due process, and (5) parent participation.

In developing the plan, LEAs may appoint a task force comprised of administrators, teachers, psychologists, school board members, state department consultants, consumers, and representatives of potential funding sources, such as county commissioners. When an opportunity to be involved in educational planning is extended to a broad group of people, support for implementing the plan is more likely to be generated.

Careful consideration should be given to providing educational services to handicapped children aged three through five and eighteen through twenty-one, even in instances where state law, practice, or court orders do not specifically require that an LEA do so. Clear evidence exists that early educational programming aimed at stimulating the development of young handicapped children can substantially contribute to increasing their learning potential and can reduce the number of children requiring long-term intervention. If public agencies provided intensive early intervention programs, they could reduce the number of children needing special education services throughout their school career. The problems of many handicapped students can not be ameliorated in full by early intervention, but they can be reduced in complexity. Thus, early intervention programs can have strong pay-offs for handicapped children, their families, and educational service providers. Incentive grants are provided to LEAs to serve the three through five age group (see Chapter 10).

In deciding whether to provide educational services to handicapped students in the age range of eighteen through twenty-one, agencies should consider vocational education programs. Research has indicated that even the most severely handicapped individuals can successfully perform job tasks associated with modern industry.[56] If a goal of education is to prepare persons to function in society to the fullest extent possible, preparation for a vocation and for the demands of everyday adult living cannot be overemphasized. School systems that provide thorough vocational training will help insure that handicapped individuals become tax-paying citizens as adults. The age range of eighteen through twenty-one is a critical transition period between adolescence and adulthood. School systems that invest extra money and resources into training during that period may realize a substantial payoff in the productivity of their handicapped graduates. The agencies should also take into account the fact that the Vocational Education Act of 1968 stipulated that a minimum of 10 percent of the Basic State Grant Programs be earmarked for the vocational training of handicapped individuals in each state.

Coverage: LEAs, IEUs, Residential Facilities, and Private Schools

Undoubtedly the private-school coverage will have a significant impact on both public and private programs. Because the costs of private placement probably will exceed the costs of public programs, the LEA may bargain-hunt for inexpensive private facilities, disregarding the quality of the programs. It may well come under great pressure to create its own programs in order to avoid the higher costs of private placement; this in turn will have implications for the financing, staffing, and administration of LEA programs. An LEA that is willing to pay private school costs to absolve itself of educating handicapped children in its own programs can do so if the parents do not object to private school placements; the "way out" is available, albeit expensive. And it is possible that parents will not object to private school placements, which are often less stigmatizing to their child than public school placements and may provide a more appropriate education.

Predictably, public control over private programs will increase. If private programs resist these controls, they may elect not to accept children for placement, which will generate even more pressure on the LEA to develop its own programs. The regulation requiring the LEA to pay the room, board, and educational costs of children placed in residential facilities will also increase the pressure on the LEA to develop its own programs or to enter into local cooperative agreements with nearby LEAs. The pressure may force SEAs to consider using the funds they receive under P.L. 94–142 (and do not pass on to LEAs) for the purpose of reducing some of those expenses. If a state has made separate appropriations to state residential facilities or the state department that operates them, those appropriations may be used to reduce the LEA's or SEA's liability for inpatient costs. If a state is not now making such appropriations, there will be pressure for it to do so, lest the drain on the public education dollar become unbearable. The private-school provisions may also discourage LEAs from placing children in such schools and encourage them to make placements in state institutions, which could run counter to deinstitutionalization efforts and create competition by institutions for "education" dollars.

Child Census

In order to receive federal aid for implementing zero reject, each SEA is required to report the following information to the Commissioner of Education [Sec. 121a.251]:

1. the number of handicapped children who receive special education and related services on October 1 and February 1 of the school year, and the average number for those two dates;
2. the number of the handicapped children who fall into each disability category as defined by the statutes; and
3. the number of handicapped children within each of the following age groups: three through five , six through seventeen, and eighteen through twenty-one.

Only children who receive special education services in a program operated or supported by a public agency may be included in the report. Children receiving special education funded in total by the federal government may not be counted unless they are in the age range of three through five and eighteen through twenty-one [Sec. 121a.753].

SEAs are responsible for devising procedures for LEAs and other educational institutions in counting handicapped children. In addition to establishing the procedure, the SEA must set timelines for the information to be reported by the LEAs, obtain certification of data accuracy, and compile the data from all LEAs into the state report [Sec. 121a.754]. Thus, the methods that LEAs should follow in identifying, locating, and evaluating all handicapped children needing special education services who reside in their respective jurisdictions are set up by the SEA. Appendix C includes an overview of the child-census model established in Idaho.

One problem of interpretation concerns what constitutes the jurisdiction of a LEA when implementing the requirement of counting all the handicapped children residing *in* the jurisdiction. Sec. 504 defines the meaning of "in" as related to jurisdiction as both domicile and actual residence. Domicile is typically interpreted as the place where the child is living. Actual residence, however, could be the parents' place of domicile, since that is the place the child will return to if his domicile is different from his parents'. This issue has become troublesome in areas where there are large group homes and nursing homes for the purpose of returning severely handicapped children to the community. These children may have one county as their domicile and another county as their actual residence. The situation may be even more complicated if the child's parents have moved several times during the period of institutionalization and are living in another state when the child is deinstitutionalized into a group home. Which LEA has responsibility for educating the child? When a significant number of severely handicapped children whose parents live elsewhere are deinstitutionalized to the same county, the financial implications for the LEA can be tremendous. This problem warrants careful analysis in determining a fair solution, which can probably best be achieved at the state level.

Service Priorities

According to P.L. 94–142, the priority groups to be served include: 1) handicapped children who are receiving no education, and 2) the most severely handicapped children within each disability who are receiving an inadequate education. Since the majority of children who are receiving no free public education fall into the severely and profoundly handicapped classifications (those residing in state institutions and home-bound situations, or who require twenty-four-hour nursing care), both priorities largely address the same target population—the severely handicapped within each disability area. Severely handicapped children typically have multiple impairments and require intensive, systematic programming in order to make continuous educational progress. In general, public schools are just beginning to address the issues of implementing programs for this population.

In responding to the service-priorities requirements, many LEAs will have to redefine the purpose of education and, hence, curriculum goals. Many severely handicapped children will never learn the traditional content of elementary and secondary school programs. The major curriculum goals for them may be in the areas of self-care, language, motor, social and vocational skills. In the past, a child who was not toilet trained was often excluded from school; now a major goal specified on the individualized education program (IEP) could include teaching the child to use the toilet (see Chapter 5).

Appropriate education requires responsiveness to the individual needs of the child. Since the curriculum for classes for the severely handicapped is radically different from that of the regular program, LEAs should consider orienting their total school faculty to the needs of severely handicapped students. This orientation would lay the foundation for faculty members to develop a positive attitude toward the inclusion of severely handicapped students in public educational facilities. Although the vast majority of severely handicapped children must be served in separated special classes, the least restrictive approach may be to locate their special classes in an elementary or secondary school attended by nonhandicapped students instead of placing them in a special school or residential institution. The attitudes of faculty members within the school are very important, especially in view of the fact that many nonhandicapped students are likely to model the attitudes and behaviors of faculty members.

At the initial faculty orientation meeting, teachers can be made aware of techniques they might use in helping nonhandicapped students develop respect for their severely handicapped peers. The majority of nonhandicapped students have probably never known or even seen a severely handicapped person. They have natural curiosities about why people are different, and are sometimes frightened or put off by the differences. In order to develop a positive social climate, open and honest communication is essential. As an outgrowth of becoming aware of the needs of the severely handicapped, nonhandicapped students might serve as tutors or advocates for the severely handicapped students. Another possibility would be for nonhandicapped students to make instructional materials for the severely handicapped, such as form boards, lacing cards, tapes of songs, and language scrapbooks.

Since severely handicapped children usually have multiple disabilities, specialists are required to plan and implement the IEPs for these students. Although there is a substantial increase in the number of college and university special education programs offering training and certification in the area of the severely handicapped, LEAs outside metropolitan areas are apt to have difficulty locating certified teachers. To be successful with severely handicapped children, teachers must be highly skilled at breaking tasks down into discrete and sequential steps, arranging a learning environment that reinforces the student for successive gains, collecting progress data to serve as an indicator of whether the teaching strategies are effective, and consulting with parents and specialists.

Professionals in special education, who are often needed to provide an appropriate education to severely handicapped students, may be trained in the area of speech, audiology, physical therapy, occupational therapy, nursing, psychology, medicine, social work, or vocational rehabilitation. The implication of this for the LEA is that problems can exist not only in paying for the services, but also in locating them even when the money has been allocated. A required component of the IEP is the specification of services that the *child* needs; not the services that are readily available in the LEA. When services are specified, the LEA, according to P.L. 94–142, is obligated to provided them.

Appropriate Education and Functional Exclusion

In order to prevent functional exclusion, schools must provide an appropriate education to handicapped students. This requirement is satisfied by the effective implementation of principles related to nondiscriminatory assessment (Chapter 4), individualized education program (Chapter 5), placement in the least restrictive alternative (Chapter 6), entitlement to due process (Chapter 7), and parent participation (Chapter 8). The implications of these principles is discussed in those chapters.

One issue that is not specifically addressed by the legislation is whether a handicapped student can be suspended from school, and if so, what limitations are placed on this type of exclusionary practice. Many systems have absolved themselves of responsibility for handicapped students, particularly seriously emotionally disturbed students, by suspending them from school for extended or indefinite periods. In *Mills*, the District of Columbia was ordered not to make any suspensions for longer than two days unless the child is furnished with a hearing prior to the suspension and his educational program is continued while he is suspended. Since P.L. 94–142 and Sec. 504 do not provide specific guidelines in regard to suspensions, LEAs should consider adopting the policy set forth by *Mills* as a way of insuring the implementation of zero reject. Case law and the federal statutes— P.L. 94–142, providing for education for handicapped persons ages eighteen through twenty-one, and Sec. 504's regulations on compensatory education [Secs. 84.33-84.38]—can be used as grounds on which the children might claim compensatory education to "make up" time lost during suspensions or expulsions.

Hiring the Handicapped

It has been predicted that one million young handicapped persons will be underemployed—they will not have jobs that require them to exercise their highest level of skills. This means that two out of every five handicapped persons will be underemployed.[57] Society does not extend the same vocational opportunities and rights to the handicapped person as it does to the nonhandicapped, even when the handicapped person's disability does not impede him from performing competently. To remedy this situation, Congress required SEAs and LEAs to advance the employment opportunities for the handicapped in P.L. 94–142 programs.

Consideration is to be given to hiring teachers who are handicapped and who have received appropriate certification. Sec. 504 requires colleges and universities receiving federal money to adapt some of their standard procedures, if necessary, to train persons with various handicaps. Other job possibilities besides teaching might be found in providing related services, like a speech clinician who has a physical handicap or a handicapped bus driver for a program. A handicapped person can also make a significant contribution by providing inservice training. If the topic of an inservice session is adapting physical education for the physically handicapped, an adult with a physical handicap who frequently participates in sports such as basketball, softball, tennis, swimming, bowling, or track and field events is undoubtedly an expert on the subject. He or she has a wealth of relevant functional information to share with educators. In addition to helping educators with instructional strategies and curriculum adaptation, the handicapped adult could significantly influence the attitudes of the inservice participants by minimizing their perceptions of the "differences" between handicapped and nonhandicapped persons. Having the "status" of inservice trainer also helps the handicapped person change the stereotypes of educators. Status positions tend to highlight abilities rather than disabilities. Thus, a potentially rich and meaningful source of inservice training can be tapped by hiring the handicapped as consultants.

The public agencies should not restrict employment opportunities for the handicapped to programs funded by P.L. 94–142. Qualified handicapped persons should also be considered for jobs primarily involved with the nonhandicapped segment of the school population. The handicapped person's abilities and competencies should be the basis for evaluating his potential for job success. Being physically handicapped and confined to a wheelchair did not keep Franklin Roosevelt from skillfully executing the duties of president of the United States.

Single-Agency Responsibility

Congress requires that a single state agency, the SEA, assume overall responsibility for assuring that P.L. 94–142 is carried out. Single-agency responsibility means that the SEA must supervise and monitor the educational programs that in the past have fallen under the responsibility of other state and local agencies, such as mental health, human resources, corrections, and social services. The bureaucratic confusion that has followed the single-agency provision may do more harm to the principle of zero reject than any other requirement of the act. Most children in correction or youth/juvenile–service facilities can be diagnosed as seriously emotionally disturbed, learning disabled, or otherwise handicapped, and therefore entitled to benefits of the act. But corrections and youth/juvenile–service agencies are unaccustomed to operating like public schools: there is relatively little due process; the "school" programs are scant in comparison with school programs for noninstitutionalized handicapped programs; other penal programs like work-release, institutional labor, vocational training, and disciplinary corrections preclude a substantial amount of special education from being offered. There are, as well, shortages of staff, classrooms, and other facilities, which are often different in degree and kind from the resources of the LEAs. The paramilitary structure of the institutions may effectively exclude the kind of parent participation that the act requires. To a lesser extent these same problems exist in human resources and social service agencies operating residential facilities for handicapped children.

The requirement to place a child in the least restrictive setting flies in the face of any institutionalization except in extreme cases. Least restrictive placement is, however, only a means for helping determine what is an appropriate placement, and it may have little or no meaning to institutionalized children unless "school release" programs can be arranged with the nearest LEA (in which event, there would be a problem in determining which agency must pay for the child's education), "less restrictive" programs can be created within the institution itself, or the children actually are deinstitutionalized to community settings and attend public schools.

The duty of the SEA to supervise special education and related services furnished by other state agencies to handicapped children makes it necessary that the SEA's standards for programs and personnel be imposed on the other agencies. This could cause substantial disruption to state or local personnel qualifications, among other things. Must employees serving as educators at a state center for the mentally ill meet the same standards (including, where applicable, certification) as LEA employees? If so, are they entitled to the same terms and conditions of employment (including wages, tenure, union representation, pay steps, and leave)?

It is routine, and sometimes required by Title XX of the Social Security Act Amendments, for human resource, mental health, and public health agencies to charge for their services. But P.L. 94–142 and Sec. 504 entitle a handicapped child to a free public education. Undoubtedly, the human resource agencies will have to itemize their "education" costs and distinguish them from "noneducation'' costs. Both human resource agencies and the SEAs will be on guard to insure that only the pure ''education costs'' are allowed as charges against the public instead of the client. This may not be easy. Is a ''cottage parent'' an educator, in the sense of carrying out an institutionalized child's treatment plan or individualized program? When does ''education'' end and ''training'' or ''custodial care'' begin in an institution that serves a child twenty-four hours a day? It is clear that the SEA or LEA must pay for all costs of institutional care, including medical services performed for diagnostic or evaluation purposes. (Medical services are defined as services performed by a licensed physician to determine a child's needs for special education and related services [Sec. 121 a.4]). The SEA or LEA need not pay for medical services performed for other purposes. The problem of what constitutes an allowable educational expense in institutional settings remains, however, unanswered by the act and its regulations.

Finally, the SEA and LEA may want to develop their own services instead of purchasing them from existing mental health or public health agencies. By the same token, mental health agencies may want to develop their special education and related services instead of purchasing them from existing school-based services. The problems of agency competition and the resulting dilution of limited financial and personnel resources are not fully answered by the single-agency requirement. It speaks directly only to standards and supervision over programs, not to interagency relationships.

Elimination of Architectural Barriers

Both P.L. 94–142 and Sec. 504 require the elimination of architectual barriers. LEAs do not have to make each existing school accessible to the handicapped if programs ''as a whole'' are accessible. Schools can instead redesign equipment, reassign classes or other services to accessible buildings, and make aids available to students. Although each building in a school district need not be completely accessible, the district may not make only one facility or part of a facility accessible if the result is to segregate handicapped students. All nonstructural changes must have been completed within sixty days after the regulations went into effect.

If a school district finds there is no possible way to make its education program accessible other than by structural changes, those changes must be made ''as expeditiously as possible . . . and not later than three years'' after June 1, 1977. Outside ramps, however, must have been built immediately after June 1, 1977, since they can be constructed quickly and at relatively low cost.

Six months after the regulations went into effect, schools should have developed a transition plan outlining the steps necessary to make the structural changes. The plan was to be developed in consultation with ''interested persons,'' including handicapped persons or organizations representing them, and a copy of the transition plan was to be made available for public inspection. The plan must, at minimum, identify physical obstacles, describe the methods to make facilities accessible, and set out the schedule for taking the necessary steps to remove obstacles.

Schools must make information available to all citizens, including the hearing and visually impaired, about the location of accessible services and facilities. To obtain information on state and regional services, LEAs can contact the consultants for the education of handicapped children in the SEA.

Right to Sue

P.L. 94–142 granted to handicapped children the right to sue in federal or state courts to enforce their claim to a free appropriate public education. Sec. 504 does not grant this right, although the courts have permitted such suits. Usually litigation should be considered only after administrative remedies have been exhausted. A punitive case decision may not be the best motivation for LEA officials, but it is important to know that legal action is a possibility if a handicapped child is totally or functionally excluded from schools. To prevent involvement in legal suits, LEA officials are encouraged to implement the legislative regulations according to a systematic plan. They are to provide written documentation and justification of all major decisions, involve consumers in decision making, and establish careful monitoring procedures for providing data on problems in their initial stages so that immediate intervention can prevent them from reaching crisis proportions.

P.L. 94–142 and Sec. 504 essentially require educators to do what they should have been doing all along: provide an appropriate education to public school children, handicapped as well as nonhandicapped. Legal action can most easily be prevented by the acceptance of the challenge of educational responsibility and accountability by all concerned.

IMPLICATIONS FOR HIGHER EDUCATION

With the number of handicapped children to be served expanding under the zero-reject principle, the number of personnel to serve those children must increase in proportion. Maintaining a reasonable balance between supply and demand will require substantial changes in college and university training programs. The successful implementation of the concept of zero reject will rely, in part, on the responsibilities assumed by institutions of higher education. Some of the major implications include: (1) coordinated planning among colleges, universities, and SEAs; (2) an increased supply of personnel for the handicapped; (3) reexamination of certification requirements; and (4) continued research.

Coordinated Planning Among Colleges, Universities, and SEAs

The SEA is required to submit an inservice training and personnel development plan to HEW [Sec. 121 a.380]. It must conduct a needs assement for staff development training and then devise a plan to meet the assessed needs. The plan should include the type of training to be offered, incentives planned to insure participation, the target group for the training, the estimated number of trainees, the funding sources, the cost of training, the time-frame, and methods for evaluating program objectives [Sec. 121a.382]. The regulations state that the SEA *may* enter into contracts with institutions of higher education or other agencies for conducting training programs, developing or modifying instructional materials, and disseminating the results of research and demonstration projects.

The SEA must insure that all public and private institutions of higher education interested in the education of handicapped students have an opportunity to fully participate in the development, review, and updating of the personnel development system [Sec. 121a.381]. Coordinated planning leads to the phase of coordinated implementation: the SEA might work with colleges and universities to conduct a statewide assessment of training needs. This data could have rich implications for colleges and university preservice programs, as well as their inservice program development. Colleges, universities, and the SEA might also develop a cooperative plan of delivering inservice training. Considering the geographical distribution of colleges and universities within a state and the distribution of state and regional staff development centers, target areas for inservice training might be "regionalized" so that a given staff development center, college, or university assumes responsibility for training in their particular locale. This would cut down tremendously on the transportation costs and logistical problems of one agency or institution criss-crossing a state to deliver training. Collaboration can also promote shared resources and training materials. If the energies and efforts of a wide range of trainers can be capitalized on and their expertise shared, the quality of the training programs is likely to be enhanced. There is a saying to the effect that "all of us is smarter than one of us." The saying certainly applies to the idea of coordinating services of colleges, universities, and the SEAs.

On the basis of the needs assessment data, coordination can be focused on the type of training programs needed to supply appropriately trained teachers for implementing zero-reject regulations. A state may find, for example, that there is an oversupply of persons being trained to teach mentally retarded children and an undersupply of teachers qualified to teach blind students. Coordinated planning would insure that program development in colleges and universities minimized redundancies and filled in categorical gaps.

If some remote or rural areas of the state are having a particularly difficult time recruiting qualified teachers for their handicapped population, the SEA might provide incentive grants to local colleges and universities to provide inservice training for regular education faculty from the area who wish to change their certification to special education. Special education students might be provided tuition waivers or scholarships during their preservice training if they agree to teach in a remote or rural area of the state for a specified number of years after graduation.

Providing an Increased Supply of Personnel for the Handicapped

To provide appropriate educational services for some one million handicapped students excluded from schools, thousands of additional personnel will be needed. Even more personnel will be needed to serve students who have been inadequately served in the past. Programs in colleges and universities in the areas of special education, regular education, school psychology, counseling, educational administration, speech therapy, physical therapy, and occupational therapy must be responsive to this need and appropriately train an adequate number of students.

Many special education departments in colleges and universities have initiated resource consultant training programs. One of the major thrusts of the programs is teaching individuals how to deliver inservice training to teachers in the field. They are models for training trainers. Considering the tremendous personnel development needs that exist, the resource consultant model may well prove to be cost and time efficient.

Reexamination of Certification Requirements

Implementing the principle of zero reject (and least restrictive placement) will probably result in a reexamination of certification requirements. Since handicapped children representing a wide variety of handicaps and broader degrees of disability are to be educated in the public schools, personnel will need a broader array of skills. Most public schools cannot afford specialists in every categorical area. Serving children in the least restrictive setting will also mean that regular teachers will have to deal with a variety of handicaps in one class. It is unrealistic to expect the regular teacher to work with a different specialist for each categorical condition; the time spent in teacher conferences alone would be overwhelming.

Another issue that could force reexamination of certification requirements is the fact that many handicapped children previously excluded from school are multihandicapped. Providing appropriate education for a deaf-blind child requires a person with the combined skills of an educator of the deaf and a teacher of the blind. There is already a trend to reduce the number of different certificates in special education. Reynolds[58] has reported on the DELPHI survey which was conducted as part of the Professional Standards and Guidelines Project of the Council for Exceptional Children. The survey indicated that leading professionals in the field of special education predicted that the types of special education certificates would decrease from seven or eight to approximately four. The implementation of the zero-reject regulations will probably increase the pace of declining certificate categorizations and result in educators being trained to meet the needs of a wider variety of handicapped children.

Research

There is a dire need for more research on the implementation of zero-reject requirements and their effects on educational programming for severely handicapped students, child-census procedures, administrative arrangements related to single-agency responsibility, social integration of handicapped and nonhandicapped individuals, and inservice training models. Those who work closely with public school personnel in identifying researchable questions and carrying out research projects can make a significant contribution to the effective implementation of P.L. 94–142 and Sec. 504. Since the concept of zero reject is so new and implementation is in its infancy, research data gathered by faculty members could provide a rational basis for future policy decisions on implementing the legislation. It is hoped that college and university faculty will assume the responsibilities of data collection, data analysis, and policy recommendations.

IMPLICATIONS FOR CONSUMERS

It was through the efforts of consumers—largely the parents of mentally retarded children—that the first litigation was brought (*PARC, Mills*) which resulted in the assertion of the right to free appropriate public education for all handicapped children. Zero-reject policies have paid off for consumers by entitling them to the educational opportunities they fought to achieve. However, the implications of zero reject are not only in the category of "pay-offs." There is still a need for monitoring and advocacy to insure that the principle of zero reject is implemented in a fashion equal to the promise. Some of the major implications of zero reject for consumers include: (1) enactment of right to education; (2) participation in the SEA and LEA planning process; and (3) advocacy.

Enactment of the Right to Education

Parents have a responsibility to present their handicapped child to the LEA so that he may receive an appropriate education. Parents should participate in the child census activities by completing all necessary forms to register their child. Further, some parents might choose to assume an active role, working with the LEA to plan and implement child-identification procedures. Consumer leadership can be valuable in child-identification, because it encourages other consumers to bring the needs of their handicapped children to the attention of the LEA.

After the handicapped child has been identified, his parents need to cooperate with LEA representatives to insure that the child is provided with an appropriate education. This is typically done through involvement with the processes of nondiscriminatory assessment (see Chapter 4) and IEP development (see Chapter 5). The IEP serves as the basis for making the placement decision. The parents and other IEP committee members should agree on the most appropriate educational placement for the child. If placement is in a private school or an agency other than the LEA, the parents should be sure that the LEA is going to assume financial responsibility. At any point in the process of identification, evaluation, and placement, parents can enact their due process rights (see Chapter 7) if they believe their child is being totally or functionally excluded from the education he is entitled to under P.L. 94–142 and Sec. 504.

Participation in the SEA and LEA Planning Process

As previously discussed in this chapter, LEAs are responsible for writing two kinds of plans: (1) the full-service goal plan, and (2) a plan to specify the deadlines and exceptions for providing a free appropriate public education. LEAs should extend the opportunity to a representative group of consumers to participate in the process of developing these plans. Participation could involve task force or committee membership with significant responsibility for the planning process. Consumers who are not formal members of the planning groups should be encouraged to attend public meetings concerning the plans, to read the plans, and to comment on them.

In the absence of LEA encouragement, it may be necessary for consumers to insist on having this type of involvement (see Chapter 8). They can make a request for active involvement to the director of special education, to the superintendent, to a member of the board of education, or to the local or state advisory panel. Whether they request active participation or are invited to take part, it is important for consumers to follow through on their responsibility. A planning task force can require an incredible amount of hard, tedious work. It can be a time-consuming and frustrating experience. If educators and consumers are to overcome the ill effects of their adversary encounters of the past, it is important to start immediately to establish a partnership based on respect and shared responsibility. Respect and shared responsibility grow out of positive experiences of productively working together.

Advocacy

There are still issues related to zero reject that require further advocacy. Some states have "mandatory" legislation that should be strengthened as a basis for appropriating increased state dollars to special education or as a hedge against emasculating amendments of federal law. For example, advocacy efforts might be directed at amending P.L. 94–142 and Sec. 504 to eliminate the state law exceptions to the requirements for the provision of preschool educational services to handicapped children and the provision of services to handicapped individuals within the ages of eighteen through twenty-one.

Consumers have been extremely successful with legal and legislative advocacy; their efforts should be continued. Consumer organizations like the National Association for Retarded Citizens and the National Society for Autistic Children are good vehicles for this type of advocacy. There is strength in numbers, and large organizations that speak with a single voice can be extremely strong sources of social change. Consumers who see a need to expand the zero-reject policies are encouraged to become actively involved in the political process through advocacy efforts.

NOTES

1. *E.g.*, Brown v. Board of Education, 347 U.S. 483 (1954) (school segregation), Shapiro v. Thompson, 394 U.S. 618 (1969) (discrimination against the poor in right to interstate travel), Weber v. Aetna Cas. & Sur. Co., 406 U.S. 164 (1972) (discrimination against illegitimates), Wisconsin v. Constantineau, 400 U.S. 433 (1971) (discrimination against alcoholics), and Robinson v. California, 370 U.S. 660 (1962) (discrimination against narcotics addicts).

2. 347 U.S. 483, 493 (1954).

3. *E.g.*, Frontiero v. Richardson, 411 U.S. 677 (1973), Graham v. Richardson, 403 U.S. 365 (1971), Levy v. Louisiana, 391 U.S. 68 (1968), and Loving v. Virginia, 388 U.S. 1 (1967), to the effect that, respectively, race, alienage, illegitimacy, and race (again) are suspect classifications.

4. *E.g.*, Mills v. D.C. Board of Education, 348 F. Supp. 866 (D.D.C. 1972) and Maryland Ass'n. for Retarded Children v. Maryland, Equity No. 100/182/77676 (Cir. Ct., Baltimore Cty., April 9, 1974).

5. 334 F. Supp. 1257 (E.D. Pa. 1971) and 343 F. Supp. 279 (E.D. Pa. 1972).

6. 348 F. Supp. 866 (D.D.C. 1972).

7. Rodriguez v. San Antonio, 411 U.S. 1 (1973).

8. *See* Harper v. Vir. State Bd. of Elections, 383 U.S. 663 (1966) (voting) and Douglas v. California, 372 U.S. 353 (1963) (access to courts).

9. Equity No. 100/182/77676 (Cir. Ct., Baltimore Cty., April 9, 1974).

10. 269 F. Supp. 401 (D.D.C. 1967), *aff'd. sub. nom.* Smuck v. Hobson, 408 F. 2d 175 (D.C. Cir. 1969).

11. 348 F. Supp. 866, 875 (D.D.C. 1972).

12. 535 P. 2d 200 (Colo. S. Ct., 1975).

13. *See, e.g.,* Wyatt v. Stickney, 325 F. Supp. 781 (M.D. Ala. 1971) and 344 F. Supp. 387 (M.D. Ala.), *aff'd. sub. nom.* Wyatt v. Aderholt, F.2d (5th Cir., 1974); Welsch v. Likens. 373 F. Supp. 487 (D. Minn. 1974); and N.Y.A.R.C. v. Rockefeller, 357 F. Supp. 752 (E.D.N.Y., 1972).

14. No. C74-587 (N.D. Ohio, April 5, 1976).

15. 409 F. Supp. 148 (D. Md. 1976).

16. For other zero reject cases not discussed elsewhere in this chapter, *see* Ass'n. for Mentally Ill Children v. Greenblatt, Civ. No. 71–3074–J (D. Mass., filed Dec. 30, 1971); Beauchamp v. Jones, No. 75–350 (D. Del., filed Oct. 23, 1975); Brandt v. Nevada, Civ. No. R–2779 (D. Nev., filed Dec. 22, 1973); Burnstein v. Kipp, No. R–19266 (Super. Ct., Contra Costa, Cal., filed Dec. 31, 1970); Calif. A.R.C. v. Riles, No. 77–0341–ACW (N.D. Cal., filed 1977); Catholic Social Services, Inc. v. Bd. of Ed. (administrative proceeding, State Bd. of Ed of Del., filed Aug. 24, 1971); Doe v. Bd. of Sch. Directors, Civ. No. 377–770 (Cir. Ct., Milwaukee Cty., filed 1970); Eaton v. Hinton, Civ. Act. No. 10326 (Super. Ct., Ariz., filed Dec. 10, 1974); Freeman v. Brooks, No. A–5104 (Ch. Ct., Davidson Cty., Tenn., filed March, 1975); Kekahuna v. Burns, Civ. No. 73–3799 (D. Hawaii, filed Apr. 12, 1973) and *refiled sub. nom.* Silva v. Bd. of Ed., Civ. Act. No. 41768 (1st Cir. Ct., Hawaii, filed Apr. 8, 1974); Marcombe v. Dept. of Ed., No. 73–102 (M.D. La., filed Oct. 31, 1973); N.C. Ass'n. for Retarded Children v. N.C., No. 3050 (E.D.N.C., filed May 18, 1972); and Swain v. Barrington School Bd., No. Eq. 5750 (Super. Ct., N.H., Mar. 12, 1976).

17. For other "tuition" cases not discussed elsewhere in this chapter, *see* Crowder v. Riles, No. CA 00384 (Super. Ct., Los Angeles, Cty., Cal., filed Dec. 20, 1976); Davis v. Wynne, No. CV—176—44 (S.D. Ga., filed May 21, 1976); Dembrowski v. Knox Community School Corp., Civ. Act. No. 74–210 (Starke Cir. Ct., Indiana, filed May 15, 1974); Kivell v. Nemoitan, No. 143913 (Super. Ct., Fairfield Cty., Ct., July 18, 1972); St. of Wisconsin ex rel. Warren v. Nussbaum, 219 N.W. 2d 577 (Sup. Ct., Wisc., 1974); W. E. v. Bd. of Ed. of City of Chicago, Civ. Act. No. 73–CH–6104 (Cir. Ct., Cook Cty., Ill., filed 1973, appeal pending in Ill. Sup. Ct.)

18. Reid v. Bd. of Ed. of City of N.Y., No. 8742, 13 Ed. Dept. Rep. (Comm'r. of Ed. of St. of N.Y., decided Nov. 26, 1973), federal abstention order, 453 F.2d 238 (2d Cir. 1971).

19. Davis v. Wynne, CV–176–44 (S.D. Ga., filed May 21, 1976) and Matter of Young, 377 N.Y.S. 2d 429 (Family Ct., St. Lawrence Cty., 1975).

20. Weintraub and Abeson, *Appropriate Education for All Handicapped Children*, 23 SYR.L. REV. 1037, 1056 (1972).

21. 60 F.R.D. 135 (E.D. La., 1973) and 417 F. Supp. 169 (E.D. La., 1976).

22. See Ch. 4 for more complete discussion of issues of racial discrimination in special education.

23. 414 U.S. 563 (1974).

24. No. 14,948, Mass. Super. Ct., Suffolk Cty., consent decree, June 23, 1976; supplemental consent decree, Sept. 17, 1976; motion for contempt finding, October 27, 1976. Similar claims are made in Burnstein v. Kipp, No. R–19266 (Super. Ct., Contra Costa, Cal., filed Dec. 31, 1970) (challenge to exclusion from appropriate education); Fletcher v. Bd. of Ed., No. A–741–00530–AW (Cir. Ct., Kalamazoo Cty., Mich., filed March 14, 1974) (plaintiffs seek to enforce state-law right to appropriate education); Catherine D. v. Pittenger, C.A. No. 74–2435 (E.D. Pa., filed Sept. 20, 1974 and consent order entered, 1975) (claim to appropriate education under equal protection doctrine of Fourteenth Amendment settled by consent decree); and Dembrowski v. Knox Community School Corp., Civ. Act. No. 74–210 (Starke Cty., Indiana, filed May 15, 1974) (claim for appropriate education settled by placement of plaintiff in school program, but claim for damages is pending).

25. Cal. Super. Ct., Los Angeles Cty., filed Dec. 20, 1976.

26. 405 F. Supp. 946 (E.D. Pa. 1975).

27. No. 74–52 (E.D. Pa., Aug. 2, 1976), aff'd., F.2d., 46 U.S. L.W. 2008 (3rd Cir. 1977).

28. Civ. Act. No. 5081 (D.R.I., stipulations signed Sept. 19, 1975).

29. No. 787938 (Super. Ct., King Cty., Wash., stipulations signed Sept., 1976).

30. No. 21350–75 (N.Y. Sup. Ct. App. Div., filed Jan. 21, 1976).

31. No. CV–176–44 (S.D.Ga., filed May 21, 1976).

32. *See e.g.,* Rios v. Read, C.A. No. 75–C–296 (E.D.N.Y., Jan. 14, 1977); Hernandez v. Porter, No. 571532 (E.D. Mich., filed Aug. 15, 1975); Guadalupe Org., Inc. v. Tempe Elementary School Dist., Civ. No. 71–435 (D. Ariz. 1972); Ruiz v. St. Bd. of Ed., No. 218294 (Super. Ct., Sacramento Cty., Cal., filed Dec. 16, 1971); and Bilingual Education Act, 20 U.S.C. 880b–880b–13 and regulations at 41 Fed. Reg. 23860 (June 11, 1976), 45 C.F.R. 123.

33. Mills v. Bd., 348 F. Supp. 866 (D.D.C 1972); LeBanks v. Mills, 60 F.R.D. 135 (E.D. La. 1973) and 417 F.Supp. 169 (E.D.La. 1976); and Donnelly v. Minn., Civ. No. 3–72–141 (D. Minn., filed May 2, 1973) (dismissed as moot upon passage of state "mandatory education" law for exceptional children).

34. MARC v. Md., Equity No. 100/182/77676 (Cir. Ct., Baltimore Cty., Apr. 9, 1974) and Reid v. Bd. of Ed. of City of N.Y., No. 8742, 13 Ed. Dept. Rep. (Comm'r. of Ed. of St. of N.Y., decided Nov. 26, 1973), federal abstention order, 453 F.2d 238 (2d Cir. 1971).

35. *See, e.g.,* Doe v. Colburn, Mont., 555 P.2d 753 (S. Ct. Mont. 1976); PARC v. Commonwealth, 334 F. Supp. 1257 (E.D.Pa. 1971) and 343 F. Supp.

279, 302 (E.D. Pa. 1972); Mills v. Board of Education of District of Columbia, 348 F. Supp. 866, 878 (D.D.C. 1972); and MARC v. Maryland, Equity No. 100/182/77676 (Cir. Ct., Baltimore Cty., May 3, 1974).

36. Civ. No. 75–0622–R (E.D. Va., filed Dec. 1, 1975, interim order, Mar. 23, 1976); see also Mielke v. Redmond, Civ. Act. No. 75–C–473 (N.D., Ill., filed 1976), challenging limitation of $2500 on tuition grants for children placed in private schools because no appropriate programs are available.

37. 391 F. Supp. 872 (E.D.Pa., 1975).

38. 396 F.Supp. 1291 (D.N.H. 1975).

39. In Re Held, No. H–2–71 and H–10–71 Family Ct., Westchester Cty., N.Y., Nov. 21, 1971); In Re Downey, 72 Misc. 772, 340 N.Y.S. 2d 687 (Family Ct., N.Y. Cty., N.Y. 1973); In Re Kirshner, 74 Misc. 2d 20, 344 N.Y.S. 2d 164 (Family Ct., Monroe Cty., 1973); and In Matter of Kaye, 379 N.Y.S. 2d 261 (Family Ct., Rockland Cty., 1975).

40. In Re Levy, 370 N.Y.S. 2d 351 (Family Ct., Westchester Cty., 1975).

41. In Re Levy, 345 N.E. 2d 556 (1976).

42. In Re Tracy Cox, Civ. No. H4721–25 (Family Ct., Queens Cty., Apr. 8, 1976).

43. In Re Young, 377 N.Y.S. 2d 429 (Family Ct., St. Lawrence Cty., 1975).

44. 411 U.S. 1 (1973).

45. No. 75–C–383 (N.D. Ill., Aug. 19, 1975).

46. 405 F. Supp. 946 (E.D. Pa. 1975).

47. 423 F. Supp. 180 (S.D. W.Va. 1976). *Accord*, Lloyd v. Regional Transp. Auth., 548 F.2d 1277 (7th Cir. 1977).

48. Civ. Act. No. DC–75–31–S (N.D. Miss., filed April 25, 1975); see also Connecticut A.R.C. v. State Bd. of Ed., No. H77122 (D. Conn., filed 1977), claiming that the Board violates Sec. 504 by denying institutionalized children an education.

49. 424 F. Supp. 1341 (E.D. N.C. 1976).

50. 411 F. Supp. 982 (E.D. Pa., 1976), *aff'd*. F.2d (3rd Cir., April 25, 1977).

51. 553 F.2d 296 (2d Cir., 1977).

52. 383 N.Y.S. 2d 518 (Super.Ct., Nassau Cty., 1976).

53. No. 38357 (E. Mich., Oct. 30, 1972).

54. No. 72–L–461 (D.Wis., Feb. 21, 1974) and 390 F. Supp. 611 (D.Wis., 1974) (on issue of placement in private or non-neighborhood schools, discussed in Ch. 6).

55. Civ. Act. No. 730250–CIV–NCR (S.D. Fla., 1973).

56. G.T. Bellamy, L. Peterson, and D. Close, "Habilitation of the severely and profoundly retarded: Illustrations of competence," *Education and Training of the Mentally Retarded*, 10 (1974): 174-186.

57. Council for Exceptional Children, "Full educational opportunities for handicapped individuals" (An Awareness Paper prepared for the White House Conference on Handicapped Individuals), in J. Jordan (ed.), *Exceptional Children Education at the Bicentennial: A Parade of Progress* (Reston, Virginia: Council for Exceptional Children, 1976).

58. M.C. Reynolds, *DELPHI Survey – A report of rounds I and II*, conducted for the Professional Standards and Guidelines Project (Reston, Virginia: The Council for Exceptional Children, 1973).

1978 Supplement

n. 13. See Halderman v. Pennhurst, 466 F. Supp. 1293 (E.D. Pa. 1977), appeal filed, holding that residents of a state mental retardation facility were denied equal protection of the laws (in violation of the federal constitution), rights to education and treatment (in violation of the Fifth and Fourteenth Amendments to the federal constitution and Sec. 504), and rights to the least restrictive environment (in violation of the federal constitution and Sec. 504) by reason of being committed to the state facility, where they could not receive adequate treatment, education, and habilitation. The district court's order required, among other things, the deinstitutionalization of Pennhurst residents, not reform of the institution (unlike other right-to-treatment cases).

In another deinstitutionalization case having direct right-to-education bearings, a state court held in N.Y. Association for Retarded Citizens v. Carey (No.   ), that the New York City Board of Education may not exclude from public school programs, segregate from other students, and require the reinstitutionalization of approximately 50 students who were carriers of Hepatitis B (42 of those students had been discharged from Willowbrook Hospital, a state facility for the mentally retarded, where they contracted Hepatitis B). The U.S. Public Health Service Guidelines for dealing with Hepatitis B carriers, said the court, adequately safeguarded other students, were able to be complied with by the city board of education, but were superseded by city board regulations that were more stringent and resulted in excluding the students and requiring them to be readmitted to Willowbrook. The court held that the board was violating P.L. 94–142 (zero reject and least restrictive placement provisions) and Sec. 504 (similar provisions in the regulations), as well as the Willowbrook consent decree, N.Y. Association for Retarded Children v. Rockefeller, *supra* n. 13. See also Woods v. N.Y. City Board of Education, No.,   , E.D. N.Y., filed August 3, 1978, digested in *Insight*, Council for Exceptional Children, Vol. 12, Dec. 22, 1978, pp. 3, 4, raising similar issues concerning the exclusion of Hepatitis B-carrying students from public school placement.

n. 14. The court's opinion is reported at 411 F. Supp. 46 (N.D. Ohio 1976).

n. 16. See also Kenneth J. v. Klein, No. 77–2257 (E.D. Pa. 1977) and Martin Luther King, Jr., High School Children v. Michigan Board of Education,   F. Supp.   , 46 U.S.L.W. 2628 (E.D. Mich. 1978).

A consent order has been entered in North Carolina Association for Retarded Citizens v. North Carolina, 420 F. Supp. 451 (E.D. N.C., 1976, consent order entered July 31, 1978), providing for the plaintiffs to monitor LEA compliance with P.L. 94–142, Sec. 504, and state special education law, creating a three-member monitoring review panel, and planning for compensatory education of retarded children.

n. 17. Crowder v. Riles has been refiled as Kopsco v. Riles, but the docket file number remains the same.

n. 18. The State Commissioner of Education has required the New York City Board of Education to place handicapped children in appropriate programs in the public schools or, if none are available, in private schools at the Board's expense; not to withdraw Board-financed students already in private schools unless the private school programs are no longer appropriate for the children; to submit annually to the commissioner a list of students receiving homebound instruction and reasons why they are in such a program; to prepare a comprehensive plan for educating all handicapped children; to report to the Commissioner on its child-find efforts; and to submit to the Commissioner a plan to eliminate delays in diagnosis and placement of handicapped children. Order of September 2, 1977.

n. 22. Add in text after n. 22 but before the section entitled "Appropriate Education": In North Carolina Association for Retarded Citizens v. North Carolina, *supra*, n. 16, another use of equal protection seems to be the parties' agreement in a consent order to plan to give compensatory education to retarded youths who are more than 17 years old at the time of the consent decree. The consent decree is ambiguous concerning such details of compensatory education as how long a 17-year-old retarded youth is entitled to be in compensatory education.

Finally, state competency testing programs may violate handicapped students' equal protection rights. Cases challenging such programs because of their disproportionate adverse effect on handicapped children have not yet been filed, but the outlines of the litigation are set out in *School Law News*, November 10, 1978, page 12, and March 3, 1978, page 8, and are suggested by litigation challenging the tests because of their disproportionate adverse effects on racial minorities, Debra P. v. Turlington, No.   (M.D. Fla., filed October 16, 1978) and Green v. Hunt, No. 78-539-C10-5 (E.D. N.C., filed December, 1978).

n. 25. The case has been renamed Kopsco v. Riles, but the docket file number remains the same, *supra*, n. 17. The state court held that the state violated the plaintiffs' rights to equal protection under the *state* constitution by failing to fund fully the tuition-grant program, and it ordered the state to pay all the tuition, transportation, and maintenance costs of private-school placement when appropriate public school programs are not available. The court did not rule on the allegations that P.L. 94–142 and Sec. 504 were violated. Thus, the holding is limited to state law grounds.

n. 27. Affirmed, 557 F. 2d 373 (3d Cir. 1977).

n. 31. The case was filed May 23, 1976.

n. 36. 431 F. Supp. 180 (E.D. Va. 1977), reversed 434 U.S. 808 (1977); see also Kopsco v. Riles, *supra*, n. 17.

n. 39. See also Brown v. Union Free School District, 398 N.Y.S. 2d 710 (App. Div. 1977).

n. 42. Funding for preschool costs has been ordered in *In The Matter* of J.F., 398 N.Y.S. 2d 125 (Fam. Ct. 1977), the court ordering an LEA to pay transportation and tuition costs of a preschool child, reasoning that the state Family Court Act., Sec. 236, was enacted so that state law would conform to P.L. 94–142 and that the state legislature intended to have such costs reimbursed.

n. 47, 48, and 49. Having agreed to hear the *Davis* case (Southeastern Community College v. Davis, No. 78-711, certiorari granted, Jan. 8, 1979), the Supreme Court probably will resolve the following issues: (1) who is an "otherwise qualified" handicapped person as defined by Sec. 504 and the implementing regulations for postsecondary institutions, Sec. 84.3(k)(3); (2) whether a handicapped person must exhaust his administrative remedies before being permitted to sue in federal court to enforce his rights under Sec. 504; and (3) whether a handicapped person has a right of action in federal courts to enforce his rights under Sec. 504. The court of appeals reversed the district court, 574 F. 2d 1158 (4th Cir. 1978), and the appeal to the Supreme Court is from the appeals court decision that Davis was a qualified student, was discriminated against, has a private right of action under Sec. 504, and is not required to exhaust her administrative remedies.

These are important issues for handicapped students, ones on which there is now no unanimity among the courts. With respect to the first issue, the courts have held that deaf students in postsecondary institutions are entitled to interpreters, Barnes v. Converse College, 436 F. Supp. 635 (D. S. Carolina, 1977) and Crawford v. University of North Carolina, 440 F. Supp. 1047 (M.D.N.C. 1977). Likewise, Mattie T. v. Holladay, No. D.C. 75-31-S (N.D. Miss., July 28, 1977), sustains the rights of elementary and secondary handicapped children to a nondiscriminatory education.

In *Mattie T.* v. *Holladay*, F. Supp.   (N.D. Miss., 1978), the district court has held (1) the Federal Educational Rights and Privacy Act (the so-called "Buckley Amendment") does not entitle a state or local school board to refuse to comply with a subpoena that calls for it to deliver to the plaintiffs in a right-to-education suit brought under Sec. 504 the school records of handicapped children so long as those records do not personally identify any handicapped children, and (2) the state and LEA officials had violated the rights of handicapped children under Sec. 504 by failing to adopt policies and procedures that ensure the plaintiffs their due process safeguards, that are sufficient to locate and identify all handicapped children needing special education, that assure nondiscriminatory evaluations, and that provide for children to be placed in the least restrictive educational setting. The court also ordered the defendants to develop a state plan to comply with appropriate education under Sec. 504.

(continued on page 279)

4

Testing, Classification, and Placement

CONSTITUTIONAL FOUNDATIONS

The constitutional arguments against certain types of educational evaluations and the resulting classifications of children turn on the Fifth and Fourteenth Amendments. Both provide that a person shall not be deprived of life, liberty, or property without due process of law. Denying an education is arguably tantamount to denying an opportunity to develop the ability to acquire property.[1] Misclassifying children as handicapped when they are not, or classifying them inaccurately with respect to their handicaps, can result not only in denying them their rights to an educational opportunity[2] (not to mention their rights to an appropriate education), but also in unjustifiably stigmatizing them. It follows, then, that substantive due process has been violated when a pupil is misclassified on the basis of invalid criteria and thus placed in an inappropriate "track" in school.[3]

The Fourteenth Amendment is involved in still another way. By requiring that states treat citizens equally (the "equal protection" clause), the Fourteenth Amendment has become the traditional bulwark against state-imposed racial discrimination. Inasmuch as special education classes (particularly for the mildly handicapped) have been filled with a disproportionate number of minority students (racial minorities—principally blacks—and cultural minorities—principally Latin Americans), there is at least an arguable claim of discrimination based on race or cultural background. The following discussions will show how the "substantive

85

due process'' rights under the Fifth and Fourteenth Amendments and the ''equal protection'' rights under the Fourteenth come into play in school testing and classification.

Criticisms of Testing

The alleged violations usually involve the use of IQ or aptitude tests. These tests supposedly are objective and allegedly do not depend on irrelevant variables like teacher prejudice or social class, but they are nevertheless subject to criticism, particularly when test results are the primary basis for assigning a disproportionate number of minority pupils—blacks or non-English speaking—to special education programs for the educable mentally retarded (EMR) or the trainable mentally retarded (TMR). The reestablishment of racially dual systems of education is threatened by such assignments, but the constitutional doctrine of equal protection under the Fourteenth Amendment comes into play to prohibit segregation by race in any school program, including special education.

One basis for criticizing the tests is that they have been used to determine the intelligence of children unfamiliar with the language or with the white middle-class culture that underlies the test questions.[4] In short, it is argued that tests based on a white middle-class socioeconomic group should not be used on persons not of that group because the test put them at an initial disadvantage and may lead to their mistakenly being classified as handicapped. There have been other criticisms of the tests or the ways in which they are administered or used. In some cases, they have not been administered in the child's native language (e.g., Spanish).[5] And they generally do not measure a child's adaptive behavior—his ability to cope and get along in his *own* cultural environment.[6]

Misclassification due to inappropriate testing arguably imposes on a student the stigma of being retarded or different; it can isolate him from normal school experiences and cause him to be rejected by students and adults alike; sometimes it sets up stereotyped expectations of behavior and can lead to self-fulfilling prophesy; all of this to his irreparable harm.[7] Often, the label is permanent and cannot be escaped, outgrown, or rebutted. Moreover, the label can limit (or increase) the resources available to the child, since public and private agencies tend to serve only those persons identified as belonging within their categorical clientele. A misclassified child might be placed in a special education program whether he needs it or not, or he might be placed in an inappropriate special education program or be inappropriately institutionalized. Being placed in a special education program does not necessarily ensure that the child will receive training that will be effective in overcoming the disadvantages of being classified as handicapped. Assignment to a special education program can become permanent, despite an original intention to make it temporary.[8]

Testing alone is not sufficient for developing an accurate picture of a child's abilities and handicaps, but it has often been treated as if it were, and in some cases a single test has been used as the sole criterion for classification and placement.[9] Testing results, when not supplemented by other evaluation techniques (e.g., medical information, parent conferences), are particularly subject to misinterpretation. Parent conferences to determine adaptive behavior have been rare, and parent participation in classification decisions has been negligible. Procedural due process concerning evaluation and periodic review of the placements has been the exception, not the rule.[10] Misclassification tells a child that he is deficient; the injury to self-esteem is incalculable.

Court-ordered Remedies

Given these criticisms of the nature, administration, and use of classification and testing procedures, it is not surprising that *recent* judicial response, based on substantive due process (Fifth Amendment) and equal protection (of the racial or cultural minorities under the equal protection doctrine of the Fourteenth Amendment), has been massive. The key word is "recent" because only in the last several years (1972–1978) have the courts become embroiled in the classification of issues. Their traditional posture had been to find that "mere classification . . . does not of itself deprive a group of equal protection"[11] and that "it goes without saying that there is no constitutional prohibition against an assignment of individual students to particular schools on a basis of intelligence, achievement or other aptitudes upon a uniformly administered program."[12] It is because of the criticisms of testing—criticisms centering on the permanent and stigmatizing consequences of being labelled as "mentally retarded" and on the racial differentiation that results from testing—that courts in the early and mid-1970s began to make inroads on the testing practices and procedures of the schools.

Accepting the argument that intelligence tests bear little relationship to the intelligence they are supposed to measure when there is a language or cultural unfamiliarity, some courts have held that IQ tests may no longer continue to be used to place children in ability tracks.[13] They have forbidden schools to use biased (unvalidated) tests that do not properly account for the cultural background and experiences of the children being tested.[14] They have enjoined school authorities from placing minority students in classes for the educable mentally retarded on the basis of IQ tests if using the tests brings about racial imbalance in the composition of such classes. They also ordered the dismantling of EMR classes in which Chicanos were over-represented.[15] They have given the schools the burden of proving that a test is a valid measure of intelligence and does not discriminate because of race or culture if the test is the primary basis for classifications that are resulting in racial imbalance.[16] In addition, they have ordered that pupils be tested or retested in their primary language or given bilingual instruc-tion.[17] By ordering these remedies, the courts have made it clear that they have adopted as fact the presumption that statistical imbalance (racial imbalance) would not occur unless there is some sort of discrimination based on race.[18]

The courts have ordered that factors like socioeconomic background, social adaptation, and adaptive ability be considered in making an evaluation for appro-priate placement.[19] The use of IQ test alone was found to violate substantive due process, since the basis for the school's action—the IQ score—was not reasonably related to the purpose for which it was used; namely, to determine a pupil's ability and what would be a "suitable" or "appropriate" education for him.

Just as the criteria must be related to what they are supposed to measure—that is, that they not be arbitrary—the standard for evaluation may not be arbitrarily applied. Thus, when white and minority students with similar abilities are as-signed to "remedial" classes and classes for the educable mentally retarded, it is discriminatory to put the white students in the remedial classes and the minority students into the classes for the retarded. Accordingly, schools have been prohi-bited from having a disproportionate number of minority students in classes for the educable mentally retarded[20] and, must justify their reliance on tests that have resulted in an imbalance.[21]

Still other remedies have been ordered. Schools are now required to furnish handicapped children with intensive training to help them attain their peers' skill levels. The courts also have ordered compensatory education for adults who were improperly classified, thus being denied an equal educational opportunity as children.[22] In pending litigation, they are being asked to order schools to expunge from a student's records references to his being handicapped (educable mentally retarded) when that evaluation was solely based on IQ tests.[23] They are also being asked to order that students be retested,[24] that they be tested in their native language,[25] and that Latino tutors be furnished to Latino students.[26] Thus, the equal protection clause is being used to seek redress for school practices that discriminate against non-Anglo minorities, just as it has been used to prevent discrimination against the black racial minority.

Why Testing is Required

It is obvious that testing, classification, and placement in special education programs must be continued for at least three reasons. The schools must be able to identify and evaluate handicapped children (1) in order to plan, program, and appropriate funds for them; (2) in order to provide appropriate services for them; and (3) in order to comply with federal and state law requiring that handicapped children be counted and served.

Classification can assist in measuring the results of special education efforts.[27] It can also create educational opportunity for the handicapped, supply a common denominator to create and stimulate activities of volunteer or professional interest groups, assist in the enactment of legislation to assist individuals in a specific category, furnish structure to governmental programs, and serve as a basis for financial appropriation decisions.[28] Classification is useful for determining incidence and prevalence data, which is helpful in planning how many professionals will be needed for a wide variety of services, and assures accountability in programs and services. Some of the reasons students perform poorly on standardized tests—such as slow work habits, emotional insecurity, low motivation, lack of interest, and culturally related conditions—also account for their below-average performance in school; thus, testing can provide an early warning of probable or possible future problems.

However, classification remains a powerful political tool,[29] capable of regulating people, degrading them, denying them access to educational opportunity, excluding them as "undesirables," and, in the case of minority persons, forcing dominant cultural values and mores on them. For all of these reasons, it is important to establish procedures to protect children from improper testing, misclassification, and inappropriate placement. That is the principal thrust of current federal legislation.

The label of "handicapped" often has the effect of excluding a person so labelled from an appropriate education and, in some instances, from any education at all. The label itself emphasizes the handicap and serves to underscore the differences between "them" (the handicapped) and "us" (the nonhandicapped). It creates not only a dual system of services but also a dual system of law—law for "them" and law for "us." For these reasons, federal legislation seeks to minimize labelling and to ensure that labels, when necessary, accurately describe the handicaps and become useful devices for appropriately serving handicapped children.

FEDERAL LEGISLATION

P.L. 94–142

A school's failure to detect handicaps can prevent children from receiving an appropriate education [Sec. 601(b)(5)]. Misuse of classification data can result in discrimination, and an erroneous classification represents a major obstacle to a child's receiving an appropriate education [U.S. Senate, Report No. 94–168, Education for All Handicapped Children Act, June 2, 1975, pp. 26–29]. Recognizing these problems, Congress sought to accomplish "nondiscriminatory testing." Its effort is broad-based and multifaceted.

Nondiscriminatory testing procedures. Congress required that three strategies be followed to assure nondiscriminatory testing. The SEAs and LEAs must establish procedures to assure that testing and examination materials and procedures used for evaluating and placing handicapped children will be selected and administered so as not to be racially or culturally discriminatory [Sec. 612 (5) (C) and 614 (a) (7) and Sec. 121a.530]. Next, each SEA and LEA must provide and administer such materials or procedures in the child's native language or mode of communication unless it is clearly not feasible to do so [Secs. 612 (5) (C) and 614 (a) (7) and Sec. 121a.530]. Finally, no single procedure may be the sole criterion for determining an appropriate educational program for a child [Secs. 612 (5) (C) and 614 (a) (7)]. The term "nondiscriminatory testing" applies to evaluation materials and procedures used with all handicapped children, as the regulations make clear (Sec. 121a.530–.534), and the P.L. 94–142 regulations (Sec. 121a.530–.534) are identical with the Sec. 504 regulations.

In response to the requirement for racially and culturally nondiscriminatory testing and evaluation, Sec. 121a.532 requires that:

> (a) Tests and other evaluation materials
> > (1) Are provided and administered in the child's native language or other mode of communication, unless it is clearly not feasible to do so;
> > (2) Have been validated for the specific purpose for which they are used;
> > (3) Are administered by trained personnel in conformance with instructions from the producer;
> (b) Tests and other evaluation materials include those tailored to assess specific areas of educational need and not merely those which are designed to provide a single general intelligence quotient;
> (c) Tests are selected and administered so as best to insure that when a test is administered to a child with impaired sensory, manual or speaking skills, the test results accurately reflect the child's aptitude or achievement level or whatever other factor the test purports to measure, rather than reflecting the child's impaired sensory, manual, or speaking skills (except where those skills are the factors which the test purports to measure);
> (d) No single procedure is used as the sole criterion for determining an appropriate educational program for a child and placement;
> (e) The evaluation is made by a multidisciplinary team or group of persons, including at least one teacher or other specialist with knowledge in the area of suspected disability;
> (f) The child is assessed in all areas related to the suspected disability, including, where appropriate, health, vision, hearing, social and emotional status, general intelligence, academic performance, communicative status, and motor abilities.

Sec. 121a.531 requires that before a child is initially placed in a special education program, a complete and individual evaluation of his educational needs must be conducted in accordance with Sec. 121a.532.

Sec. 121a.533 regulates placement procedures and the use of evaluation results. Public agencies must:

> (1) Draw upon information from a variety of sources, including aptitude and achievement tests, teacher recommendations, physical condition, social or cultural background, and adaptive behavior;

(2) Insure that information obtained from all of these sources is documented and carefully considered;

(3) Insure that the placement decision is made by a group of persons, including persons knowledgeable about the child, the meaning of the evaluation data, and the placement options; and

(4) Insure that the placement decision is made in conformity with the least restrictive environment rules in Secs. 121a.–550–121a.554.

Reevaluation must occur at least every three years or more often if "conditions warrant" or the child's parent or teacher requests it [Sec. 121a.534].

The regulations require parental consent for a preplacement evaluation only; in the event the parents withhold consent, a due process hearing may be held at the request of the school. They do not require such consent for subsequent evaluations [Sec. 121a.504 (b) (1) and (2)].

Ceiling. Congress placed a ceiling on the number of children a state may count for the purpose of receiving federal funds under P.L. 94–142 [Sec. 611 (a) (5)(A)(i) and (ii)]. The limit is twelve percent of the number of all children aged five through seventeen. The ceiling reflects Congress' concern that recipients might have counted children who were not in fact handicapped in order to receive more federal funds. More than 12 percent of the school population may be classified as handicapped, but federal funding will only be available for up to 12 percent.

"Learning disability" narrowly defined. Congress carefully defined "children with specific learning disabilities" [Sec. 602 (15) and *Fed. Reg.*, Dec. 29, 1977, pp. 65082–5] so that children who do not satisfy the definition will not be classified as handicapped. (See Chapter 2 for the full definition.)

Service priorities. Congress also established the "service priorities." (See Chapter 3 for a discussion of the priorities.) Like the ceiling, the service priorities are intended to stop an LEA from miscategorizing children as handicapped in order to increase the amount of federal funds it may receive. Serving the "first-priority" (previously excluded) and "second-priority" (most severely handicapped not receiving an appropriate education) children makes it unlikely that the LEAs will soon have Part B funds free to spend on handicapped children who do not fall in either category. There is little risk that LEAs will unnecessarily classify children as handicapped, since many of them are still a long way from satisfying the needs of the first and second-priority children.

Recoupment. Congress required the SEAs to adopt procedures for recouping funds from LEAs in order to furnish services for children who were erroneously classified and thus were not eligible for federal funds [Sec. 613 (a) (5)]. This requirement is intended to prevent misclassification; the desire for federal funding, after all, does make it tempting to count a child as handicapped.

Accounting. Congress provided that SEAs and LEAs must report and account for the receipt and expenditure of P.L. 94–142 money. It granted the Commissioner of Education the power to audit those agencies and check the accuracy of their data with regard to the number of handicapped children the state is actually educating [Secs. 613 (a) (1) and (7) and 614 (a) (3)]. The commissioner's power to trade federal dollars is intended to help enforce the service priorities and thereby prevent misclassification.

Due process hearing. Congress granted procedural safeguards—essentially a due process hearing right—to children who have been identified, evaluated, and placed in programs for the handicapped [Sec. 615 (a), (b) (1) (A) and (C)]. These safeguards give protection against misclassification by furnishing a forum for investigating whether a misclassification has occurred. (See Chapter 7 for further discussion of due process.)

Sanctions. Congress provided that federal funds be withheld from any SEA that is alleged to be or found to be in violation of the provisions of P.L. 94–142 [Sec. 616 (a)]. These sanctions contain an element of overkill not evident in the other enforcement measures described in the paragraphs above. For that reason, the other measures should be used before the sanction of withholding is invoked. There is an undoubtedly counterproductive element in the withholding sanction; it can penalize the handicapped (by cutting off federal dollars) in the name of aiding them.

Sec. 504

Like the proposed regulations of P.L. 94–142, the regulations of Sec. 504 acknowledge that failure to furnish handicapped students with an appropriate education is usually the result of misclassification or incorrect placement. Accordingly, Sec. 84.35(a) requires an evaluation of any person who needs or is believed to need special education or related services because of his handicap. The evaluation must be completed before a school takes any action (including denial of placement) with respect to *initial* placement in a regular or special education program or any subsequent significant change in placement. But a full reevaluation is not obligatory every time a lesser adjustment in the child's placement is made.

Sec. 84.35 (b) and (c) set out procedures to ensure that children are not misclassified, unnecessarily labeled as handicapped, or incorrectly placed because of inappropriate selection, administration, or interpretation of evaluation materials. As the Department of Health, Education, and Welfare's (HEW) comments on Sec. 84.35 make clear, the regulations are "aimed primarily at abuses in the placement process that result from misuse of, or undue or misplaced reliance on, standardized scholastic aptitude tests."

Sec. 84.35 (b) requires schools to establish standards and procedures for evaluation and placement to ensure that tests and other evaluation materials are validated for the specific purpose for which they are used and are administered by trained personnel in conformance with the instructions of their producer. Tests and other evaluation materials are to include those tailored to assess specific areas of educational need and not merely those designed to provide a single general intelligence quotient. And, in addition, tests are to be selected and administered to students with impaired sensory, manual, or speaking skills, so that the test results accurately reflect the student's aptitude or achievement level—or whatever other factor the test purports to measure—rather than the student's impaired skills, except where those skills are the factors that the test seeks to measure. Sec. 84.35 (b) drives home the point that tests should not be misinterpreted, that undue reliance on general intelligence tests is undesirable, and that tests should be administered in such a way that their results will not be distorted because of the student's handicap.

Sec. 84.35 (c) requires schools to draw upon information from a variety of sources, including aptitude and achievement tests, teacher recommendations, physical conditions, social or cultural background, and adaptive behavior when evaluating and placing students. Schools must establish procedures to insure that information obtained from all such sources is documented and carefully considered; and the placement decision is to be made by a *group* of people, including those knowledgeable about the child. The meaning of the evaluation data and the placement options must be made clear to all concerned, and placement decisions are to conform with the doctrine of least restrictive ("most integrated") setting.

Sec. 84.35 (d) requires periodic (though not necessarily annual) reevaluation, and makes it clear that reevaluation procedures consistent with P.L. 94–142 (P.L. 94–142 allows reevaluation at three-year intervals unless more frequent reevaluations are requested) are a means of meeting the requirement of reevaluation.

Sec. 85.36 requires schools to provide for due process in the evaluation procedures: notice, right of access to records, impartial hearing, right to counsel, and appeal procedures (see Chapter 7).

IMPLICATIONS FOR PUBLIC SCHOOLS

Prior to the passage of P.L. 94–142 and Sec. 504, school systems were required by the Office of Civil Rights (OCR) to follow certain classifications practices in order to comply with Title VI of the Civil Rights Act of 1964. The OCR has issued regulations concerning the types of information to be considered in classifying a student as mentally retarded, the need to obtain parental permission for evaluations, the development of educational plans, the compilation of records, and the creation of an assessment advisory board comprised of parents and educational professionals representing the racial and cultural composition of the school. P.L. 94–142 and Sec. 504 are the legislative confirmation of the OCR regulations, and expand on most of them. Some of the major implications of these legislative requirements include: (1) redefinition of evaluation; (2) sensitivity to cultural factors; (3) use of appropriate and multifaceted measures; (4) attention to the qualifications of personnel administering and interpreting tests; and (5) consideration of due process requirements.

Redefinition of Evaluation

In P.L. 94–142 and Sec. 504, evaluation is viewed not as an end in itself, but rather as a means for providing an appropriate and individually tailored education to handicapped students. Evaluation is defined in the statutes as ''procedures used in accordance with Secs. 121a.530–121a.534 to determine whether a child is handicapped and the nature and extent of the special education and related services that the child needs. The term means procedures used selectively with an individual child and does not include basic tests administered to or procedures used with all children in a school, grade or class'' (*Fed. Reg.*, Aug. 23, 1977, p. 42494).

Evaluation is conducted at various points in the educational process. These points include initial classification to find if the student does in fact have an educational handicap, specification of the current level of performance in regard to developing the student's individual education plan, and continuous assessment of the short-term objectives specified on the student's individual education plan that determine the scope and sequence of his curriculum. Thus, evaluation has the major purposes of classification, individual program planning, and daily or weekly measurement of student progress. Diagnostic, prescriptive, and monitoring functions are inherent in properly conceptualized and administered evaluation procedures. The legislative requirements previously outlined in this chapter speak largely to the classification or diagnostic functions of evaluation; the prescriptive and monitoring functions are considered part of the process of developing and implementing the student's individualized educational program in Chapter 5.

The new definition of evaluation represents a radical change from that applied in many school systems. In the past, arbitrary and rigid normative standards have resulted in evaluation procedures being used primarily to determine if a student's IQ fell below a certain point. If the IQ score happened to fall in the EMR range, it was considered sufficient evidence to warrant special education placement. Evaluation has traditionally been viewed as a tool for educational *placement* rather than an aid to *individual program planning*.

The rigidity of the placement standards can be illustrated by a situation that occurred in one school system in the late 1960s. A student in the EMR program was reevaluated through the use of an IQ test, and scored two points below the basal cut-off for EMR classification. Since there was no TMR program in the system, the psychologist who administered the test recommended that the student be removed from the EMR program and placed back in the regular class. The recommendation was implemented with no consideration for the student's individual education needs. Under the new legislative requirements evaluation information must be drawn from a variety of sources, results are to be analyzed and recommendations made by a team of persons rather than by an individual, and tests aimed at assessing educational need (as opposed to IQ) must be administered. School systems need to pay careful attention to this redefinition of evaluation. Reorienting faculty away from practicing faulty habits can be a difficult task. Educational change in evaluation procedures will most likely require clearly defined policy statements prepared by school personnel and officially adopted by the board of education.

Sensitivity to Cultural Factors

The cultural and socioeconomic bias of classification procedures has become a civil rights issue. (We reviewed the resulting litigation earlier in the chapter.) In addition to judicial and legislative guidelines, professional organizations like the American Psychological Association and the National Association of Educators have adopted policies to minimize the bias against cultural and socioeconomic diversity inherent in many standardized tests.[30] The American Psychological Association adopted two sets of standards pertaining to the assessment of minority children. These include the Ethical Standards of Psychologists[31] and Standards for Educational and Psychological Tests.[32] (See these documents for the specific guidelines set forth by the American Psychological Association.) The administrator responsible for evaluation procedures within each public agency should obtain copies of these standards and encourage all school personnel who conduct formal evaluations to become familiar with them.

Research has shown that testing practices in schools have penalized students from culturally diverse backgrounds and caused an unbalanced proportion of them to be placed in special education classes.[33] The new legislative requirements related to classification force schools to redesign evaluation programs and procedures to minimize cultural bias. Legislative guidelines aimed at minimizing bias include the requirements to: (1) administer tests in a child's native language or other mode of communication, unless it is not feasible to do so, and (2) use tests that are valid for the purpose for which they are being used [Sec. 121a.532].

Native language is defined in P.L. 94–142, as in the Bilingual Education Act, as follows:

> The term "native language," when used with reference to a person of limited English-speaking ability, means the language normally used by that person, or in the case of a child, the language normally used by the parents of the child. (*Fed. Reg.*, Aug. 23, 1977, p. 42479)

A comment inserted in the regulations states that if there is a difference between the language normally used by the child and that used by the parents, communication should be in the language normally used by the child. Thus, if a child normally speaks Spanish, his evaluative tests should be administered in Spanish. If a person is deaf or blind and has no written language, his typical mode of communication (sign language, speech, braille) must be identified and used for testing [Sec. 121a.9].

School systems that incorporate a range of cultural diversity should consider hiring psychologists and teachers who reflect the cultural make-up of the school. The faculty of the school would then be able to speak the languages of the students. School systems might also hire or contract the services of professionals specializing in communicating with blind and deaf persons. Although there is no empirical evidence that pairing racial-ethnic background of examiner and examinee will improve test performance,[34] the problem of diverse language patterns can be minimized by following such a strategy. Another strategy would be to hire interpreters for examiner and examinee. This might be the best strategy for schools with an extremely low incidence of a particular racial, ethnic, or disability group. Of course, translating a test into a different language does not necessarily eliminate all bias; even translation can violate linguistic patterns. However, until less culturally biased tests are developed, translation is a useful intermediate strategy to consider.

What is important is minimizing the unjust effects of language barriers on a child's evaluative test results. Systems should carefully interpret the phrase "unless it is clearly not feasible to do so" in regard to testing the student in his native language. Feasibility must be defined in the student's interest rather than in the system's interest. Just because a system does not have ready solutions for minimizing language barriers (such as a bilingual faculty or money to hire interpreters) it cannot then assume that it is not "feasible" to test the child in his native language. Meeting the spirit and letter of P.L. 94–142 and Sec. 504 means making student-centered educational decisions.

The second major legislative requirement calls for the use of tests that have been validated for the specific purpose for which they are to be used. This is an extremely difficult requirement to implement, since few tests have been constructed and validated for the purpose of assessing handicapping conditions in minority-group children. Factors like speed, item content, and verbal content can place minority children at a disadvantage on formal and informal tests.[35] If a test has been standardized on a white, middle-class population, it probably will not be valid for minority children. If a test is to be valid for all children, the standardization sample must represent children from diverse educational experiences and cultural patterns. The more similar minority children are to the standardization sample, the more valid the results will be and the better the educational decisions made on their behalf will be.

The norms for some tests, such as the 1972 Stanford-Binet and the WISC-R, are generally adequate.[36] However, it can be argued that these tests do not lend themselves directly and specifically to individual program planning. Basically, school systems have a very limited pool of validated measures for minority children that they can draw from. Legislation places the burden of proof on the public agency to show that evaluation measures are appropriately selected for racial-ethnic differences. School systems can help if they encourage institutions of higher education and test publishers to develop tests standardized on and recommended for use with minority children. Neither school systems nor agencies can solve the classification dilemma alone. Strategies which might serve as intermediate measures include the use of culture-specific tests, the establishment of regional and ethnic norms, the test-train-retest model,[37] pluralistic evaluation,[38] and the use of multifaceted assessment techniques.

In regard to culture-specific tests, measures specifically designed for subcultural groups can be used. One such measure is the Black Intelligence Test of Cultural Homogeneity, comprised of vocabulary items from the Black culture.[39] Some tests have been designed to be *culture-fair* rather than culture-specific. Culture-fair tests are supposedly designed to be appropriate for persons from a variety of subcultural groups. Examples of such tests are the Leiter International Performance Scale and Cattell's Culture-Fair Intelligence Test. These tests have unfortunately not succeeded in being free of bias.

School systems would probably find it difficult to develop regional and ethnic norms for particular tests that have not been sufficiently standardized on minority individuals. There is a shortage of qualified test examiners, and already strong demands are made on their time. School systems might consider collaborating with institutions of higher education, research agencies, and test publishers on the development of norms representative of their student bodies. Although this strategy would be time-consuming, it does hold the potential for creating more valid assessment measures.

The test-train-retest model proposed by Budoff[40] emphasizes pretesting a student on specified skills and concepts, providing a period of instruction, and then testing the student again to determine how much improvement has occurred. (This model has strong similarities to the criterion-referenced tests that will be discussed later in the chapter.) Budoff asserts that students demonstrate their learning potential—as measured by the student's achievement gains as a result of instruction—when they do well on nonverbal reasoning tasks.

Another approach, proposed by Mercer and Ysseldyke,[41] is pluristic evaluation: considering a student's sociocultural, socioeconomic, and racial-ethnic background when evaluating the scores of standardized tests. Equations have been designed for the development of normative criteria and standards representative of different backgrounds. This approach to estimating learning potential has promise as a means of substantially reducing discrimination against minority children. In any event, bias can be substantially minimized through the use of multifaceted assessment. Since the use of appropriate and multifaceted measures has major implications for all students—not just minority students—we will consider those measures separately in the next section.

Use of Appropriate and Multifaceted Measures

The classification regulations of both P.L. 94–142 and Sec. 504 are intended to expand on the formal and informal assessment *tools* and the *sources* of information (other than tests) pertaining to a student's status used to make educational decisions. The regulations require: (1) that evaluation measures assess educational need rather than a general intelligence quotient and that information from sources other than tests (physical condition, sociocultural background, adaptive behavior) be used; (2) that a minimum of two tests or types of tests be used as the criteria for placement; and (3) that the test format and response style not penalize a student because of his specific handicap (impaired sensory, manual, or speaking skills). Strategies for implementing these regulations follow.

The multidisciplinary evaluation team might choose from a variety of standardized achievement tests—survey or diagnostic. Generally, the major questions to be answered by *educational* assessment involve documenting what skills and concepts the student has already mastered and what skills and concepts the student should learn next. This is the type of assessment information that leads to making informed curriculum decisions. It is also the type of information that must be included on the student's individual education plan in specifying current level of performance (see Chapter 5). Most general achievement tests (like the Metropolitan and the California tests) fail to pinpoint a student's performance level in regard to sequential skill development. The scores are expressed in grade equivalents or percentiles. Documentation that a student is performing at the 3.2 grade level does not help the evaluation team pinpoint his educational needs or discover which skills he has mastered and which ones he should learn next.

Grade equivalent scores can, however, tell how a handicapped student performs in comparison to the peer group in a particular placement alternative. If a student who reads on the second grade level is placed in a seventh grade class where the majority of the students read at their grade level, substantial curriculum adaptations will have to be made for the student. Thus, grade equivalent scores can be useful in considering the least restrictive alternative appropriate to the child's needs.

Diagnostic achievement tests are more comprehensive in their scope and sequence of questions for a particular subject area. Examples of such tests are the Woodcock Reading Mastery Test and the Key Math Diagnostic Arithmetic Test. From careful analysis of the results of these tests, a student's performance level for a particular hierarchy of skills and concepts can be pinpointed. All achievement tests (survey and diagnostic) must be chosen with attention to the standardization population (cultural bias) and the nature of the student's handicap (blind students obviously should not be given tests which require the reading of print).

Another form of assessing educational need is criterion-referenced tests. Norm-referenced tests compare a given student's performance to other individuals of the same age or grade; criterion-referenced tests compare a student with a predetermined criteria or standard of performance. To develop a criterion-referenced test educational objectives must be clearly specified, the objectives must be sequenced according to complexity, test items must be formulated for each objective, and the criteria for successful mastery of the objective must be defined. One of the strong advantages of criterion-referenced tests is the natural tie that exists with curriculum development. Once the educational objectives are specified in a sequential format and the examiner has identified the skills and concepts a student has already mastered, the skills and concepts that should be introduced next are readily identifiable. This type of assessment has particular educational relevance for the development of the IEP (see Chapter 5). Since the IEP requires that educators specify annual goals and short-term instructional objectives for handicapped students, evaluation instruments like criterion-referenced tests, which are tailored to assess specific educational need, obviously have tremendous utility.

Some educators incorrectly believe that criterion-referenced tests are free of cultural bias. This is not true. Many value decisions are inherent in the construction of the tests. Objectives deemed important for the student to master, criteria for successful performance, and the linguistic structure of the objectives and test items can easily reflect the designer's bias. (There have been attempts to develop criterion-referenced tests specifically for cultural subgroups. One example is SOBER-Espanol, an evaluation of Spanish reading developed by Cornejo.[42]) Thus, caution must be exercised with criterion-referenced tests, just as with norm-referenced tests.

The legislative requirement that information other than test scores be considered in the evaluation process is not particularly difficult to implement. Information about a student's medical and developmental background, adaptive behavior, social adjustment with peers, cultural background, and language dominance is usually not hard to come by. The student's parents are valuable sources of such information, and school systems might construct a questionnaire for them to fill out. Conferences might be held with parents who cannot read at school or in the parent's home, led by a member of the evaluation team or by a representative of another agency (such as a public health nurse or social worker) who has already had contact with the family. Parents should be involved in the evaluation process to the maximum possible extent.

Another source of information about a student's adaptive behavior, social adjustment with peers, and language dominance is observation of the student in educational settings. "Educational settings" applies to more than the classroom. Knowledge about a student's performance level and social interaction abilities can be gained from observing him on the playground, during free periods, in the cafeteria, and immediately before and after the formal school day. Checklists of behaviors to look for could be developed to answer questions the evaluation team has about the student, or anecdotal records could be kept. It is important to note that the regulations for learning disabilities (*Fed. Reg.*, December 29, 1977) requires that at least one member of the evaluation team observe the learning disabled student's academic performance in the regular classroom setting as an integral part of the evaluation process.

In regard to language dominance, much can be learned from observing a student at school and from talking to the student's parents. Also, a host of language-dominance tests have been developed. A list of these tests including addresses of the publishers, the purpose of each test, and a description of the tests is provided by Oakland.[43]

As already pointed out, no test may penalize a student because of his specific handicap. This means that deaf students who are not fluent in oral communication should not be given oral tests or test instructions, and physically handicapped students who cannot write should not be required to make written responses. Tests are to be chosen or developed that present information and require responses in channels appropriate to a student's particular sensory, manual, or speaking deficit. This means that the school must have a variety of assessment measures to draw on and that at least one member of the evaluation team should have expertise in educational adaptations for various handicapping conditions. For example, if a blind student is to be evaluated, someone on the evaluation team must know how to assess the student who cannot print or make standard written responses. When the purpose of the test is to measure the extent of the handicap or the skills associated with it (such as the degree of residual vision) rather than the student's achievement or aptitude, then the test may be directly aimed at the deficit ability.

Standardization samples must also be considered in choosing tests for students with sensory, manual, and speaking handicaps. Very few standardized tests have been normed on blind, deaf, or physically handicapped students. For example, it is widely recognized that deaf students often have more difficulty formulating abstract concepts than nonhandicapped students because of language complexities. Thus they are put at an automatic disadvantage on many standardized tests of a verbal nature. The development of multiple norms similar to the pluristic evaluation described by Mercer and Ysseldyke[44] for minority children, might also be considered for various handicapping conditions.

The requirement of using at least two tests as the criteria for placement decisions will mean changes for school systems that have traditionally used only an intelligence test as the basis for special education placements. These school systems will have to invest more time and more staff (and therefore more money) in the evaluation process.

Qualifications of Persons Administering and Interpreting Tests

The qualifications of persons administering and interpreting tests are very important. States have license requirements for examiners who administer intelligence and personality measures. Standards for Educational and Psychological Tests[45] lists specific duties of "test users," and qualifications corresponding to these duties can be inferred from the Standards.

It may be advantageous for school systems to appoint one administrator or supervisor as having overall responsibility for developing and implementing policies related to evaluation. In many school systems, evaluation coordination falls in the cracks between school psychology and special education responsibilities, and the program suffers. The administrator or supervisor with responsibility for testing should be thoroughly familiar with federal and state regulations and should be able to provide inservice training for the psychologists, teachers, and counselors who will be involved in evaluating students. Many psychologists and educators have been careless in conducting evaluations. This carelessness and haphazard approach can no longer be condoned.

P.L. 94–142 and Sec. 504 require that the interpretation of evaluation results and the decision about the student's educational placement be made by a team of persons who are familiar with the student, the placement options, and the meaning of evaluation results. The team must include at least one teacher or other specialist knowledgeable in the area of the suspected disability. The regulations pertaining to learning disabilities (*Fed. Reg.*, December 29, 1977) that came out of the special task force set up by P.L. 94–142 specify in more detail the composition of evaluation teams for learning disabled students. In addition to the requirements of P.L. 94–142 the team must also include the child's regular teacher (or a regular teacher qualified to teach the child if he does not have a regular teacher), and a person qualified to conduct individual diagnostic examinations. Thus, a variety of educators within a school system must be competent in administering and interpreting evaluations.

The make-up of IEP committees may be a means of increasing the probability of coordination between the initial evaluation process and the development of the IEP itself. According to the regulations, the IEP committee must be comprised of a representative of the public agency that is to provide or supervise special education, the teacher or teachers responsible for implementing the IEP, and the parents. (When handicapped students are evaluated for the first time, a member of the evaluation team must participate in the IEP meeting or a member of the IEP committee must be knowledgeable of evaluation procedures that have been used with the child and what the results of those procedures were.) School systems may want to consider using the same members for the evaluation committee as for the IEP committee. Having entirely separate committees for the various steps in the process of referral and provision of an appropriate education for handicapped students can create chaos and disorganize programming. The smoothness of the process should be enhanced if a stable nucleus of faculty members coordinate each case.

Consideration of the Due Process Requirements

Due process is an integral part of classification and placement; it is impossible to imagine a classification process that is not intertwined with due process procedures. Since due process is fully discussed in Chapter 7, it will not be repeated here, but the close relationship between classification and due process should be kept in mind when reading that discussion.

IMPLICATIONS FOR HIGHER EDUCATION

Colleges and universities traditionally have been involved in evaluation through their training and research programs, and often have provided testing services for the public schools. Under P.L. 94–142 and Sec. 504, the roles and responsibilities of institutions of higher education will probably need to be expanded in order to implement the law effectively.

Research

Currently, there is a pressing demand for more research on topics such as the elimination of cultural bias; the elimination of bias attributable to particular handicapping conditions; the development of criterion-referenced tests; the development of procedures to collect information on the handicapped student's physical condition, adaptive behavior, social adjustment, sociocultural background, and language dominance; and methods by which parents can be meaningfully involved in the evaluation process. The complexity of the task warrants the expertise of an interdisciplinary faculty. Trained personnel are needed in the fields of psychology, special education, educational administration, sociology, law, medicine, linguistics, physical therapy, occupational therapy, and social work. Faculty at institutions of higher education are in a unique position to collaborate in interdisciplinary research; their efforts can help minimize or eliminate some of the obstacles to valid and reliable evaluation of handicapped students.

The application of research efforts will be enhanced if university faculty work closely with school systems to design and implement evaluation programs. Collaboration will allow college and university researchers to observe problems firsthand and test solutions that are realistic in view of such factors as time, competency of staff, and amount of paperwork. The combination of realism and empirically documented evaluation strategies holds a great potential for helping to insure that handicapped students are provided with an appropriate education.

Preparation of Students for the Evaluation Process

College and university students who plan to teach or provide direct services to handicapped students should receive training related to the legislative regulations for evaluation. College and university faculty members have a responsibility to provide such training. However, when this was suggested to one professor of an assessment course for education majors, he replied that he did not plan to include information on nondiscriminatory assessment of minority children in his course, and, furthermore, that it violated his academic freedom to be told what content might be appropriate for his course. This response has alarming implications. Public schools are being held accountable by the SEAs and by HEW for implementing P.L. 94–142 and Sec. 504. Colleges and universities prepare and certify the students who will work in those systems. How can colleges or universities graduate students who are not competent to operate within federal and state law requirements? Legislative requirements and academic freedom may well be on an inevitable collision course if many share such negative attitudes. Colleges and universities that make the decision not to prepare students according to the requirements of P.L. 94–142 and Sec. 504 should be prepared to accept the consequences dealt out by professional education organizations, public school officials, consumers, and the courts.

Educators certainly need to understand the nature of evaluation and the proper administration of a variety of measures; they also need training as evaluation team members who interpret results, make placement decisions, and plan individual programs. Colleges and universities could structure practicum arrangements so that students from special education, regular education, counseling, and school psychology can work together in the formal and informal assessment of handicapped students. In addition, the students might attend a weekly seminar to discuss their individual perspectives on evaluation, the roles and responsibilities of various team members, strategies for reaching consensus, and other issues related to conducting and interpreting evaluations within a group situation.

Providing Testing Services

A frequent practice of colleges and universities has been to have a testing center on campus staffed by faculty and graduate students, or to have arrangements for faculty and graduate students to go into the schools to test children. Traditionally, most of the testing has been oriented toward individual intelligence tests, with graduate students doing the testing to fulfill practicum requirements under the supervision of faculty members who meet state licensing requirements. This arrangement has provided much needed services to school systems that were understaffed. Such arrangements could be continued and, in addition to intelligence testing, faculty members and graduate students could offer a valuable service by introducing new tests to the schools. These new tests might be culture-specific, criterion-referenced, or measures of adaptive behavior or language dominance.

IMPLICATIONS FOR CONSUMERS

The evaluation regulations of P.L. 94–142 and Sec. 504 are sensitive to the importance of involving consumers in the process of classification and testing. The courts found consumer involvement to be essential, particularly in cases in which the child's family was a member of a different racial-ethnic group than the majority of the faculty at the school. Some of the major implications for consumers in regard to the development and implementation of evaluation procedures include: (1) participation in the collection and interpretation of evaluation data; (2) enactment of due process rights; and (3) creation of a consumer advisory board.

Participation in the Collection and Interpretation of Evaluation Data

The legislation does not specifically require a student's parents be members of the evaluation team; however, the parents *are* required members of the IEP committee (see Chapter 5). If the parents believe they have not been provided with appropriate opportunities to contribute to the evaluation process—providing data on their child or interpreting the meaning of particular test information—they should follow-up at the IEP committee. The starting point for IEP development is documenting the student's current level of performance. This information should be a direct outgrowth of the classification process. Evaluation and IEP development cannot really be separated into two discrete processes. During the initial evaluation phase parents should be encouraged to provide and interpret information. They can ask to be a member of the evaluation team if the team does not invite them to participate actively in the classification process. Whether or not the parents are formal team members, they should be asked to provide information on their child's sociocultural background, language dominance, adaptive behavior, and social adjustment at an interview or through a detailed questionnaire. Often parents feel intimidated by those who teach and evaluate their children. One way to minimize this intimidation is for educators to approach parents as partners in the evaluation process and to let them know that their insights and opinions are extremely important in formulating a program for their child's educational needs. Parents should be encouraged to provide information and to ask questions, and all communication should be in the parents' native language.

Enactment of Due Process Rights

Due process rights have strong consumer implications in regard to evaluation. Parents must be notified of all proposed evaluation procedures, their consent must be obtained prior to conducting a preplacement evaluation, a description of any action proposed or refused must be provided with reasons why the particular decision was made, and all procedural safeguards available to the parents must be fully explained. Chapter 7 includes a review of these regulations and an analysis of consumer implications. Again, it is impossible to separate evaluation and due process; because of the due process requirements, parents must be informed of every procedure and decision in the evaluation process.

Creation of a Consumer Advisory Board

The Office of Civil Rights (OCR) issued a memorandum entitled "Elimination of Discrimination in the Assignment of Children to Special Classes for the Mentally Retarded" (U.S. D/HEW, Office for Civil Rights, 11–28–72), which was viewed as the most comprehensive set of federal guidelines on educational and psychological evaluation prior to the passage of P.L. 94–142 and Sec. 504. One of the suggestions in this memorandum was that school districts should establish an assessment board including parents representing the ethnic and cultural composition of the student body. This board would take responsibility for recommending policy in regard to nondiscriminatory assessment and monitor assessment practices. P.L. 94–142 and Sec. 504 do not require public agencies to create such advisory boards with consumer representatives. The legislation does require, however, that the public agencies submit a plan to the SEA, which must in turn present a plan to HEW containing assurances that compliance with the statutes and regulations has been achieved. One strategy to insure that assessment does not discriminate against minority children is to establish an advisory board similar to that proposed by the OCR. This type of board can provide both direction and protection to the LEA. Adversary relationships can be prevented or overcome if consumers and educators practice shared responsibility and experience shared accountability.

NOTES

1. Brown v. Board of Education, 347 U.S. 483 (1954).
2. Larry P. v. Riles, 343 F. Supp. 1306, *aff'd*. 502 F.2d. 963 (9th Cir. 1974).
3. *Id*.
4. Larry P. v. Riles, *supra* n. 2; Mattie T. v. Holladay, Civ. No. DC–75–31–S (N.D. Miss., filed Apr. 25, 1975); and Hobson v. Hansen, 269 F. Supp. 401, 514 (D.D.C. 1967), *aff'd. sub nom*. Smuck v. Hobson, 408 F.2d 175 (D.C. Cir. 1969).
5. Guadalupe Org., Inc. v. Tempe Elementary School District No. 3, Civ. Act. No. 71–435 (D. Ariz. 1972); and Diana v. State Board of Education, Civ. No. C–70–37 RFP (N.D. Cal., Jan. 7, 1970 and June 18, 1973); Ruiz v. St. Bd. Ed., No. 218294 (Super. Ct., Sacramento Cty., Cal., filed Dec. 16, 1971); Hernandez v. Porter, No. 571532 (E.D. Mich., filed Aug. 13, 1975).
6. LeBanks v. Spears, 60 F.R.D. 135 (E.D. La. 1973) and Larry P. v. Riles, *supra* n. 2.
7. Stewart v. Phillips, Civ. Act. No. 70–1199–F (D. Mass., filed Sept. 14, 1970); Larry P. v. Riles, *supra* n. 2; and Hobson v. Hansen, *supra* n. 4.
8. Hernandez v. Porter, *supra* n. 5; Stewart v. Phillips, *supra* n. 7; Diana v. Bd., *supra* n. 5; Guadalupe Org. v. Tempe, *supra* n. 5.
9. Larry P. v. Riles, *supra* n. 2 and Stewart v. Phillips, *supra* n. 7.
10. LeBanks v. Spears, *supra* n. 6.
11. Carrington v. Rash, 380 U.S. 89, 92 (1965).
12. Stell v. Savannah-Chatham County Board of Education, 333 F.2d 55, 61 (5th Cir.), *cert. denied*, 379 U.S. 933 (1964); Miller v. School District No. 2, Clarendon County, 256 F. Supp. 370 (D.S.C. 1966); and Hobson v. Hansen, 269 F. Supp., *supra* n. 4. at 511–12.
13. Hobson v. Hansen, *supra* n. 4.
14. Larry P. v. Riles, *supra* n. 2; Diana v. Board, *supra* n. 5; and Mattie T. v. Holladay, *supra* n. 4.
15. Larry P. v. Riles, *supra* n. 2, and Diana v. Board, *supra* n. 5.
16. Larry P. v. Riles, *supra* n. 2, and Diana v. Board, *supra* n. 5.
17. Diana v. Board, *supra* n. 5; Guadalupe Org. v. Tempe, *supra* n. 5; Lau v. Nichols, 414 U.S. 563 (1974); U.S. v. Texas, 342 F. Supp. 24 (E.D. Tex. 1971), *aff'd*. 466 F.2d 518 (5th Cir. 1972); and Serna v. Portales, 499 F.2d 1147 (10th cir. 1974).
18. Larry P. v. Riles, *supra* n. 2.
19. LeBanks v. Spears, *supra* n. 6.
20. Larry P. v. Riles, *supra* n. 2; *cf*. Carmical v. Craven, 457 F.2d 582 (9th Cir. 1971), *cert. denied*, 409 U.S. 929 (1972), on use of intelligence tests to screen jurors.

21. Larry P. v. Riles, *supra* n.2.
22. LeBanks v. Spears, *supra* n. 6; Mills v. D. C. Board of Education, 348 F. Supp. 866 (D.D.C. 1972); Hernandez v. Porter, *supra* n. 5; North Dakota Ass'n for Retarded Children v.Peterson, (D.N.D. filed Nov. 1972); and Rockafellow v. Brouillet, No. 787938 (Super. Ct., King City, Wash., 1976).
23. Hernandez v. Porter, *supra* n. 5.
24. *Id.*
25. *Id.*
26. *Id.*
27. N. Hobbs (Ed.). *Issues in the Classification of Children* ((2 vols.). San Francisco: Jossey-Bass, 1975, at p. 100.
28. *Ibid.* at 101.
29. *Ibid.*
30. T.D. Oakland and L.M. Laosa, "Professional, legislative, and judicial influences in psychoeducational assessment practices in schools," in T. Oakland (ed.), *Non-biased assessment of minority group children, with bias toward none* (Lexington, Kentucky: University of Kentucky, CORRC, no date).
31. American Psychological Association, *Ethical Standards of Psychologists* (Washington, D.C.: 1972).
32. F. Davis, *Standards for educational and psychological tests* (Washington, D.C.:American Psychological Association, 1974).
33. L.M. Laosa, "Reform in education and psychological assessment: Cultural and linguistic issues," *Journal of the Association of Mexican American Educators*, 3 (1973): 214-224; J.R. Mercer, "Implications of current assessment procedures for Mexican American Children," *Journal of the Association of Mexican American Educators*, 1 (1973): 25-33; T.E. Newland, "Assumptions underlying psychological testing," in T. Oakland and B.N. Phillips (eds.) *Assessing minority group children: A Special Issue of Journal of School Psychology* (New York: Behavioral Publications, 1973), 315-322; and T.D. Oakland, "Assessing minority group children: Challenges for school psychologists," in T. Oakland and B.N. Phillips (eds.), *Assessing minority group children: A Special Issue of Journal of School Psychology* (New York: Behavioral Publications, 1973).
34. T.D. Oakland and P. Matuszek, "Using tests in nondiscriminatory assessment," in T. Oakland (ed.), *Non-biased assessment of minority group children, with bias toward none* (Lexington, Kentucky: University of Kentucky, CORRC, no date).
35. L.M. Laosa, "Historical antecedents and current issues in nondiscriminatory assessment of children's abilities," in T. Oakland (ed.), *Non-biased assessment of minority group children, with bias toward none* (Lexington, Kentucky: University of Kentucky, CORRC, no date).
36. Oakland and Matuszek, "Using tests in nondiscriminatory assessment."

37. M. Budoff, "Measuring learning potential: An alternative to the traditional intelligence test," in G.R. Gredler (ed.), *Ethical and Legal Factors in the Practice of School Psychology* (Philadelphia, Pennsylvania: Temple University, 1972).

38. Jane R. Mercer and J. Ysseldyke, "Designing diagnostic intervention programs," in T. Oakland (ed.), *Non-biased assessment of minority group children, with bias toward none* (Lexington, Kentucky: University of Kentucky, CORRC, no date).

39. R. Williams, "The BITCH-100: A culture specific test" (Paper presented at the 80th Annual Convention of the American Psychological Association, Honolulu, September, 1972).

40. Budoff, "Measuring learning potential."

41. Mercer and Ysseldyke, "Designing diagnostic intervention programs."

42. R. Cornejo, "A criterion referenced assessment system for bilingual reading," *California Journal of Educational Research*, 25 (1974): 294-301.

43. T.D. Oakland (ed.), *Non-biased assessment of minority group children, with bias toward none* (Lexington, Kentucky: University of Kentucky, CORRC, no date).

44. Mercer and Ysseldyke, "Designing diagnostic intervention programs."

45. Davis, *Standards for educational and psychological tests.*

1978 Supplement

n. 2. The trial on the merits is proceeding as this supplement is being prepared, No. C-71-2270 (M.D. Cal.).

Individualized and Appropriate Education

CONSTITUTIONAL FOUNDATIONS

In its finding of facts in P.L. 94–142, Congress zeroed in on individualized education, characterizing it in terms of "appropriate" education and stating in Sec. 601 (b) (2) and (3) that:

1. the special educational needs of handicapped children are not being fully met; and
2. more than half of the handicapped children in the United States do not receive appropriate educational services and are thus denied full equality of opportunity.

These claims are well grounded on the constitutional principles of substantive due process under the Fifth and Fourteenth Amendments and on equal protection under the Fourteenth. The common element of substantive due process and equal protection, in the context of individualized or appropriate education, is exclusion. Total exclusion from any type of educational opportunity violates both constitutional principles (see Chapter 3 on zero reject). Functional exclusion from a meaningful educational opportunity likewise violates both principles, since education that lacks meaning or significance for the pupil is tantamount to no education at all.

Case Law

The courts have certainly realized this important aspect of equal educational opportunity. *MARC*, for example, took the proposition that if all handicapped children are to be furnished with an education the purpose of that education must be redefined, since many of them are inherently unable to master even a modified regular academic program. The goal of their education must be to develop their capabilities to the highest possible level of achievement for each child.[1] *Mills* required a handicapped child's education to be "suited to [his] needs,"[2] and *PARC* ordered that it be "appropriate to his learning capacities."[3]

MARC, Mills, and *PARC* addressed the substantive due process aspects of appropriate education (a meaningful education in order to prevent functional exclusion); *Lau* v. *Nichols*[4] skirted the issue but arguably gave comfort to it (see Chapter 3). Equal protection is the other constitutional foundation for claims to an appropriate education for handicapped children. A federal district court has ruled that learning disabled children have made a viable claim under the equal protection principles that they are the victims of unconstitutional discrimination when they are not given instruction specially suited to their needs although nonhandicapped and mentally retarded children are being furnished with an *appropriate* free public education. The discrimination exists in learning disabled children being treated differently than nonhandicapped or mentally retarded children.[5] Another federal court has denied a state's motion to dismiss a case alleging that two multiply handicapped persons have been denied equal protection because the nature of the educational programs offered to the plaintiffs is such that no chance exists that the programs will be of benefit to them.[6] Both cases rely on equal protection concepts to argue discrimination in the provision of meaningful (i.e., appropriate or suitable) education.

Other recently filed cases are pushing the claim to an appropriate education even farther. One case is based on the assertion that, even in the absence of federal law, a handicapped child has a right to an individualized education program.[7] Another claims that an emotionally disturbed child has a right to psychological counseling,[8] and yet another alleges that a child's constitutional rights to substantive due process (freedom over one's self under the "liberty" and "property" phrases of the Fifth and Fourteenth Amendments) have been violated when a school requires him to take certain psychotropic medication (to prevent or alleviate hyperactivity) as a condition of his being allowed to attend school.[9] And another case contends that a child placed in a separate program for emotionally disturbed youths, searched by staff for contraband, and put into programs segregated by race and sex, has also been denied an appropriate education.[10]

Court Remedies

None of the courts have yet defined "appropriate" or "suitable." The most they have done is discuss the special educational opportunities that should be made available. *Mills*[11] and *LeBanks*[12] required compensatory or adult education to overcome the effects of prior exclusion. Although "early intervention" (that is, preschool training) for handicapped children has not been ordered by the courts, legislatures often find, as a matter of state policy, that early education is desirable.[13]

Zero-reject policy does not mean that all children must be placed in regular classrooms within the public school system. "Suitable education" may mean homebound instruction for physically handicapped children unable to attend school. In some instances, however, homebound or in-hospital instruction is permissible only if the pupil is physically unable to attend school.[14] A child who cannot benefit from a program of instruction within the public school system may be assigned to the state department that oversees state institutions, but he is nevertheless entitled to an appropriate program of education and training.[15] *MARC* also required that transportation to alternative forms of education be provided by the state.[16]

Another alternative to classroom instruction within the public schools is a program of tuition and maintenance subsidies for children whose special needs cannot be met by the public school system. Many states have provisions for tuition subsidies in cases where a private school or institution is providing a child with suitable education and training.[17] *Mills, PARC,* and *MARC* all order that tuition grants be made available if suitable education must be obtained from a private school or institution.[18] These cases also noted, however, that a state has not discharged its duty to provide education if it refers a child to a private facility where he is only placed on a waiting list.[19] (See Chapter 3 for a fuller discussion of the tuition cases.)

Clearly, alternatives to regular classroom education are recognized as sometimes being the most appropriate form of education for a child. Some courts, however, have stated that regular classroom instruction (with auxiliary services if necessary) is preferable to separate special classes, which in turn are preferable to homebound instruction.[20] This preference for mainstream placement is based on the belief that children with special problems benefit from contact with nonhandicapped children and suffer less from the stigma of difference attached to children separated from the regular program. (See Chapter 6 for a discussion of the "least restrictive" and "mainstream" issues.)

There may also be a new challenge to appropriate education being developed in the courts. A case recently filed alleged that handicapped children are not given an appropriate education if their separate programs experience a decrease in the number of teachers and staff and if an exception to class size—larger classes than prescribed by local school board regulation—is allowed.[21] One theory of this case is perfectly obvious: appropriate education depends on a minimum staff-to-student ratio. Another theory may be in the offing: handicapped children should not be subjected to decreased staff and increased class size if nonhandicapped students are not also subjected to enlarged staff-class ratios. This theory is well grounded in the equal protection doctrine and finds support in P.L. 94–142 and Sec. 504, which measure an appropriate education for the handicapped in terms of equal standards and equivalency to education for the nonhandicapped. *MARC*[22] also made it clear that an appropriate education depends on students being enrolled in programs that meet accreditation standards. Sec. 121a.4 duplicates this requirement.

FEDERAL LEGISLATION

P.L. 94–142

In the cases, the requirement that a handicapped child's education be appropriate or suitable to *his* needs is simply a requirement that it be individually appropriate or suitable; in the language of P.L. 94–142, the requirement of an appropriate education [Sec. 612 (1)] boils down to a requirement that his education be individualized [Sec. 612 (4)] to redress problems found by the Congress [Sec. 601 (b) (2) and (3)]. The policy of providing an *appropriate* education [Sec. 601 (c)] is achieved principally by the device of the individualized education program (IEP).

> The term "individualized education program" means a written statement for each handicapped child developed in any meeting by a representative of the local educational agency or an intermediate educational unit who shall be qualified to provide, or supervise the provision of, specially designed instruction to meet the unique needs of handicapped children, the teacher, the parents or guardian of such child, and whenever appropriate, such child, which statement shall include (A) a statement of the present levels of education performance of such child, (B) a statement of annual goals, including short-term instructional objectives, (C) a statement of the specific educational services to be provided to such child, and the extent to which such child will be able to participate in regular educational programs, (D) the projected date for initiation and anticipated duration of such services, and appropriate objective criteria and evaluation procedures and schedules for determining, on at least an annual basis, whether instructional objectives are being achieved.

The SEA and the public agency must assume responsibility for implementing a child's IEP in a private or parochial school. This responsibility includes initiating a meeting to develop an IEP before the child is placed in the private or parochial school and insuring that a representative of the school attends the meeting or that other methods, such as individual or conference telephone calls, are used to insure participation. Meetings must be held to review or revise the IEP after a child is placed in a private or parochial program. A representative of the public agency must be involved in any decisions made at these meetings and must agree to proposed IEP changes. The public agency is also responsible for insuring that an IEP is developed and reviewed for each child placed in a private or parochial school by the agency before October 1, 1977 (the effective date of the regulations) [Sec. 121a.341, .347 and .348].

The IEP. Each LEA must establish, or revise if appropriate, an IEP for each handicapped child at the beginning of each school year. The provisions must be reviewed and, if appropriate, revised at regular intervals, but not less than annually [Sec. 614 (a) (5) and Sec. 121a.343]. Similarly, each SEA is required to assure the Bureau for Education of the Handicapped (BEH) that each LEA will maintain records of the IEP for each handicapped child and that the program will be established, reviewed, and revised as required in Sec. 614 (a) (5) [Sec. 612 (4) and Sec. 121a.341]. The state plan must contain procedures for the SEA to evaluate—at least annually—the effectiveness of LEA programs in meeting the educational needs of handicapped children. The evaluation is to include an evaluation of IEPs [Sec. 613 (a) (11)]. If a child is placed in a private program by the SEA or an LEA, he is still entitled to an IEP in the private school [Sec. 613 (a) (4) (B) (i) and (ii) and Secs. 121a.341 (b), .347 and .348].

Sec. 121a.346 requires the IEP to include the following elements:

(a) A statement of the child's present levels of educational performance;

(b) A statement of annual goals, including short term instructional objectives;

(c) A statement of the specific special education and related services to be provided to the child, and the extent to which the child will be able to participate in regular educational programs;

(d) The projected dates for initiation of services and the anticipated duration of the services; and

(e) Appropriate objective criteria and evaluation procedures and schedules for determining, on at least an annual basis, whether the short term instructional objectives are being achieved.

The regulations make it clear that the IEP is not a legally binding contract and that no agency, teacher, or other person may be held accountable if the child does not achieve the projected progress based on the annual goals and objectives [Sec. 121a.349]. This section does not relieve agencies and teachers from making good faith efforts to teach the child (there are no cases on this point); nor does it prevent parents from using due process procedures for problems related to the IEP, the agencies or the teachers.

Developing an IEP. The following people must be involved in developing the IEP: a representative of the public agency (other than the child's teacher) who is qualified to provide or supervise the child's special education; the teacher; one or both of the child's parents; the student, when appropriate; and other individuals at the discretion of the parents or agency. When a child is first evaluated, an IEP committee member must be a member of the team that evaluates him, or the public agency representative, the teacher, or some other person attending the IEP meeting knowledgeable about the evaluation procedures used and able to interpret the results. Either the agency representative or the teacher should be "qualified" in the area of the child's suspected disability [Sec. 121a.344].

Since parent participation in the child's education and particularly in planning the IEP is a high priority under P.L. 94–142, public agencies are to take specified steps to insure that one or both of the child's parents have a chance to attend the IEP conference. These steps include advance notice of the meeting, mutually convenient scheduling of the meeting, and arranging for interpreters for deaf or non-English speaking parents. If the parent(s) cannot attend the meeting, they may still participate through individual or conference telephone calls. The agency may have an IEP meeting without parent participation only when it can document that it unsuccessfully attempted to have the parents participate. The documentation should include detailed records of telephone calls, copies of letters to or from the parents, and the results of visits to the parents' home or places of work. The agency must give the parents a copy of the IEP if they ask for it [Sec. 121a.345].

Timing of IEP. The statute mandates that an IEP for each child must be established, or revised if appropriate, at the beginning of each school year. Exactly when must the conference be held? The regulations specify that the planning conferences for a handicapped child already receiving special education and related services must be conducted early enough to insure that the child's IEP is developed (or revised) by the beginning of the next school year. To meet this provision, a local educational agency should conduct the meeting at the end of the school year or during the summer [Sec. 121a.343 (b)]. If a handicapped child is not receiving special education, an IEP committee meeting must be held within thirty days of the determination that the child needs special education and related services [Sec. 121a. 343 (c)].

Rationale for the IEP. The IEP is justified on many grounds:

1. The IEP is, of course, a method for assessing the child and prescribing an appropriate program for him (thereby overcoming objections based on substantive due process or equal protection—claims of functional exclusion or discrimination).

2. The IEP enables the teacher and other educators to better help the child develop his full potential, as required by *MARC*. It is one of the most important elements of his success in school.

3. It enables the school and the parents to monitor the child's progress in school, measure his development, identify his areas of weakness, and concentrate on remediating those weaknesses.

4. It recognizes that each child is unique and should be treated in light of his own needs.

5. It is a safeguard not only for the child but also for his parents, inasmuch as they are legitimately concerned about misclassification, inappropriate placements, and inadequate programs.

6. The requirement of parental involvement not only recognizes the legitimate concerns of the parents to have their child protected against potential wrongs, but also strengthens the child's educational program by linking his parents' views of his needs and their needs with the school's and parents' ability to train the child. Parents have a wealth of information about their child that can enhance the child's schoolroom training and be carried over into the child's family life if it is shared with school personnel and incorporated in the IEP. The "six-hour handicapped child" (one who is seen as handicapped only when he is at school) is too familiar, but parental involvement in the IEP has the potential of relegating them to history. Quite simply, what happens to the child in school is relevant to his home life, and vice versa.

7. The IEP is a technique for sharing decisions and decision-making powers among school personnel and parents; it is another step along the line toward achieving participatory democracy in public education.

8. It is also a powerful device for assuring accountability. It makes the schools accountable to the child for what they do to train him by requiring an assessment of achievement; a statement of goals, services, and timetables; and procedures and criteria for determining if the goals are being met. It makes schools accountable to the parent as a taxpayer and as a participant in developing the individualized program. Parent involvement in curriculum decisions also promotes accountability on the part of the parents. As an outgrowth of the IEP development, parents may come to assume specific responsibility for teaching or reinforcing particular skills and concepts at home.

9. By securing parent participation, the IEP also helps forestall the possibility of a due process protest and hearing under Sec. 615. It is not a device of cooption, although some may see it that way. Rather, it is a positive force that assures parent/school decision-sharing, contributing to a collaborative relationship between parent and school personnel instead of an adversarial confrontation.

10. IEPs are, of course, necessary to accomplish the zero-reject principles; they tend to assure that no handicapped child is overlooked once he is identified as handicapped. They enable school authorities to plan services for the handicapped and to provide those services; in addition, they furnish a basis for BEH evaluation of school programs. They are a way to focus the capacity of a school system on the child. Like procedural due process, the IEP is child-centered, not system-centered.

11. IEPs reflect the best current thinking of special educators; in the words of the Report of the House of Representatives [Report No. 94–332, Education of All Handicapped Children Act of 1975, June 26, 1975, p. 13], "(t)he movement toward the individualization of instruction, involving the participation of the child and the parent, as well as all relevant educational professionals, is a trend gaining ever wider support in educational, parental, and political groups throughout the nation."

12. Finally, the policy of the IEP, individualization, is reflected in P.L. 94–142 and in two other federal laws affecting the handicapped, P.L. 93–112, the Rehabilitation Act Amendments of 1973 and P.L. 93–380, the Education Amendments of 1974 (Title 1). The latter two require individualized rehabilitation or education programs for handicapped persons.

Other statutory provisions. Although the IEP is the principal means in P.L. 94–142 for assuring an appropriate education, it is not the only one.

1. Procedures to assure nondiscriminatory testing serve as safeguards against inappropriate placement and resulting inappropriate education [Sec. 612 (5) (C)].

2. The requirement of placement in the least restrictive appropriate program also protects against inappropriate placement and unsuitable programs [Sec. 612 (5) (B)]. It advances the concept of appropriate education by insuring appropriate placement.

3. The rights of parents to see and comment on LEA records enables them to hold the school accountable for providing an appropriate education [Secs. 614 (a) (4) and 615 (b) (1) (A)].

4. The due process hearing is yet another method for accountability and compliance with the requirements of appropriate education [Sec. 615].

5. The early childhood incentive grants [Sec. 619] and the inclusion of children aged three to five in the act [Sec. 612 (2) (B)] are intended to make elementary education, especially in the least restrictive setting, appropriate for the child upon his attaining elementary-school age.

6. The "exclusion" (not more than 12 percent of a state's children aged five through seventeen may be counted as handicapped for the purpose of receiving federal funds under the act) is also a device for appropriate education. It tends to prevent overcategorization and miscategorization of children as handicapped, thereby preventing inappropriate identification, evaluation, placement, and unsuitable programs [Sec. 611 (a) (5)].

7. State educational agencies must develop and implement a "comprehensive system of personnel development," a means for disseminating to school personnel "significant information derived from educational research, demonstration, and similar projects" [Sec. 613 (a) (3) (A)]; and, where appropriate, "promising educational practices and materials development through such projects" [Sec. 613 (a) (3) (B)]. These requirements are intended to improve the schools so that they can provide appropriate education to handicapped children. BEH and SEA evaluation, particularly for IEP compliance, will also help LEAs provide appropriate programs [Secs. 618 (d) (2) and 613 (a) (11)].

Determining what is appropriate. There are no statutory definitions of "appropriate education." P.L. 94–142 seeks to define "appropriate education" by a *process*, not by language cast in stone. The "definition" of appropriate education looks first to the child and second to the means by which an appropriate education is to be provided. It is child-centered and process-oriented, not system-centered or result-oriented; it takes account of educational "inputs," not educational "outputs." For example, assume a nine-year-old child is moderately mentally retarded and school personnel (and his parents) are concerned about what kind of education, what kind of placement, is "appropriate" for him. How do they answer their question? They do it by adhering to the following process: (1) they make a nondiscriminatory evaluation; (2) they develop an individualized education program; (3) they attempt to place the child in the least restrictive appropriate program; (4) throughout this process, they see that the parents have access to the child's school records; and (5) if the parents wish to protest the placement or any other action related to the child's right to a free appropriate education, they call a due process hearing. The act's technique for defining "appropriate," then, is to require that a process be followed, in the belief that a fair process will produce an acceptable result—an appropriate education. The regulations do, however, define "free appropriate education" for special education and related services in terms of standards and conformity with IEPs [Sec. 121a.4]. Thus there are two techniques in P.L. 94–142 for determining what is appropriate.

Sec. 504

The regulations under Sec. 504 [Sec. 84.33 (b)] provide a third way to define "appropriate" education by requiring the school to provide the handicapped child with special education and related aids and services designed to meet his educational needs as adequately as the needs of nonhandicapped children are met (an "equivalency" definition). The program must be based on the "least restrictive placement" principles and include a full and individual preplacement evaluation, a nondiscriminatory test, an annual reevaluation of special educational placement, and procedural due process. Implementing an IEP is one way to provide an appropriate education; but Sec. 504 does not require an IEP, nor do its regulations. Like P.L. 94–142, Sec. 504 addresses the requirement of appropriate or individualized education by requiring that schools follow a process and requires equivalency between the handicapped and nonhandicapped. In commenting on Sec. 84.33, HEW said [*Fed. Reg.*, May 4, 1977, p. 22690–91]:

> Section 84.33 (b) concerns the provision of appropriate educational services to handicapped children. To be appropriate, such services must be designed to meet handicapped children's individual educational needs to the same extent that those of nonhandicapped children are met. An appropriate education could consist of education in regular classes, education in regular classes with the use of supplementary services, or special education and related services. Special education may include specially designed instruction in classrooms, at home, or in private or public institutions and may be accompanied by

such related services as developmental, corrective, and other supportive services (including psychological, counseling, and medical diagnostic services). The placement of the child must however, be consistent with the requirements of Sec. 84.34 and be suited to his or her educational needs.

The quality of the educational services provided to handicapped students must equal that of the services provided to nonhandicapped students; thus, handicapped student's teachers must be trained in the instruction of persons with the handicap in question and appropriate materials and equipment must be available. The Department is aware that the supply of adequately trained teachers may, at least at the outset of the imposition of this requirement, be insufficient to meet the demand of all recipients. This factor will be considered in determining the appropriateness of the remedy for noncompliance with this section. A new Sec. 84.33 (b) (2) has been added, which allows the full implementation of an individualized education program developed in accordance with the standards of the EHA [Education of the Handicapped Act].

IMPLICATIONS FOR PUBLIC SCHOOLS

Developing IEPs is a major concern for administrators and teachers. It is difficult to argue with the principle of an individualized and specified education program, jointly developed by a multidisciplinary team including the parents and the student, and based on the student's present level of performance and identified needs. Educators probably should have been assuming such responsibilities all along. On the other hand, the requirements for IEPs are difficult to implement. For many school systems, they represent a radical change from the curriculum practices of the past. If the IEP requirements are implemented in a systematic and sound fashion, they have the potential of significantly changing educational decision making and programming. Major implications for public schools include: (1) development of system policies and procedures; (2) attention to curriculum development; (3) inservice training; (4) allocation of time; and (5) monitoring and documentation.

Developing System Policies and Procedures

The requirements of the IEP, which have been previously discussed in this chapter, are massive, covering the following areas:

1. required components (e.g., level of performance, goals, and objectives);
2. timing (IEPs must be completed at the beginning of the school year or within thirty days after the student is classified as handicapped);
3. participants (the team must include an individual responsible for providing or supervising special education, the teacher, the evaluator, parents, and possibly the student); and
4. scope (IEPs must be written anytime instruction needs to be specially designed or altered to meet the needs of the handicapped student).

The effective implementation of these requirements cannot be assumed to occur in school systems in an incidental fashion. It is essential that policies and procedures be planned and specified in writing by the LEA. It is also important for persons involved in writing and implementing IEPs to participate in developing policies for IEPs.

The starting point for developing policies might be to establish a system-wide task force comprised of the following individuals or groups: curriculum supervisors, special education directors, principals, special education teachers (resource and self-contained), regular classroom teachers, school psychologists, counselors, special therapists employed by the school (speech, physical), parents of handicapped students, and representatives from the Parent-Teacher Association. Although the size of this group would of necessity be large, it is important to include a broad array of school personnel in policy development, since they all are likely to be involved to some extent in IEP implementation. The person who will have ultimate administrative and supervisory responsibility for IEP development and implementation in the school system should be designated as early as possible. In most school systems, this person will probably be from the central administrative office. Meeting the IEP requirements within the specified timelines is a formidable task, and assigning the responsibility for policy development and implementation to a single person with task force support facilitates the process of getting the job done. It also provides school personnel with a single contact person to approach with their questions or concerns. The qualifications of the chosen person should be examined very carefully, and might include competency in skills related to curriculum development and individualized instruction, a positive attitude toward the provision of individualized programs for handicapped students, interpersonal skills in working with colleagues who have opposite points of view, organizational skills, and a generally positive and enthusiastic approach to educational tasks. The quality and comprehensiveness of the system's planning and the way the IEPs are initially introduced to school personnel will greatly influence the system's success or failure to meet the intent and spirit of the law. The individual with the ultimate administrative and supervisory responsibility for IEPs has a unique opportunity to provide positive leadership.

When the responsible person is designated and the task force convenes for the first time, everyone should have written copies of the legislative requirements for IEPs. The requirements provide the "givens"; the policies for implementing the requirements are the "negotiable" items. It is important to keep energies and comments focused on viable areas; it is unproductive to just argue the pros and cons of IEPs. It would be far more constructive to concentrate on identifying factors already existing in the school system that might facilitate or obstruct IEP development and implementation. After identifying the "assets" and "liabilities," the group can develop strategies to strengthen the assets and minimize or eliminate the liabilities. Naturally, the particular combination of assets and liabilities will vary from system to system.

Prior to developing policy, the task force members may want to break into small groups and write an IEP for an already identified handicapped student. Working through the task from beginning to end can give the members insights into a desirable format, the time involved, the curriculum resources that are needed, the nature of IEP parent conferences, the necessary coordination among individuals, and other relevant factors. This strategy can be especially informative if each small group develops an IEP for a student of a different age and type of handicap, using different IEP formats.

Task force members should also consider bringing in consultants from school systems that have already developed an effective implementation plan or some other knowledgeable persons who have had experience with initiating IEP policies. The task force should study a variety of models before formulating policy, if possible within the constraints of the timelines. Soliciting comments and ideas from other members of the system not represented on the task force can also be a wise step to take, because the final policies will then represent the viewpoints of everyone responsible for implementing the program.

After all the necessary information has been gathered, the task force must set a policy and write procedural statements on the following topics:

1. the administrative/supervisory role and its responsibilities;
2. the IEP format to be adopted;
3. the method of introducing it to school faculty;
4. procedures for parent involvement;
5. curriculum development considerations;
6. inservice training;
7. allocation of time; and
8. monitoring and documentation.

They should present their recommendations to the LEA's board of education for review and adoption. The first four of the above topics will be discussed in this section; the last four topics are dealt with in later sections. (For more information, see NASTE,[23] Torres,[24] and Turnbull, Strickland, and Brantley.[25])

The administrative/supervisory role and its responsibilities. The importance of assigning overall administrative and supervisory responsibility to a single individual has already been discussed. If this recommendation is followed, the policy statement should include a job description for this individual.

Format. P.L. 94–142 specifies components that must be included in the IEP. The LEA, working with the SEA, is responsible for adopting a particular format. Some SEAs might strongly recommend that all LEAs use a uniform format, since uniformity will simplify the SEA's job of monitoring the procedures of the LEA. Other SEAs merely suggest a model that might be followed; but encourage the LEAs to design an IEP format that is best suited to their personnel. When recommending policy on this topic, LEAs and SEAs should work together closely. A major consideration is choosing a format that is educationally meaningful. If the IEP is to be relevant to the handicapped students' educational programs, the format must allow for specifying a meaningful educational program. Some formats presently being used are so short that it is impossible to include short-term instructional objectives that would lead to mastery of annual goals. "Paper compliance" with IEP requirements is a waste of everyone's time and is probably legally insufficient. The format can immediately convey to school personnel the value the system places on IEP development; a format that helps teachers plan in a systematic and detailed fashion also contributes to successful implementation of IEP requirements .

Method of introduction to school faculty. The way school faculty members are informed of IEP requirements, policies, and procedures is critical to effectively implementing IEPs. Many faculty members have only heard bits and pieces of information about them and have distorted impressions of what actually is involved. In some school systems, the anxiety level is high regarding IEP expectations, and the teachers generally want to know *exactly* what is expected of them.

The initial presentation to the faculty should be as substantive, organized, and positive as possible. Since the principal is the local leader, his or her endorsement can be vital. It might be advisable for special education teachers not to be actively involved in the initial presentations. If they are, classroom teachers may see the special educators as having "imposed" the IEP requirements on them.

Written policy statements should be given to all faculty members. Timelines are short, and educators want to know what the P.L. 94–142 requirements mean; clearly stated policies and procedures will certainly help them. Plans for inservice training (discussed later in this section) should be announced at the initial IEP meeting. Again, teachers should be provided with as much support as possible and given assurance that the task of IEP development and implementation is manageable and has the potential to increase the quality of education for handicapped students.

Procedures for parental involvement. The nature of parental involvement in IEP development and approval is probably more extensive than the traditional teacher-parent relationships in the majority of school systems. The attitudes of some educators toward such joint educational decision making may require altering and their skill in interviewing parents may need strengthening. Strategies for informing parents of their role in IEP development, as specified in P.L. 94–142, must be planned and carried out: the location of the conference, its timing, and the nature of parental participation must be specified. Methods of providing documentation of parents' unwillingness to be involved must also be designed; and a due process procedure for resolving conflicts of teacher-parent opinions should be set forth. All of these issues should be addressed by the task force and included in the written policies and procedures that are recommended.

Attention to Curriculum Development

The IEP essentially specifies a systematic and coordinated curriculum for a handicapped student. It requires educators to pinpoint the skills and concepts the student has achieved, the sequential skills and concepts he should learn by the end of the school year, and the means of evaluating his progress. The IEP is based on a diagnostic-prescriptive model of instruction, and educators must be able to plan step-by-step instruction based on a hierarchy of skill and concept development.

Many educators are not accustomed to planning instruction in a sequential fashion. At a conference in which IEP requirements were discussed, a teacher commented that he had no idea what skills and concepts he would cover next week in his physical education class, much less next month or by the end of the school year. Many teachers plan instruction from day-to-day and may be reluctant to try a systematic and logical sequence of presenting new information. Take, for example, the concept of addition. Although it may seem like a simple skill, it can be an extremely difficult process for students with learning problems. Writing short-term objectives for the IEP means specifying what the sequence of addition skills and concepts will include. Thus, the task for school systems is not just the mechanical development of IEPs; it is also training teachers in the process of curriculum development with emphasis on task analysis skills (breaking tasks down into sequential steps). IEPs can be written with far more facility and in significantly less time when teachers have these curriculum competencies or have resource material with skill sequences already developed.

Considering the timelines for IEP development, school systems should immediately start collecting reference materials that specify skill sequences. Figure 5-1 shows a sample sequence for beginning subtracting. For teachers who are

Figure 5-1: SKILL SEQUENCE IN BEGINNING SUBTRACTION

1. **Demonstrates understanding of the concept/operation of subtraction with concrete objects.**
2. **Demonstrates understanding of the concept/operation of subtraction with pictures.**
3. **Demonstrates knowledge of the *meaning* of the "−" symbol.**
4. **Demonstrates understanding of the proper use of the "−" symbol in a pictorial sentence.**
5. **Demonstrates understanding of the proper use of the "−" symbol in a numerical sentence.**
6. **Solves simple subtraction problems with minuends of 5 or less using concrete objects.**

7. Solves simple subtraction problems with minuends of 5 or less using pictures.
8. Solves simple *vertically*-presented numerical subtraction problems with minuends of 5 or less.
9. Solves simple *horizontally*-presented numerical subtraction problems with minuends of 5 or less.
10. Can supply the missing *term* in a subtraction equation (minuends of 5 or less), with and without picture cues.
11. Solves simple *orally*-presented subtraction word problems using concrete objects, minuends of 5 or less.
12. Solves simple *written* subtraction word problems (picture clues provided), minuends of 5 or less.
13. Solves simple orally-presented subtraction word problems (no object cues provided), minuends of 5 or less.
14. Solves simple *written* subtraction word problems (no picture clues provided), minuends of 5 or less.
15. Masters basic subtraction facts for minuends of 5 or less by rote.
16. Solves simple subtraction problems, minuends of 10 or less, using concrete objects.
17. Solves simple subtraction problems, minuends of 10 or less, using pictures.
18. Solves simple *vertically*-presented (i.e. columnar) numerical subtraction problems, minuends of 10 or less.
19. Solves simple *horizontally*-presented numerical subtraction problems, minuends of 10 or less.
20. Can supply the missing *term* in a subtraction equation (minuends of 10 or less), with and without picture cues.
21. Solves simple *orally*-presented subtraction word problems using concrete objects, minuends of 10 or less.
22. Solves simple *written* subtraction word problems (picture clues provided), minuends of 10 or less.
23. Solves simple *orally*-presented subtraction word problems (no object cues provided), minuends of 10 or less.
24. Solves simple *written* subtraction word problems (no picture clues provided), minuends of 10 or less.
25. Masters basic subtraction facts for minuends of 10 or less by rote.

---

unfamiliar with breaking skills and concepts into smaller steps, this sort of checklist can be extremely helpful. If the school system can provide teachers with a variety of curriculum sequences in different subject areas, they can use these reference materials to write IEPs and refine their own task analysis skills by familiarizing themselves with existing skill hierarchies. Skill and concept sequences can be collected from curriculum guides, commercial instructional programs, textbooks on curriculum, state and regional staff development centers, and education departments of colleges and universities. Another strategy for obtaining reference materials is to have committees of faculty members work on the specification of specific curriculum skills and concepts. When the skills and concepts are written in behavioral form, they are easily transferrable to the IEP. In fact, one approach is to develop a format that includes a skill and concept checklist (Figure 5-2). Using this format, IEP committee members could simply check the appropriate skills and write in the level of accuracy the student would be expected to reach. The major advantage of this checklist format is that it can be a tremendous time-saver for the IEP committee members. A danger of this approach might be the tendency to fit the student into a preset curriculum rather than designing the curriculum to the needs of the student. This danger can be minimized by recognizing that every listing of skills and concepts should be interpreted with flexibility.

Although checklists can be helpful to educators for planning curriculum, consideration should also be given to providing inservice training on refining curriculum skills related to the instruction of both handicapped and nonhandicapped students. All students benefit from an indivdualized approach to curriculum development.

Inservice Training

Effective implementation of IEP requirements will be facilitated by inservice training. School personnel may need training in assessment, curriculum development, knowledge of instructional materials, parent interviewing, and coordinated planning (working in teams). The *development* of IEPs is only the first step in the process; the real test for improving the quality of education for handicapped students is *implementing* the IEP. A substantial number of workshops on the mechanics of IEP development are currently being planned and conducted; there is not nearly as much attention being focused on how to implement the IEP once it has been developed. It is one thing to write objectives for language development for hearing impaired students; it is quite another to plan and use instructional strategies to meet those objectives.

Time is at a premium in regard to inservice training. It is important to get the maximum benefit from every training hour. Since IEP development and implementation requires shared responsibility, perhaps one of the more effective methods of providing training is through small groups working together and actually "walking through" the steps of developing an IEP. As a beginning point, the coordinator for IEP development might provide training or locate a consultant

Fig. 5-2: IEP Incorporating a Vocational Skills Checklist (High School Level)

Skills	Accuracy	Materials	Individual Responsible	Evaluation
1. Practices filling out various application forms reading and spelling all words independently				
2. Can role play interview situation engaging in proper behavior				
a. Introduction				
b. Proper conversation				
c. Courtesy and politeness				
d. Eye-contact and general alertness				
e. Well-groomed				
f. Relates proper personal and vocational information				
g. "Sells" self in appropriate and postiive manner				
3. Reads want ads in newspaper to locate jobs				
4. Makes contacts and takes advantage of services from following agencies:				
a. Vocational Rehabilitation				
b. Public employment agencies				
c. Private employement agencies				
d. Personnel offices of plants and businesses				
5. Applies for and possesses social security card				

Fig. 5-2 Continued

_____ 6. Writes letters of application

_____ 7. Makes phone calls concerning job information
        and making job applications

_____ 8. Knows the importance of having patience while
        looking for a job

_____ 9. Can explain some of the laws controlling
        employment

        _____ a. Work certificate
        _____ b. Restrictions
        _____ c. Birth certificate

_____ 10. Identifies the common causes of unemployment
         and firing

_____ 11. Explains wage and hour laws

_____ 12. Identifies the rights of the worker

        _____ a. Right to fair wages
        _____ b. Right to no discrimination on an unfair basis
        _____ c. Right to be treated with dignity and respect
        _____ d. Right to terminate employment

_____ 13. Identifies responsibilities of worker to employer

        _____ a. Loyalty
        _____ b. Working at a competitive pace all day
        _____ c. Giving appropriate notice before termination
               of a job

to provide training for a nucleus of educators from each school in the system. Representatives should include the principal, the school psychologist, the counselor, special education resource teachers, and classroom teachers. Other interested individuals might also be included. The groups might work together as an ''IEP Committee'' in simulated tasks with the trainer providing information and practice on each component of the IEP. Reference materials like the ones described in the previous section should also be made available.

After these groups have developed skills in IEP development, they can plan strategies for training their respective school faculties, based on a similar procedure of small working groups actually developing an IEP. It is preferable to have an inservice training day set aside on which students would not come to school; faculty members need to be able to devote their full attention and energy to the task of learning new skills. Many commercial companies have IEP training programs and provide materials for various stages of development. In the near future, school systems will have a wide array of commercial training resources to choose from for inservice training.

Again, educators must also be trained to implement IEPs. This training should be part of inservice sessions on preparing teachers to educate handicapped students in the least restrictive setting. The inservice training described in Chapter 6 should provide instruction on the methods and materials for providing an appropriate education to handicapped students. The provision of an appropriate education should be synonymous with the implementation of the handicapped student's IEP if the IEP is to meet the intent of P.L. 94–142 and Sec. 504.

The Allocation of Time

Another major issue in developing IEPs is time. When are IEP committees going to get together for planning? How can time be found for parent conferences? When will committee members actually write the plan? Will time be available to conduct the annual review? When all the tasks of IEP development are considered, one wonders if teachers will have time to teach.

What happens to the nonhandicapped students while classroom teachers are meeting with the IEP committee, conducting parent conferences, and writing IEPs? Will they be provided with an unequal education opportunity in the process? To minimize the possibility of penalizing nonhandicapped students, systems must plan for the most efficient use of faculty members' time.

Several strategies for time allowances might be considered. One is to set aside a day or two approximately two weeks after the school year has started. The two-week period is to allow time for initial assessment to pinpoint a student's current level of performance. After obtaining this information, IEP meetings and parent conferences can be held on the designated workdays. Parents who work may only be able to meet in the evenings; in that instance, faculty members might attend school for half of the regular workday and come back in the evening for necessary parent conferences.

IEP committees might also decide to assign portions of IEP development to individual members and submit their plans to the committee for review. For example, one committee member might have primary responsibility for math and another might be assigned to social adjustment. Faculty members should be assigned to work on the IEP that best fits the time available in their particular schedules. This would eliminate the need to coordinate schedules for at least a portion of the task. After the individual assignments have been completed, the entire committee should review and approve the IEPs.

Another idea is for the system to hire a "roving" substitute teacher. The substitute could free four or five classroom teachers for periods of 1 to 1½ hours during the school day. The classroom teachers might then be able to meet with the IEP committee during regular hours.

Special education resource teachers will probably spend the majority of the first month of school on the development of IEPs. This will mean that few hours will be devoted to student instruction. It might seem unproductive to decrease the quantity of resource instruction for handicapped students, but if a comprehensive, coordinated, and systematic plan can be developed that specifies sequential skill development and identifies the responsible person for teaching each objective, the quality of instruction for handicapped students stands to gain in the long run. The advantage to early planning is that it often saves time throughout the school year in planning the steps of a handicapped student's educational program.

Once IEPs are implemented, they can often be prepared at the end of the school year for the following year. School systems might consider paying teachers for extra days immediately after the end of the school year or during the summer to develop IEPs for the next academic year. If this strategy is used, school systems will need to make tentative teacher assignments for the upcoming year in late spring, since one of the legislative requirements is that the student's teacher be a member of the IEP committee.

There are no easy solutions for creating time to do the IEPs properly. Collaboration and skillful use of financial resources by the school system are prerequisites to solving the problem, however.

Monitoring and Documentation

P.L. 94–142 requires that IEPs be monitored by the SEAs and LEAs. Thus, LEAs must work closely with the SEA in defining IEP policies and procedures. Issues that should be considered include the completeness of the IEP relative to the required components, the nature of parent involvement, the delivery of specified

IEP services, student progress within the plan, obstacles preventing the student from making anticipated progress, the teacher's ability to implement the IEP, and periodic evaluation of objectives. The IEP administrator might wish to develop a checklist for monitoring purposes. The checklist should set forth the factors to be monitored; it could also serve the purpose of providing written documentation of monitoring activities.

One procedure for implementing monitoring activities is to appoint a faculty member in each school to be the IEP coordinator for that school. This person could monitor practices within the school by completing the checklist on each IEP developed. This checklist review could be done in conjunction with the committee that developed the IEP. The coordinator for each school should work directly with the system IEP administrator, who should monitor practices at each school on a first-hand basis, particularly in the initial stages of IEP development. Correcting errors at the beginning can prevent the establishment of faulty habits. Monitoring is essential as a means of ensuring that IEP development proceeds on an educationally sound basis.

Documentation of need can be an outgrowth of monitoring if sufficient records are maintained. (This is the purpose of the checklist mentioned earlier in this section.) When data indicate that particular needs or gaps exist in providing handicapped students with an appropriate education, the IEP administrator can use this information as a basis for responding to the need. For example, if data from the review of IEPs indicate that the speech therapy services of the system are insufficient to serve all students who need speech therapy, this information can be used to make a case to the LEA for expanding services. IEPs can be the vehicles through which educators can specify the numbers of students needing a particular educational alternative, service, or instructional material. Specific information makes a much stronger case than an estimation based on someone's intuition or opinion. Monitoring and documentation of need should be viewed as positive and facilitating functions, rather than as negative and punitive.

IMPLICATIONS FOR HIGHER EDUCATION

College and university faculty members have long advocated the need to provide handicapped students with an individualized and appropriate education. A significant number of the expert witnesses in right-to-education cases have been on the faculties of higher education institutions. With the passage of P.L. 94–142 and Sec. 504, the legislative requirements regarding the provision of an appropriate education have clear implications for colleges and universities, as well as for public schools. These implications include: (1) training for the development of IEPs; (2) research; and (3) consultation with public schools.

Training for the Development of IEPs

Based on the legislative requirements to prepare an IEP for each handicapped student, colleges and universities have a clear duty to teach their students how to prepare IEPs. Students majoring in special education, regular education (early childhood, elementary, and secondary), school psychology, counseling, supervision, and administration should all receive IEP training. Various competencies related to IEP development and implementation could be integrated into courses on assessment, curriculum, methods, parent counseling, and school law. Although instruction can be spread over several courses, it is important that students have the experience of pulling all of their training together to create an IEP that meets the legislative requirements.

Since IEPs are to be developed by committees in the public schools, preservice students should learn to work with fellow students on an interdisciplinary basis. For example, students from special education, regular education, and school psychology programs could be assigned to work together to develop an IEP for a handicapped student. This could be done easily and effectively in a practicum site. The students should experience the entire process of IEP development, including the parent conference. They should work under the close supervision of college and university faculty and cooperating supervisors at the practicum site.

Many preservice programs focus almost exclusive effort on preparing educators to work with children. In fact, many college and university students make the decision to major in education because of a desire to work with children. IEP development is one important example of the need for educators to develop skills in working with other adults as well. These skills cannot be expected to develop automatically; they must be systematically taught. One method is to provide opportunities for college and university students from different areas of specialization to work together during their training programs. IEP development and implementation can provide a basis for group work and can help teach preservice students skills related to shared responsibility for the education of handicapped individuals.

Another training consideration is the documentation of modeling as an effective learning strategy. Education faculty members might prepare an IEP on each student in the class. They could pretest the students on knowledge related to competencies to be covered in the course, write semester goals for each student, specify short-term objectives, describe instructional materials to be used, and explain the method of evaluation. College and university students probably would welcome the specific goals and individual attention to their own needs. Having experienced the benefits of an IEP from the student point of view, they should develop more positive attitudes toward the concept of IEPs. At the very least, they would develop greater respect for a faculty member who actually "practiced what he preached."

Research

The total process of IEP development and implementation has not been empirically tested. Will the development of an IEP enhance the instructional progress of handicapped students? How well can teachers predict at the beginning of a school year how much progress the student will make by the end of the year? Is there a type of inservice training that is more effective than others for preparing school personnel to develop and implement IEPs? What types of assessment tools are the most reliable and conducive to IEP development? What questions do parents most frequently pose? What methods are most successful in obtaining parental involvement? These are but a few of the unanswered questions that need to be investigated. There are tremendous opportunities for college and university faculty members and graduate students to get involved in applied research in these areas. The results of this research could be invaluable for designing and redesigning IEP policies and procedures.

Consultation with Public Schools

In addition to collaborative research efforts, education faculty members in institutions of higher education should consider working with public schools in tasks associated with the IEP. They might be very helpful in policy development, designing formats, conducting inservice training, providing curriculum reference materials, and devising monitoring procedures. Collaboration with the public schools on IEP development is an excellent way for education faculty to prepare themselves to train preservice students. It is one thing to discuss the merits of preparing IEPs; it is quite another to solve the difficult problems associated with implementation. Several faculty members who have been involved with public schools as IEP consultants have commented that they learned more from the experience than they contributed to it.

IMPLICATIONS FOR CONSUMERS

The legislative requirements for providing handicapped students with an individualized education also have important implications for consumers. The groundwork has been laid for partnerships between parents and education professionals based on cooperation and collaboration. Some of the implications of this partnership are: (1) shared decision making; and (2) the assumption of educational responsibility.

Shared Decision Making

P.L. 94–142 requires schools to give parents an opportunity to be involved in developing their child's educational program. Parents must be involved in IEP conferences, except in cases where documentation can be provided to show that parents refused all invitations to be involved. The clear legal preference supports the concept of professional-parent alliances.

It is important for parents to take advantage of this opportunity for shared decision making. The first step toward obtaining active parent involvement is to inform parents of their legal rights related to the IEP and to explain the importance of exercising this right. If consumer groups in the community (like the Association for Retarded Citizens or the Association for Children with Learning Disabilities) determine that a school system has not done an adequate job of informing parents and encouraging their participation, they might choose to assume the responsibility of providing more detailed information to the parents through newspaper articles, community forums, newsletters, telephone calls, and personal visits. Consumers are often more likely to be influenced by other consumers than by the school system.

When parents participate in conferences, it is important for them to state their concerns and their priorities in regard to their child's development and education. Parents usually want their children to learn skills and concepts that will make home adjustment and routines easier. For example, the parent of a retarded child might want the child to learn to tie his shoes. Parents should express these opinions openly, with confidence that they are important members of the team. Consumer groups or the PTA could help prepare parents for these conferences by showing them a videotape of an IEP conference or by giving them a list of issues to think about, such as:

- What skills would you like your child to learn?
- Are there problems with your child's home adjustment that could be helped by work at school?
- What are your child's likes and dislikes?
- Has your child expressed any career interest?
- What types of peer relationships does your child have in the neighborhood?
- What are your child's hobbies?
- What does your child consider to be a special privilege or punishment?
- What type of contact would you like to have with your child's teacher?
- Are you interested in following up on school activities at home?
- When you have a question or concern about your child's educational program, what is the most convenient way for you to inform the teacher or someone else at the school?

This type of advance information can help parents gain confidence in their new roles as educational decision makers. Educators on the IEP committee should realize that some parents may feel anxious, insecure, and awkward in specifying curriculum goals and objectives for their child. They can help the parents by setting a relaxed tone for the conference so that parents are not put on the spot. They can also provide feedback to parents to let them know that their comments and opinions are respected and valued.

The IEP conference is an opportunity for parents to advocate for the special services their child needs, such as physical therapy. If the assessment information indicates a deficit in physical development and coordination, the parents may request that physical therapy services be provided to provide an *appropriate* education tailored to the child's needs. The regulations require that the services specified on the IEP should be those the student needs, not just what is available in the system. Parents can withhold their approval of the IEP (not sign it) until the service arrangements have been made or planned for their child. If parents do not exert this pressure during the initial developmental process, the need for physical therapy may be overlooked as educators get busy with other IEPs.

Sometimes parents and other IEP committee members will be unable to agree on what curriculum constitutes an appropriate education for the child. If the conflict cannot be resolved through negotiation and consensus, either party may initiate a due process hearing (see Chapter 8).

Assuming Educational Responsibility

Parental participation in IEP development could result in a more active parental role in implementing the IEP. If parents state their interest in working with their child at home on particular skills and following up on what the teacher did during the day, the IEP plan should include the parents' contribution. For example, parents of a severely retarded child may be interested in working on the development of feeding skills. The parents and the teachers should work together to plan a consistent program for teaching self-feeding skills. The discussion of goals and objectives at the IEP conference provides an opportunity for parents to learn exactly what they can do to help their child. If parents are inclined to active roles, school personnel should provide all the support and help they can to make the parents successful in their training efforts.

Not all parents are interested in assuming responsibility for teaching some of the objectives. This disinterest may be related to a lack of time, a desire to be involved with their child in other ways, or an unsuccessful past experience of trying to teach a skill or concept. Sometimes older siblings, members of the extended family, or tutors might be available to work with the child in the afternoon and evenings. In any case, the IEP conference provides an opportunity to coordinate training between home and school, involving the parents to the maximum extent appropriate for them.

NOTES

1. Equity No. 100/182/77676 (Cir. Ct., Baltimore Cty., May 3, 1974).
2. 348 F. Supp. 866, 878 (D.D.C. 1972).
3. 343 F. Supp. 279, 307 (E.D. Pa. 1972).
4. 414 U.S. 563 (1974).
5. Frederick L. v. Thomas, Civ. Act. No. 74–52 (E.D. Pa., Memorandum Order, Aug. 2, 1976), aff'd., 557 F.2d 373 (3rd Cir 1977). 4 U.S. L.W. 2008 (July 5, 1977); for earlier opinion, see 408 F. Supp. 832 (E.D. Pa. 1972).
6. Fialkowski v. Shapp, 405 F. Supp. 946 (E.D. Pa. 1975).
7. Allen v. McDonough, No. 14948 (Super. Ct., Suffolk Cty., Mass., filed June 23, 1976).
8. Davis v. Wynne, No. CV–176–44 (S.D. Ga., filed May 21, 1976).
9. Benskin v. Taft City School District, No. 136795 (Super. Ct., Kern Cty., Cal., filed Sept. 8, 1975).
10. Lora v. The Board of Education of the City of New York, No. 75 Civ. 917 (E.D. N.Y., filed June 11, 1975).
11. *Supra* n. 2.
12. LeBanks v. Spears, 60 F.R.D. 135 (E.D.La. 1973).
13. *See* FINAL REPORT, SPECIAL EDUCATION IN THE STATES: LEGISLATIVE PROGRESS REPORT, HANDICAPPED CHILDREN'S EDUCATION PROJECT, EDUCATION COMMISSION OF THE STATES (Denver, 1974).
14. Pennsylvania Ass'n. for Retarded Citizens v. Commonwealth, 343 F. Supp. 279, 287 (E.D. Pa. 1972).
15. Maryland Ass'n. for Retarded Citizens v. Maryland, Equity No. 100/182/77676 (Cir. Ct., Baltimore Cty., filed May 3, 1974).
16. *Id.*
17. *Supra* n. 13.
18. *Supra* n. 2, 3, and 15.
19. *Id.*
20. Pennsylvania Ass'n. for Retarded Citizens v. Commonwealth, 343 F. Supp. 279, 311 (E. D. Pa. 1972) and LeBanks v. Spears, 60 F.R.D. 135 (E.D. La. 1973).
21. McWilliams v. New York City Board of Education, No. 21350-75 (Sup. Ct. App. Div., filed Jan. 21, 1976).
22. *Supra* n. 15.
23. National Association of State Directors of Special Education, *Functions of the placement committee in special education: A resource manual* (1976).

24. Scottie Torres (ed.), *A primer on individualized education programs for handicapped children* (Reston, Virginia: The Foundation for Exceptional Children, 1972).

25. Ann P. Turnbull, Bonnie Strickland, and John C. Brantley, *Developing and implementing individualized education programs* (Columbus, Ohio: Charles E. Merrill Publishing Co., 1978).

1978 Supplement

n. 5. The appeals court opinion is reported at 557 F. 2d 373 (3d Cir. 1977).

n. 10. The federal district court agreed in part, holding that the plaintiffs have federal equal protection rights to adequate treatment, including diagnosis and classification procedures and adequately equipped and staffed special day schools, and that they are entitled to an appropriate education under state and federal laws (P.L. 94–142), to due process hearings under both state and federal laws, and to periodic reevaluation of their placement. Lora v. N.Y. Board of Education, F. Supp. , 46 U.S.L.W. 2683 (E.D.N.Y. 1978). Other "appropriate education" cases claim handicapped children are entitled to education twelve months a year, not just nine, so that they will not regress (Armstrong v. Kline, No. 78-172, E.D. Pa., filed Jan. 17, 1978); allege that the schools' failure to write IEPs and to make student discipline rules understandable to them deny them an appropriate education (P-1 v. Shedd, No. 78-58, D. Conn., filed Feb. 27, 1978); and argue that an inadequate number of special education teachers denies handicapped children an appropriate education (Doe v. Grille, Civ. No. F 77-108, N.D. Ind., 1978).

Insert at p. 197—BEH Chief Edwin W. Martin has issued an opinion that the IEP must set out all the services a child needs without regard to whether they are available or not (Letter, Nov. 17, 1977, reported in *Insight*, Council for Exceptional Children, Vol. 12, p. 5, Dec. 19, 1977).

Insert at p. 198—BEH is of the opinion that, unless the student's parents consent, teacher union representatives may not participate in an IEP conference without violating a student's privacy rights under P.L. 94–142 and the Buckley Amendments (Letter from HEW Deputy Assistant Secretary for Management Thomas McFee to Pennsylvania Secretary of Education Earyl Kline, January 3, 1978, reported in *School Law News*, p. 8, Jan. 20, 1978).

6

Least Restrictive Appropriate Placement

CONSTITUTIONAL FOUNDATIONS

Functional Exclusion

No requirement of the right-to-education movement is as likely to generate more heat than light as the requirement that handicapped children be placed in the least restrictive appropriate program. Given the inaccurate code name "mainstreaming," this requirement has the potential for encountering the same levels of opposition, misunderstanding, and ill will as the requirement for racial desegregation of the schools. It also has the potential for significantly improving the education of handicapped children, redressing some of the wrongs they have been subjected to, and contributing to the education of all pupils and the training of all educators. It is popular nowadays to say that "mainstreaming" is an admirable concept improperly executed, and that may be true. If so, it should be instructive to analyze the requirement of least-restrictive appropriate placement in the context of substantive due process—denying equal educational opportunity to handicapped children by placing them in special education programs that are inappropriate for them—the practice of functional exclusion.

Case Law: The Preference for the Mainstream

In *PARC, LeBanks,* and *MARC,* there was ample evidence of, among other things, functional exclusion, misclassification resulting in inappropriate placement, and general inadequacy of special education programs (in terms of financing, programs, and personnel). There was, as well, other evidence of the indisputable denial of equal educational opportunities for handicapped children in violation of equal protection and procedural due process principles (see Chapters 3 and 7). Like Hamlet, a court faced with such overwhelming evidence might have been inclined to say, "There is something rotten in the State of _____; oh, cursed spite that I was born to set things right."

Court remedies. Given the facts, the courts had to fashion remedies. One remedy, particularly appropriate for the practice of functional exclusion, was stated as follows (in *PARC*):

> It is the Commonwealth's obligation to place each mentally retarded child in a free, public program of education and training appropriate to the child's capacity, within the context of the general educational policy that, among the alternative programs of education and training required by statute to be available, placement in a regular public school class is preferable to placement in a special public school class and placement in a special public school class is preferable to placement to any other type of program of education and training.[1]

So far as the case law initially was concerned mainstreaming reflected a judicial preference for students to be placed or tracked in a regular "normal" track rather than in a special education track and for students to be educated in the regular school environment rather than in the confines of a special school. Mainstreaming was no more than a *preference* in favor of regular educational placement; it was not an inflexible rule. It was a guide for conduct, not a rule of conduct, and as a guide, it did not prohibit alternatives to regular class and regular school placement.

Some of the more recently filed cases have asserted that handicapped children are still being denied an equal educational opportunity because they have been placed outside the mainstream. Not all of these cases have been decided. In one case, however, the Wisconsin Supreme Court upheld the power of the state school superintendent to place a handicapped child in a nonsectarian private school when no local appropriate special education is available.[2] In another case, in the face of an equal protection and due process challenge, a United States District Court upheld the power of the state superintendent to make an out-of-state placement of a handicapped child when no appropriate special education program is available within the state.[3] The court rejected the parents' claim that the statute under which the superintendent acted required their child to live far away from home even though a private facility with an appropriate program was nearby. The court said:

The requirement of the Wisconsin State Department of Public Instruction that the various options set forth in the statute for providing handicapped children with specialized instruction at public expense are to be considered sequentially, and not alternatively, is a rational one, and, though the state must provide each child with an equal educational opportunity in accordance with the equal protection guarantee, it is not necessarily required to do so in the context of a "neighborhood" or conveniently accessible setting, especially where a virtually infinite range of special educational needs must be met with limited resources.

Because the two Wisconsin cases were decided before P.L. 94–142 became effective and did not rely on Sec. 504, it is unlikely that they stand for any principle other than that the placement alternatives fixed by statute are not unconstitutional under the Fourteenth Amendment because they are rationally related to a legitimate state purpose—providing appropriate education without seriously jeopardizing the state's fiscal resources. Even within this limited application, the cases may still have a bearing on more recently filed cases. For example, the practice of the New York City Board of Education of placing socially maladjusted and emotionally disturbed children in programs that segregate by race and sex is under challenge on equal protection grounds, the failure of the Board to give a due process hearing opportunity in these cases is under attack on due process grounds, and the Board is alleged to have violated the students' Fourth Amendment rights to privacy and freedom from unreasonable searches and seizures.[4] The merits of the case have not been decided pending an appeal from the Second Circuit Court of Appeals' order refusing to certify the case as a class action.

The practice of placing handicapped children in special classes segregated from the regular class population was challenged, but never decided, in a Massachusetts case.[5] The children claimed that being segregated from the "regular class" population was causing them to receive a substantially different education than the children in the "regular classes." The special class placement, they alleged, resulted in educational, psychological, and social harm; moreover, the longer they were kept in special classes, the greater the damage they suffered. They also claimed that they were stigmatized by the special placement and that when they were returned to the regular class they were so far behind their "mainstream" peers that they could not catch up, and thus were irreparably harmed. The case was not decided on its merits because the state passed a "mandatory special education act" and the decision was postponed while the act was being implemented.

Until *Mattie T. v. Holladay*[6] was filed in a United States district court, none of the "least restriction" cases relied on federal statutes. That case, however, squarely raised the "least restrictive placement" issue by relying on P.L. 94–142 (20 U.S.C. Sec. 1411), Sec. 504 (29 U.S.C. Sec. 794) and T. 1, ESEA of 1965 (20 U.S.C. Sec. 421e). The case focused on the provision of inadequate educational services to handicapped children placed in self-contained special education classes that isolated them from nonhandicapped children and allegedly failed to meet their educational needs. A decision on these issues has not been reached yet. A similar case, *California Association for Retarded Citizens*,[7] filed more recently, challenges placement in nonmainstream programs on the same federal statutory grounds. No decision on the merits has been reached in that case either.

The equal protection grounds relied on in the Wisconsin cases permit the state greater latitude in placing handicapped children outside of regular programs in the public schools in the districts in which they reside. However, P.L. 94–142 and Sec. 504 seriously circumscribe that latitude, as will be explained below.

A Legal History and a Legal Tactic

Why is mainstreaming a judicial preference? The reasons are many. The preference is a reaction to the exclusion of children with special needs from both the opportunity for education (placement in a school system) and the opportunity for a meaningful education (placement in an appropriate program). It addresses total and functional exclusion, with an emphasis on the latter.

Mainstreaming is also a reaction to the view traditionally accepted by many educators (and institutionalized in school practices) that children with special needs are different from, and therefore should be excluded from education with, nonhandicapped children. Mainstreaming is an attempt to protect exceptional children from the stereotype that they are different and deficient. It speaks to the stigmatizing effects of special educational placement—the effects that such placement has on the child's self-image and on the school's and his peers' image of him.

Mainstreaming is a method for individualizing an exceptional pupil's education, since it prevents a child being placed in special programs unless it is first determined that he cannot profit from regular educational placement. It simultaneously addresses the requirements of an appropriate education—an individualized education—and nondiscriminatory classification. It promotes the concept that curriculum adaptations and instructional strategies tailored to the needs of exceptional children can occur in regular classrooms, as well as in special classrooms.

Mainstreaming is preferred because the existence of separate, self-contained special education programs and schools was found to be equivalent to the establishment of separate but unequal systems of education. Separate has generally meant unequal, and special education has not been equated with equal educational opportunities. Some commentators have argued that the pattern and practice of some schools has been to assign the "worst" children, typically those with special needs, to the least capable teachers, putting them in the most inferior facilities, with less than adequate educational materials. Often special education programs were funded less generously than normal "mainstream" programs. In face of such biased treatment, mainstreaming has adopted some of the strategies used to bring about racial integration of the schools.

One strategy for racial integration was integrating a racial minority into the racial mainstream. The hope behind the strategy was that the racial majority would not neglect its children's education in integrated schools, and the continued attention of the white majority to "quality education" would assure the black minority of the same quality education as the white majority. Similar hopes underlie the preference for mainstreaming handicapped children. It is undoubtedly true that special education and other systems imperfectly serving, or indeed discriminating against, the handicapped are the new civil rights battlefield.

Mainstreaming has more than a civil rights aspect; it is imbued with a sense of desperation. A court wishing to redress the manifold wrongs of functional exclusion, misclassification, and inadequate special education programs could (and we suspect they did) easily contrast "regular" education with special education; see that nonhandicapped children were not excluded, misclassified, or shortchanged; and reach the conclusion that the quickest remedy was to order placement, to the maximum extent appropriate, with the nonhandicapped. The remedy was sure—the "regular" programs were already in existence and could accommodate some nonhandicapped children without extensive revision. Extensive revision of special education programs was hardly certain to be achieved satisfactorily despite court orders for revision—the courts fired with buckshot, not single rounds—and revision undoubtedly would not be quick. Mainstreaming, then, gained popularity as an easy and readily available remedy.

Mainstreaming is a reaction to the terminal aspects of special education. The placement of an exceptional child in a self-contained special education program has usually been the last step in a child's development; it was often the terminal placement. The preference for mainstreaming rests on the hope that the self-fulfilling prophesies and the self-limiting characteristics of special educational placement will not be the end result for children with special needs.

Mainstreaming is also preferred because it is widely and forcefully advocated by many educators. They argue that the handicapped child will learn more, and more easily, by being educated with the nonhandicapped child. They contend that there are serious doubts about the educational efficacy of special (separate) programs; and they say that the nonhandicapped child needs the educational and experiential benefits of coming into contact with handicapped children.

Finally, mainstreaming—or, more precisely, placement in the least restrictive appropriate school program—cannot be divorced from two related legal developments. One is the application of the "least-restrictive" principle to at least two other areas of state action: (1) criminal law and placement in the least restrictive placement, and (2) civil commitment of persons dangerous to themselves or others. The other is the trend toward deinstitutionalization—preventing mentally disabled persons from being placed in institutions except as a final resort, and discharging as many as possible from institutions. In one sense, the deinstitutionalization movement is part of a more generalized application of the "least-restrictive" doctrine. But it is different because of its implications for the public schools. Deinstitutionalization prevents many handicapped children from being placed in institutions; instead, they remain "in the community." By requiring that all children be given a free appropriate public education, the cases (and P.L. 94–142) have put pressure on the public schools, particularly in terms of the zero-reject principle. In responding to this pressure, the schools will have to begin training the more severely handicapped children, who are, after all, the most apt candidates for institutionalization and have traditionally been most excluded from school. They may choose not only to create new (or more extensive) programs for the severely handicapped, but also to broaden the range of the nonhandicapped by placing the mildly handicapped children in the "main-stream." Thus, although the least restrictive placement doctrine was born in non-school contexts as part of the constitutional requirement of substantive due process, it has significant implications for the public schools.

FEDERAL LEGISLATION

P.L. 94–142

It is not surprising that many of Congress' findings reflected in P.L. 94–142 are identical to the conclusions of the courts and the reasons the courts required children to be placed in least-restrictive educational settings. These findings include the following: handicapped children have been inappropriately educated [Sec. 601 (b) (3)]; they have been denied the opportunity "to go through the educational process with their peers" [Sec. 601 (b) (4)]; there is a lack of adequate services available to them within the schools [Sec. 601 (b) (6)]; and educators have the ability to provide effective special education and related services, including, presumably, education and services in the "regular" program [Sec. 601 (b) (7)]. Legislative requirements will be examined in this section in regard to: 1) least restrictive appropriate placement, 2) other statutory provisions, and 3) Sec. 504 of the Rehabilitation Act.

Least restrictive appropriate placement. It was predictable that Congress would require SEAs [Sec. 612 (5) (B)] and LEAs [Sec. 614 (a) (1) (C) (iv) to follow a policy of least-restrictive placement [Sec. 121a.550]. They must develop procedures to assure that, to the maximum extent appropriate, handicapped children—including children in public agencies, private institutions, or other care facilities—will be educated with children who are not handicapped. Further, the requirements stipulate that special classes, separate schooling, or other removal of handicapped children from the regular educational environment will occur only when the nature or severity of a child's handicap is such that his education in regular classes with the use of supplementary aids and services cannot be achieved satisfactorily.

The regulations prohibit placement outside the mainstream program except under two conditions. One is that the integration of handicapped children into the mainstream should occur "to the maximum extent appropriate." It is clear from the legislative history and a proper interpretation of the act that "appropriate" is to be defined in terms of what is appropriate for the handicapped child, not whether the school system can conveniently absorb him into the mainstream or whether he will have beneficial or detrimental effects on his nonhandicapped peers. This is inescapable in light of the policy of P.L. 94–142 to provide handicapped children with an appropriate education. The other condition is that a handicapped child may not be "removed" from the "regular educational environment" unless the nature or severity of his handicap is such that education in regular classes, even with supplementary aids and services, cannot be achieved satisfactorily. This condition also focuses on the nature or severity of the child's disability, as opposed to the convenience for the school or the consequences for nonhandicapped children. Conditions for a particular placement are inexorably linked to the concept of appropriate education and are to be child-centered, not system-centered.

The regulations [Secs. 121a.550–556] speak to one of the most potentially troublesome aspects of placement in the least restrictive environment, placing handicapped children into regular programs without regard for their individual needs. Sec. 121a.552 of the regulations makes it clear that each handicapped child's educational placement must be determined at least annually, be based on his or her individualized education program, and unless the IEP requires special alternative arrangements, the child must receive his education in the same school he would attend if he were not handicapped. In selecting the least restrictive environment, any potential harmful effect on the child or on the quality of services he receives is to be taken into consideration [Sec. 121a.552]. Comments on the regulation make it clear that if the child disrupts nonhandicapped students in the regular classroom to the degree that he significantly impairs their education, his needs cannot be met in that classroom and placement there is inappropriate.

Sec. 121a.551 puts pressure on public agencies to develop appropriate alternative placements by requiring that the options must include instruction in regular classes, in special classes, in special schools, home instruction, and instruction in hospitals and institutions. The agency must also provide supplementary services such as resource rooms and itinerant teachers in conjunction with regular class placement.

Handicapped children must be given a chance to participate in nonacademic and extracurricular services and activities. They are to have access to meals, recess periods, counseling services, athletics, transportation, health services, recreational activities, special interest groups, and clubs. They should be referred to agencies that give assistance to handicapped persons, and be employed in and outside of the public agency [Sec. 121a.553 and .306].

SEAs must make suitable arrangements with public and private agencies to insure that the least restrictive placement rules are effectively carried out [Sec. 121a.554]. They are to provide technical assistance to the other agencies to help them implement the rules [Sec. 121a.555], and must monitor programs and assist public and private agencies in correcting noncompliance with the rules [Sec. 121a.556].

Other statutory provisions. The policy of least restrictive appropriate placement, like most of the P.L. 94–142 directives, is indivisible from other policies. It is a method for assuring an appropriate education, a technique of individualized education, a way of preventing misclassification, and, ultimately, a trigger for a due process hearing. Its success will depend, in part, on personnel development [Sec. 613 (a) (3)], and it is advanced by the requirement that schools spend P.L.94–142 federal funds, first, for the education of handicapped children who are not receiving an education, and, second, for the most severely handicapped children within each disability who are receiving an inadequate education [Sec. 612 (3)]. Since federal funds may not be spent on mainstream (regular) programs until the other priorities have been met, schools will be required to spend their own funds (state or local funds, or federal funds from other sources) for mainstream purposes.

The "ceiling" on the number of handicapped children will have the same effect. No more than 12 percent of all children may be counted as handicapped. If there are, in fact, more handicapped children than an LEA can accommodate within the ceilings, the LEA may tend to count as handicapped only those who fit the two service priorities, and count the less handicapped children as nonhandicapped. As a result, the less handicapped children will be served in the "mainstream" or be served (outside the mainstream in some cases) in state or locally funded programs.

Sec. 504

Sec. 504 regulations are substantially similar to those of P.L. 94–142. Sec. 84.34 requires schools to provide each qualified handicapped student in its jurisdiction with a mainstream education to the maximum extent appropriate to the handicapped person's needs. The school must place handicapped students in the regular educational environment operated by the school unless the school can demonstrate that a student's education in the regular environment with the use of supplementary aids and services cannot be achieved satisfactorily. Whenever a school places a student in a setting other than the regular educational environment, it must take into account the proximity of the alternate setting to the student's home.

Although the handicapped student's needs determine what is a proper placement, the comments on Regulation Sec. 84.34 make it clear that if a handicapped student is so disruptive in a regular classroom that other students' education is significantly impaired, the handicapped student's needs cannot be met in that placement and regular-setting placement is not appropriate or required [*Fed. Reg.*, May 4, 1977, p. 22691].

Handicapped children are also to be provided with nonacademic services in as integrated a setting as possible. This requirement is especially important for children whose educational needs require them to be solely with other handicapped children during most of each day. To the maximum extent appropriate, children in residential settings are also to be provided with opportunities for participation with other children. In providing or arranging for the provision of extracurricular services and activities, including meals, recess periods, and nonacademic services and activities as set forth in Sec. 84.37 (a) (2), a school must ensure that each handicapped student participate with nonhandicapped students to the maximum extent appropriate for the student in question.

If a school operates a facility for handicapped students, the school must insure that the facility and the services and activities it provides are comparable to its other facilities, services, and activities. This section is not intended to encourage the creation and maintenance of such facilities. A separate facility violates Sec. 504 unless it is indeed necessary for providing an appropriate education to certain handicapped students. When special facilities are necessary (as might be the case for severely retarded persons), this provision requires that the educational services provided be comparable to those provided in the recipient's regular facilities.

Among the factors to be considered is the need to place a child as close to home as possible. Under Sec. 84.34, schools must take this factor into account. The parents' right to challenge the placement of their child extends not only to placement in special classes or separate schools but also to placement in a distant school and, in particular, to residential placement. If an equally appropriate educational program exists closer to home, the parent or guardian may raise the issue under the "least restrictive" placement doctrine through a procedural due process hearing.

Commenting on the proposed Sec. 504 regulations (which are comparable to the ones adopted as final regulations), HEW took the position that, within the requirements of the regulation, schools must show that the needs of the individual handicapped child would, on balance, be furthered by placement outside the regular educational environment. According to HEW, for many handicapped children, "the most normal setting feasible is that which combines the use of special and regular classes." Education of handicapped children, including those in public and private institutions and other care facilities, in the most normal setting feasible means educating them with nonhandicapped persons "to the maximum extent appropriate." It also means educating them as close to home as possible. Thus, as HEW conceived it, the requirement for placement in "the most normal setting feasible'' was intended to encompass the same concept as placement in "the least restrictive alternative setting." HEW chose to use the "most normal" rather than the "least restrictive" terminology because placement alternatives "cannot, in many instances, be compared on the basis of relative restrictiveness: i.e., while institutional education is indeed more restrictive than non-institutional instruction, placement in special education is not necessarily more restrictive than instruction in regular classes." Despite a change in language, it does not appear that the final regulation represents a change in policy from the proposed regulations.

As HEW's comment on the proposed regulation indicated, what is "restrictive" or "inappropriate" for one person may not be restrictive or inappropriate for another. The principle of "most normal" or "least restrictive" placement rests on the policy of individualized or appropriate education. However it is phrased, the principle is a technique for individually appropriate instruction and should be viewed in that context; this view is consistent with the case-law history and with the proper interpretation of P.L. 94–142.

HEW also said that an orthopedically handicapped child may not be placed in a classroom or school that is "primarily" for handicapped children, since that placement would violate the "most normal" principle. A school district is not, however, required to make every classroom and school building barrier-free. Hence, an orthopedically impaired child may be placed away from his neighborhood school, but not in a class primarily for the handicapped. This is not true for other handicapped children; their placement must be in the "most normal" setting possible. This appears to have been followed in the final regulation, which requires the school to take into account the proximity of the alternate setting. There does seem to have been some relaxation in the case of the orthopedically handicapped, undoubtedly because of the difficulty and cost of making all or even a majority of existing schools barrier-free.

A separate regulation [Sec. 84.37] requires schools to provide nonacademic and extracurricular services and activities in such a manner "as is necessary to afford handicapped students an equal opportunity for participation." Because they are part of a school's education program, they must be provided in the most integrated setting appropriate.

Nonacademic and extracurricular services and activities include, without limitation, counseling services, recreational athletics, transportation, health services, recreational activities, special interest groups or clubs, referrals to agencies providing assistance to the handicapped, and employment of students by the school or other employers. In giving personal, academic, or vocational counseling and placement services to handicapped students, a school may not discriminate because of handicap and must make sure that students are not counseled toward more restrictive career objectives than nonhandicapped students with similar interests and abilities.

In providing physical education courses, athletics, and similar programs to any of its students, a school may not discriminate on the basis of handicap and must provide qualified handicapped students with an equal opportunity to participate in interscholastic, club, or intramural athletics. Those activities may be separate or different from the ones offered to nonhandicapped students only if separation or differentiation is consistent with the least restrictive principle (Sec. 84.35) and only if no qualified handicapped student is denied the chance to compete for teams or to participate in courses that are not separate or different. In commenting on the physical education and athletics portion of the regulation, HEW notes that "most handicapped students are able to participate in one or more regular physical education and athletics activities. For example, a student in a wheelchair can participate in regular archery courses, as can a deaf student in a wrestling course." (See Chapter 3 for recent cases of alleged discrimination in athletics, brought under Sec. 504.)

Although the proposed regulations under P.L. 94–142 and the new regulations under Sec. 504 do not set forth other criteria for placements that can violate the integrating principle of "least restrictive," such criteria would probably include the following:

1. *The presence of nonhandicapped students in the same setting.* This criterion is perhaps the most clearly discernible and most easily applied.
2. *The extent to which the handicapped student has opportunities to interact with nonhandicapped students in the school environment.* The more handicapped students are isolated from nonhandicapped students, even though both are present in an educational setting, the more restrictive their program is.
3. *The extent to which nonhandicapped students in the educational setting are peers of handicapped students.* Peers are most often defined in terms of age equivalence. For example, the peers of a handicapped secondary-aged student would be nonhandicapped secondary-aged students. A secondary-aged student's environment is restrictive if his "peers" are elementary- or preschool-aged.
4. *The ratio of handicapped to nonhandicapped students,* As the ratio shifts to a preponderance of handicapped children, the educational environment becomes more restrictive. Thus, a school should provide a compelling justification for housing multiple classes of students with low prevalence handicaps within the same building when the services required by these students are not so unique as to be unavailable if the classes were dispersed throughout the system.
5. *The physical facilities of an educational placement.* If nonhandicapped students normally have access to libraries, cafeterias, gymnasiums, and locker room facilities, these same resources should be available to their

handicapped peers. To the extent that handicapped students are denied access to all educational facilities, their environment becomes more restrictive.

IMPLICATIONS FOR PUBLIC SCHOOLS

The day-to-day implementation of the requirements for least restrictive appropriate placement is largely the responsibility of the LEAs. As with the IEP, few educators disagree with the principle of mainstreaming, but successful implementation of the mainstreaming requirements is an extremely complex process. The following factors need to be considered when implementation strategies for least restrictive appropriate placements are devised by the LEAs: (1) providing an information base; (2) developing a system-level and school-building level implementation plan; (3) insuring the availability of a continuum of services; (4) providing inservice training; and (5) developing a procedure to document appropriate placement.

Providing an Information Base

For many educators, the concept of mainstreaming (which has become a code-word for least restrictive placement) raises red flags and ignites strong antagonism. The negativism associated with mainstreaming or the least restrictive concept largely stems from two sources. First, it is a grossly misunderstood educational concept. Many erroneously assume that regular classes will be flooded with overwhelming numbers of handicapped students and that the law requires that every handicapped student be placed in a regular education program, regardless of the severity of his handicap. Because educators often lack first-hand experience with handicapped individuals, they are fearful of them and question their competency to manage effectively a mainstreamed class. Second, the movement toward least restrictive placement has frequently been implemented in a haphazard manner. For example, in some school systems, classes for the mildly retarded have been abruptly dissolved and the students shifted to regular education programs without any preparation. Moderately and severely retarded individuals have been discharged from residential institutions, sometimes after long periods of institutionalization, and expected to make immediate community and public school adjustments. Often teachers have not been prepared through preservice or inservice training to individualize the curriculum to meet the needs of these students, and wind up feeling as if they have been "put out on a limb." When the implementation of least restriction has been approached in a random manner, everyone has suffered: students (handicapped and nonhandicapped), parents, teachers, and administrators. These situations have added fuel to the fire in regard to negative viewpoints on placing handicapped students in the least restrictive setting.

Because a backlash potential exists, school systems need to provide accurate information to all faculty members in regard to what the least restrictive concept is and what it is not. Perhaps this might most effectively be done at faculty meetings at each school. Basic facts need to be stressed, such as:

1. Mainstreaming handicapped students in regular classes is a legal preference for students who can be socially and instructionally integrated into regular classes; however, regular class placement is not the most appropriate alternative for *all* handicapped students.
2. The implementation of least restrictive placement requires shared responsibility among all educators. Classroom teachers cannot be expected to implement this requirement by themselves.
3. Least restrictive placements must be implemented in a systematic fashion; a continuum of educational alternatives and inservice training are essential.
4. The same educational principles that apply to teaching nonhandicapped students apply to teaching handicapped students. Handicapped and nonhandicapped students have far more similarities than differences.

During these meetings the anxieties of educators should be relieved as much as possible. An opportunity to express feelings and give reactions ought to be provided. Since least restrictive placements are now required, information should be presented in the context of how to solve problems or eliminate obstacles. Arguing about the validity of least restrictive placement is simply spinning educational wheels. The school system's implementation plan (discussed in the next section) should also be shared with the faculty members. They should know what to expect in terms of the future.

School faculty members are not the only ones who need accurate information on the concept of least restrictive placement; the primary decision makers—the school board members—*also* need to be accurately informed. School board members typically hear the biases of everyone. Often they do not have the time to research carefully every topic of educational relevance; they need accurate summaries of the implications of educational change. School administrators might make formal presentations to the school board on least restrictive placement or they could prepare written material for them. Financial backing is a necessary ingredient for successful mainstreaming programs, and informed board members are more likely to recognize the importance of solid implementation of P.L. 94–142.

Parents and community citizens also need information about least restrictive placements and the implementation plans for their local schools. Some parents of handicapped students may be extremely reluctant to give up the special education programs they fought so hard to establish. They may fear that their handicapped child will go back to the regular class and be socially isolated and instructionally neglected. Other parents might wish to see their child remain in a regular class even though it is clearly an inappropriate alternative due to the severity of their child's handicap. Parents who have institutionalized their handicapped child may be very reluctant to have him living at home again. Parents of nonhandicapped children will understandably be concerned about the implications of least restrictive placement. Their concerns usually center around fears that too much teacher time will be taken by handicapped students or that their children will pick up inappropriate behaviors from handicapped peers. Parents and interested community citizens could be informed about the principles of least restrictive placement through newspaper articles, community forums on the education of handicapped students, and PTA programs. School systems that are careful and systematic about keeping all constitutents informed will be more successful in implementing the requirement of least restrictive appropriate placements.

Developing an Implementation Plan

For the principles of least restrictive placement to be implemented in a systematic fashion, thorough plans need to be specified at both system level and school-building level. The system plan should include goals and objectives for moving toward the placement of all handicapped students in the least restrictive *appropriate* setting. The plan might cover a three- to five-year period. It should include the numbers of students for whom less restrictive placement might be appropriate; the continuum of services to be provided; the type and extent of inservice training to be provided; guidelines covering the referral, classification, and placement process; financial resources; a plan for removing architectural barriers; and the provision of special instructional materials, like auditory trainers for hearing impaired students. Ideally, the system plan should be developed by the administrator responsible for special education and an advisory committee composed of teachers (classroom and resource), principals, counselors, school psychologists, and parents. Shared decision making during the planning process can promote shared accountability for implementation. After the plan receives board of education endorsement, it should be available for the review of any educator or any consumer within the system. If educators and consumers know what to expect and have an opportunity to prepare for the future, there will be far less resistance and antagonism towards implementation.

The school-building plan should more specifically address the particular needs of the faculty, curriculum, and physical plant relative to placing handicapped students in less restrictive settings. These needs might be discussed and given priorities by the faculty. One procedure for conducting a needs assessment has been outlined by Paul, Turnbull, and Cruickshank.[8] After the needs of the faculty have been identified, a systematic plan should be developed that outlines objectives, resources, and methods of evaluation for each identified need. Figure 6-1 provides a sample implementation guide for providing inservice training to classroom teachers. When the school-building plan has been completed, it can facilitate the systematic development of procedures to support the successful placement of handicapped students in least restrictive settings. Systematic plans have many distinct advantages. They provide the opportunity for coordinated planning and collaboration. They prevent misunderstandings and minimize the ''rumor-mill'' by providing explicit statements of future plans. They promote a systematic approach to program development by breaking down a large task into a series of small steps, documenting the need for particular resources, and clearly spelling out evaluation procedures. Refining the system before placing handicapped students in the least restrictive appropriate setting must receive careful attention. A systematic plan can strongly contribute to successful implementation.[9]

Insuring the Availability of a Continuum of Services

The least restrictive doctrine does not mean the elimination of educational alternatives; effective implementation of least restrictive policies and regulations should actually result in the creation of new alternatives within school systems. Many school systems have erroneously interpreted the concept of least restrictive placement as signifying that all special classes for mildly handicapped students should be eliminated, and, all the former students in these classes should be placed in regular education programs.

Let's take the example of Billy, who is in the seventh grade and has been classified as educable mentally retarded. Billy has a strong core of basic academic skills, learned in the special classes he has been placed in for the past six years. In addition to some learning problems, Billy has always had difficulty in the area of behavior. He has engaged in extremely inappropriate behavior in the midst of classroom lessons, such as loudly cursing the teacher, hitting, fighting, and running out of the room. Because the school system Billy attended eliminated all EMR classes in the name of least restrictive placement, Billy was put in a regular class. His new teachers were not prepared to individualize the curriculum according to his level of performance. Due to the overload of the resource teacher, he only received instruction in the resource room for three hours a week. Billy was painfully aware of his limited ability as compared to his classroom peers. His acting-out behavior became worse, and the teasing and ridicule from his peers

FIGURE 6-1

Sample Implementation Guide: Inservice Training

Objectives	Resources	Evaluation
1. By _____, 50 percent of the classroom teachers will receive 10 hours of inservice training related to teaching handicapped children in regular classes.	1.a. Regional Staff Development Center b. State Department Consultants c. Director of Special Ed. d. Curriculum Coordinator	1. Pre- and post-test on teacher competencies to be designed by inservice instructors.
2. By _____, 50 percent of the classroom teachers, all special education resource teachers, the counselor, and school psychologist, will collaborate in small groups to write an individual education plan for a handicapped student.	2. Same as 1	2.a. Questionnaires completed by participants. b. Panel of "experts" will review and evaluate the IEPs.
3. By _____, 50 percent of the classroom teachers will work with a resource consultant in their classroom for a total of 6 school hours in refining skills of working with handicapped students.	3. Same as 1	3.a. Checklists completed by teachers on benefits of working with resource consultant. b. Questionnaire completed as to areas in which more training is desirable.

FIGURE 6-1 (continued)

Objectives	Resources	Evaluation
4. By _____, 90 percent of the classroom teachers will receive 10 hours of inservice training related to teaching handicapped children in regular classes.	4. Same as 1	4. Same as 1
5. By _____, 90 percent of the classroom teachers, all special education resource teachers, the counselor, and school psychologist, will collaborate in small groups to write an individual education plan for a handicapped student.	5. Same as 1	5. Same as 2
6. By _____, 90 percent of the classroom teachers will work with a resource consultant in their classroom for a total of 6 school hours in refining skills of working with handicapped students.	6. Same as 1	6. Same as 3

intensified. He had no friends at the junior high school; he ate by himself in the cafeteria every day, walked alone between classes, and did not join any social groups before or after school. The pressure became too great for Billy in the regular class. His parents and interested professionals from a nearby diagnostic clinic kept asking the school officials to consider other alternatives for Billy. Because there were no EMR classes, the only more structured possibility was a TMR class, even though Billy clearly did not belong there. The ending of this story is not a happy one. Billy reached the point of being unable to cope and had a severe emotional breakdown. He ended up in a residential psychiatric hospital.

Although Billy's story is an extreme example, it shows how—in the name of the least restrictive setting—a handicapped child ended up in the most restrictive setting. The question must be posed: Could the final crisis have been prevented if there had been a transitional program aimed at assisting Billy and his teachers through a gradual process toward regular class placement? If the behavioral problems could have been eliminated or minimized, positive social relationships structured, and an individualized program developed to accentuate his strengths, what would the difference have been?

The handicapped child and his family, caught in the midst of the deinstitutionalization process, often need intensive help in making new adjustments and learning new skills. A program that allows for the gradual inclusion of a previously institutionalized child in a public school setting and supports his family can be essential to later success.

P.L. 94–142 clearly requires a full continuum of services ranging from most restrictive to least restrictive placements. Figure 6-2 depicts an array of services representing the service continuum. In regard to placing handicapped students in regular classes, levels II and III are important intermediate points between the self-contained class and the regular class. Some handicapped students may require adaptations in the typical services provided by the system, involving the length of the school day, the amount of instruction provided by the resource teacher, or the amount of supplemental services provided by special therapists. To the maximum extent possible, school systems need to provide services that are flexible and adaptable to the individual circumstances of students. In the language of the statutes, the "least restrictive" (P.L. 94–142) or "most normal" (Sec. 504) setting must be provided for each handicapped student at the point on the service continuum that is appropriate to the student's needs as determined by nondiscriminating testing procedures and the IEP.

School systems that lack a sufficient number of handicapped students to warrant the full-scale development of a program might contract with other nearby school systems to develop a joint program. For example, an itinerant resource teacher might be hired cooperatively by several school systems to work with all of their visually impaired and blind students and to help their classroom teachers adapt the curriculum to the needs of these students. Many states have already

Table 6-2:
CASCADE MODEL OF SPECIAL EDUCATION SERVICE

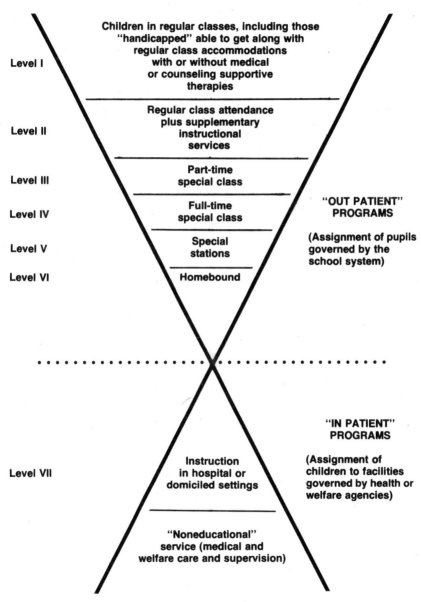

Level I — Children in regular classes, including those "handicapped" able to get along with regular class accommodations with or without medical or counseling supportive therapies

Level II — Regular class attendance plus supplementary instructional services

Level III — Part-time special class

Level IV — Full-time special class

Level V — Special stations

Level VI — Homebound

"OUT PATIENT" PROGRAMS

(Assignment of pupils governed by the school system)

"IN PATIENT" PROGRAMS

(Assignment of children to facilities governed by health or welfare agencies)

Level VII — Instruction in hospital or domiciled settings

"Noneducational" service (medical and welfare care and supervision)

From: Deno, Evelyn. Special Education as developmental capital. *Exceptional Children*, 1970, *37*, 229-237.

established cooperative service agencies to promote the concept of shared personnel as direct service providers and as supervisors of instruction. Public school
administrators interested in exploring this possibility should contact the Program
for Exceptional Children in their State Department of Public Instruction and obtain
information on established cooperative service agencies. If all LEAs are to
provide a continuum of appropriate services for handicapped students, cooperation and collaboration among systems is going to be a necessity.

Providing Inservice Training

There is no denying that the implementation of least restrictive placement is
going to require substantial inservice training efforts. Generally, the least restrictive placement requirements and their implementation in the public schools have
preceded university and college responses to provide training in regard to educating handicapped students (see the Higher Education section in this chapter).
Many, indeed the majority, of classroom teachers need inservice training related to
mainstreaming. As we pointed out in the legal interpretation section of this
chapter, mildly handicapped students do not fall under the priority groups established for P.L. 94–142 funding; therefore, a critical issue that LEAs must face is
how to fund inservice training for classroom teachers. Funding is often the biggest
factor in deciding how much inservice training can realistically be offered or
required, and whether teachers will be given release time, or if classroom follow-
up will be possible. SEAs are required to assess training needs and to submit
inservice training proposals in their annual program plans. Thus, LEAs should
insure that the SEAs are aware of the inservice training needs of their faculty.
Some states have passed legislation requiring every classroom teacher to take
a course on educating handicapped students within a specified time period. If
teachers choose not to follow this requirement, they lose their certification. States
that established this inservice requirement typically invest vast human and mone-
tary resources in the implementation of the requirement, by making training from
state and regional consultants available for a nominal fee. This is one method of
accomplishing inservice training.
Another strategy is to provide training at the system or school-building level.
Training at the school-building level is often the most effective, since it is more
likely that teachers will get assistance on their individual priority concerns. Also,
training at the school-building level might be directed at developing a systematic
basic skills curriculum for students achieving significantly below grade level,
resulting in a coordinated effort implemented across all grades. Promoting the
notion that ''we are all in this together'' can reinforce the transfer of skills learned
in inservice sessions to classroom practice. Special education resource teachers,
employed by a particular school, might also participate in the delivery of inservice

training. A particularly beneficial outcome of resource teacher involvement is that the resource teacher will be working at the school on a daily basis. Follow-up for regular education teachers—working with them in their classrooms, providing instructional materials, or assisting them in pinpointing a handicapped student's level of performance—is more likely to occur if the inservice trainer (resource teacher) is readily available.

System level or building level inservice training can also be provided by nearby college and university special education faculty with field-based training sessions. If inservice participants get certification renewal credit or graduate credit from the training sessions they are more likely to seek out such programs.

Many commercial training programs and materials are excellent for inservice sessions. Since the passage of P.L. 94–142, the increase in development of these programs and materials has been so rapid that it is difficult to keep abreast of what training materials are available. To be adequately prepared to teach handicapped students, teachers should receive training in the six major principles of the federal legislation: zero reject, classification, individualized education programs, least restrictive placement, procedural due process, and parental participation.

It is difficult to decide what to teach in inservice sessions, since the majority of inservice sessions are not long enough to cover all necessary topics. The inservice sessions that have been viewed most positively by teachers are those that generally provide relevant and practical assistance in solving problems the teacher is "likely to face on Monday morning." Since many teachers have negative attitudes about the principle of least restrictive placement and may not be enthusiastic about inservice training, it is particularly important to make these sessions responsive to the priority needs of the teachers. One way of doing this is to give teachers a checklist of possible skills that could be covered from the six areas enumerated above. Figure 6-3 provides a sample checklist of competencies in the areas of least restrictive placement and individualized instruction. Teachers could rank-order their preferences for training or check their three top choices. Training sessions could then be based on the compilation of teacher preferences. Training based on data from teachers increases the likelihood that teachers not only will attend, but also will welcome the opportunity to receive assistance in areas that are particularly troublesome for them.

A final consideration related to providing inservice training is when the sessions should be held. Inservice training is usually provided at the end of the school day. The participants are often tired, arrive late, spend the session thinking about what they need to prepare for the next day, and anxiously look forward to leaving. Alternatives for providing release time during the school day, inservice days during the school year when students do not come to school, or summer institutes with teacher stipends should be considered. These alternatives are expensive, but it is important to get the premium benefits from the time invested in inservice training.

FIGURE 6-3

Sample Checklist of Competencies in the Areas of Least Restrictive Placement and Individualized Instruction

Least Restrictive Placement

- 1. To be able to define what the concept of least restriction is and is not.
- 2. To be able to state the rationale for least restrictive placements in regard to the following issues: efficacy studies of the academic progress of mildly handicapped students in special vs. regular classes, labeling, minority status, and deinstitutionalization.
- 3. To be able to identify the interactive roles and responsibilities of various groups of educators (regular teachers, resource teachers, school psychologists, counselors, and administrators) in promoting the approach of shared responsibility to successfully implement least restrictive policies.
- 4. To be able to assess the ancillary services (speech therapy, physical therapy, etc.) required in a school system to adequately meet the educational needs of handicapped students.
- 5. To be able to apply planning and program development principles to organizationally prepare for least restrictive placement at the school system level.
- 6. To be able to explain the requirements of federal and state legislation in regard to least restrictive placements.

Individualized Instruction

- 1. To be able to develop an individual education plan for a handicapped student:
  - a. Assessment
  - b. Long-range goals
  - c. Short-term objectives
  - d. Special services and materials
  - e. Ongoing evaluation
  - f. Obtaining parental input

- 2. To be able to demonstrate appropriate instructional strategies in the classroom with handicapped students in the areas of:
  - a. Language arts
  - b. Math
  - c. Science
  - d. Social studies
  - e. Physical education
  - f. Socialization
  - g. Other

- 3. To be able to effectively use commercial and teacher-made instructional materials in the areas of:
  - a. Language arts
  - b. Math
  - c. Science
  - d. Social studies
  - e. Physical education
  - f. Socialization
  - g. Other

- 4. To be able to develop individualized programming for handicapped students using a variety of resources, such as peer tutors, community volunteers, and self-instructional materials.

- 5. To be able to apply behavior management skills to improving the academic performance and the general classroom behavior of handicapped students.

Developing a Procedure to Document Appropriate Placement

The statutes and regulations of P.L. 94–142 stipulate that a handicapped student should be placed in the least restrictive *appropriate* environment and that integration with nonhandicapped children should occur "to the maximum extent *appropriate*." Further, a handicapped student may not be removed from the regular education program unless the nature and severity of his handicap is such that education cannot be achieved satisfactorily there, even with the use of supplementary aids. The language of Sec. 504 is similar. Essentially, the burden of proof is on the school system to document exactly what curriculum and educational environment constitutes an *appropriate* education for a handicapped student. What is the documentation procedure for specifying that a handicapped student has been mainstreamed "to the maximum extent appropriate"? When does the nature and severity of a handicap become great enough to justify placing the student in a more restricted setting? If a handicapped student is performing very poorly in a regular class, how can you factor out the teacher's possible lack of competence to teach the student versus the nature and severity of the child's handicap? At present, guidance for school systems on how to document appropriate placement is practically nonexistent. Court remedies, legislation, research, and "expert" opinion in the field are generally void of documentation procedures.

Traditionally, "appropriate" placement has been decided on the basis of answers to questions such as: Is the student making instructional progress? Does he conform with behavioral expectations? Is he socially integrated in terms of peer relationships? Certainly these questions are important, and variables in the areas

of achievement level, behavioral patterns, peer relationships, and student preferences must be strongly considered. But the success or failure of a handicapped
student in a particular placement depends heavily on variables in two other areas:
teacher and system performance. Teacher variables (for both regular and resource
teachers) include the attitudes of the teacher toward least restrictive placement and
handicapped students, the teacher's skill at individualizing instruction, the classroom environment created by the teacher, the teacher's ability to facilitate social
integration, and the amount of collaboration among regular and resource teachers
in order to meet the needs of particular handicapped students. System variables
include the support teachers receive from the principal, the teacher-student ratio,
the amount of collaboration and cooperation among all special service personnel
(like school psychologists and counselor therapists) to support the teachers and
help meet the needs of the handicapped student, the quality of instructional
materials available, and the ancillary services (like occupational and physical
therapy) provided by the school system.

Appropriate placement of handicapped students in least restrictive settings
result from an interaction of student, teacher, and system variables. There is a real
need for systematic research to discover and analyze the clustering of variables
associated with success or failure of students in various placement alternatives.
Until this research is conducted, documentation of appropriate placement will
remain "a shot in the dark." Still, the burden of proof is on the school system, and
research in this area could provide data to help school systems establish documentation procedures. Research data can also serve as a basis for making more
informed placement decisions. In order to accomplish this goal, school systems
and institutions of higher education might join together to plan and conduct major
research projects on documenting appropriate placement. School systems willing
to assume the additional responsibility of helping to collect systematic data can
make an extremely significant contribution to the field. Documentation of appropriate placement is one of the more important unresolved issues in effective
implementation of the federal legislation.

IMPLICATIONS FOR HIGHER EDUCATION

The concept of least restrictive appropriate placements has significant implications for institutions of higher education. This fact was recognized by the
Bureau of Education for the Handicapped in their funding of "Dean's Projects" in
over seventy-five colleges and universities. The "Dean's Projects" are aimed at
developing training models to prepare regular educators to teach handicapped
children in regular classroom settings. Although significant changes directly
related to the new least restrictive requirements have occurred in a number of
colleges and universities, the pace of change has generally not kept up with the

pace of implementing mainstreaming in the public schools. Thus, many regular education university students are still not receiving adequate preservice training in the education of handicapped students.

Some of the major implications of the federal legislation regarding least restrictive placement for institutions of higher education include: (1) faculty reorientation; (2) curriculum modification; (3) preparing university students in consultation skills; (4) preparing "change agents"; and (5) research.

Faculty Reorientation

With handicapped students being added to regular classes in public schools, classroom teachers must be taught skills for educating handicapped students. School psychologists, administrators, and counselors in public schools also have significant new responsibilities because of the least restrictive requirements, which has equally significant implications for the colleges and universities who train them. If all students majoring in education are to receive training that will enable them to implement the concepts of a least restrictive placement, changes must occur in the organization of college and university faculty. Education faculties in all areas, including early childhood, elementary, secondary, school psychology, counseling, administration, and supervision have new roles and responsibilities in regard to training their students. They must now prepare their students to educate handicapped as well as nonhandicapped students. The education of handicapped students is new to many faculty members, and they may well require reorientation to update their own skills.

Reorientation can be provided in a variety of ways. A formal and highly structured strategy is for faculty members to receive "inservice" training through workshops or conferences sponsored by their local college or university or by another qualified institution or agency. These types of sessions are not always favorably viewed by faculty members because of the time they take from other interests that have priority for the teacher, or because of a seeming lack of relevance to their particular area of expertise.

Reorientation approaches could personalize the training if they bring special and regular education faculty together to share expertise with each other through team-teaching and collaborative projects in the areas of curriculum, research, or media development. The team-teaching and collaborative projects should be targeted in areas related to integrating the educational programs of handicapped and nonhandicapped students. Joint efforts can help get regular education faculty interested in the education of handicapped students and can lead to the development and refinement of skills for the task.

Whatever strategy is used, faculty reorientation requires top-level administrative support and a systematic program development approach. As university faculty members from different disciplines collaborate in preparing themselves and their students for the implementation of the least restrictive requirements, they will be practicing the didactic mainstreaming concepts they are teaching. This type of modeling can be one of the most effective instructional strategies for preparing university students to perform well at the public school level.

Curriculum Modification

If training is to be provided to college and university students in the regular or general education program, the traditional curriculum must be modified to include skills related to the education of handicapped students. One strategy for doing this, which has been adopted by many colleges and universities, is to require all regular education students to take a course from the special education curriculum. This course might be a general overview of the characteristics of handicapped students, or a methods and materials course directly related to the handicapped population. There are two major advantages to this approach: it is fairly easy to implement after the initial approval of the course, and the courses tend to remain permanently required. The disadvantage of requiring a separate course is that it clearly separates training for teaching handicapped students from training for teaching non-handicapped students. If public school teachers are to provide individualized instruction to students based on a developmental continuum, it makes sense for them to be prepared for this responsibility with courses that cover the entire continuum. It is somewhat contradictory to prepare students for teaching integrated classes of handicapped and nonhandicapped students through a curriculum that segregates the necessary skills.

The alternative to separate courses is to broaden all courses in the regular or general education curriculum that could have relevance to the education of handicapped students. Thus, a course on the social foundations of education might include content on P.L. 94–142 and the forces leading to the adoption of the least restrictive requirements. A child development course is a logical place to discuss exceptional child development. Methods courses could include plans and techniques for teaching all students—handicapped and nonhandicapped. An integrated curriculum would help students assimilate information on teaching individuals who function at different levels on the developmental continuum. Content specifically related to handicapped students "mainstreamed" with content specifically related to nonhandicapped students would allow students to recognize the similarities, as well as the differences between handicapped and nonhandicapped individuals. One problem with the integrated approach is that it can cause "territorial" reactions in faculty members who are not positively inclined toward the implementation of the least restrictive requirements and who may not wish to change their courses. Another disadvantage is that it is more difficult to be sure that competencies related to the handicapped are actually included in an integrated curriculum. With so many different faculty members responsible for segments of the training, insuring that the skills are taught is a very difficult process.

Weighing the pros and cons of both strategies for curriculum modification, we advocate the integrated approach, if the obstacles mentioned can be overcome. If this alternative is chosen, faculty commitment and reorientation are absolutely essential. Competencies related to the education of handicapped students must be defined, agreed upon, and "assigned" to the corresponding course in the regular education curriculum. Faculty members responsible for that course will probably need assistance in teaching the content related to the compentencies. Arrangements might be made to team-teach that content with special education faculty members, have visiting lecturers, use media and training modules, or a more traditional lecture method might be used. When an integrated curriculum is initially planned and implemented, regular education faculty members need to be provided with the necessary back-up support to be successful in teaching the new competencies. A step-by-step approach of successive approximation toward curriculum modification may be the most effective way to proceed.

Preparing University Students in Consultation Skills

The implementation of least restrictive placement requires a great deal of shared responsibility on the part of educators. Evaluation committees composed of the school psychologist, counselor, classroom teacher, resource teacher, and possibly the principal may participate in the process of assessing a student and analyzing the results. This committee, with additional members (including the parents), might also assume responsibility for developing the handicapped student's IEP. As the plan is implemented, all educators will have to work together to provide appropriate instruction and services for the handicapped students. The role of educators will change from primarily working with children to spending significant amounts of time consulting, negotiating, compromising, and reaching consensus among adults.

What are the implications of this new public school role for schools and departments of education? In the past, colleges and universities have prepared educators strictly within their separate disciplines. The same building might have housed training programs in early childhood, elementary, special education, school psychology, counseling, and administration, but it has been rare for schools of education to provide seminars to bring educators representing various disciplines together to discuss common educational concerns. The federal legislation for the education of handicapped students provides a prime motivation for initiating such seminars. Since the implications of this legislation cut across all disciplines and the implementation of the requirement will necessitate shared responsibility, students should learn about the roles and responsibilities associated with a broad range of disciplines and learn to work together during training programs.

Preparing students from various disciplines to work together on the placement of handicapped students in the least restrictive appropriate setting can be accomplished through cooperative practicum arrangements. Rather than assigning students to a particular school with individual sets of expectations, faculty members might plan a shared experience for several students from different disciplines. For example, students from the regular education, special education, and school psychology departments might be assigned to work together as a team in one or two regular classrooms to develop jointly IEPs for handicapped students in the class. They might then implement their plans through a combination of individualized and group instructional strategies. As they learn to share ideas, divide responsibility among themselves, evaluate each other's work, compromise, and reach consensus, they will be learning valuable consultative skills. If this practicum arrangement is to succeed, supervisory faculty members from each of the respective disciplines must also engage in in-depth collaboration. If faculty members model the behaviors of shared responsibility, students are more likely to follow suit. Training university students majoring in education to work with adults is a responsibility that departments and schools of education cannot ignore.

Preparing Change Agents

The implementation of the legislative requirements for least restrictive placement will also bring about changes in school systems. Mildly handicapped students formerly placed in special classes are now candidates for regular classes, and students formerly placed in residential institutional programs are being transferred to community public school programs. Planning and implementing this shift in enrollment is a complex task requiring highly refined skills in assessing needs, specifying goals and objectives, identifying available resources, designing and delivering inservice training, conducting evaluations, and working with a wide array of constituents with varying views on the process of change. In addition to these "change agent" skills, individuals working in this area will need to have a thorough understanding of federal and state legislation and a background in education that will enable them to bridge the gap between theory and educational practice. Few colleges and universities seem to be teaching those special skills at present.

An interdisciplinary curriculum appears to be required by all this change. The "change agents" of this transitional period need to be trained in a variety of areas: special education, regular education, educational administration and supervision, psychology, sociology, public health administration, mental health administration, law, business, and city and regional planning are among the most obvious.

Other disciplines could undoubtedly be added to the list. The need for leaders who can effectively implement the complexities of the least restrictive placement policies may be the catalyst that will move college and university departments to work together to capitalize on shared expertise and strengths. Interdisciplinary studies in educational programs would represent a significant improvement over past practices.

Research

Colleges and universities have a unique role in the generation of new knowledge and the reinterpretation of existing knowledge. Faculty members might consider the need to conduct research and development activities in response to the right-to-education mandates as part of their special contribution. If they are unwilling to become involved in such research, who will do it? If the data-base for implementation of P.L. 94–142 and Sec. 504 is not established, what are the alternatives for implementing policies that *must*, by law, be implemented? Under "Implications for Public Schools" earlier in this chapter we discussed the unresolved issue of school systems developing procedures to document appropriate placement, and pointed out that the effective implementation of federal and state legislation could boil down to this one issue. Zero-reject requirements may be completely satisfied, nondiscriminatory testing and IEPs might become routine, parents may be legitimately involved in decision making and informed of their rights to procedural safeguards, and the decision on placement may be made according to informed opinions of the placement committee. But is this sufficient to document appropriate placement? If significant problems surround the case of a particular student, and if litigation arises because of the student's placement, a court is going to ask for clear documentation of *why* particular decisions were made. There is a far more basic and humane rationale for research in this area, one that is totally unrelated to the prevention of litigation. Research is needed to assist educators in making the most informed and accurate decisions they can about the education of handicapped and nonhandicapped students.

Longitudinal research efforts are needed to study the effect that least restrictive placements of handicapped students have on the academic progress and social adjustment of nonhandicapped peers. It would also be valuable to know how handicapped students who were placed in regular class settings, special class settings, or institutional settings during their school years adjusted to adult life. Documenting the positive and negative influences of each of these environments would certainly help educators strengthen educational alternatives. Research could have tremendous implications for training and program development activities. Difficult ethical considerations are also potential outcomes of this research. For example, newly collected data could conceivably support the fact that nonhandicapped students are jeopardized by mainstreaming. How can the federal legislation mandating a child-centered system accommodate this type of information? The responsibility of colleges and universities goes much further than data-gathering and statistical process; they need to help identify the implications of these studies and should work with the educational and legal system in incorporating this information into sound policies.[10]

IMPLICATIONS FOR CONSUMERS

The requirements of least restrictive placement have clear implications for handicapped students and their families. Consumers may well have more at stake than anyone regarding the success or failure of least restrictive placements. While least restrictive requirements are being implemented, consumers stand to bear much of the brunt of negative attitudes and training gaps of teachers. Some of the major implications for consumers include: (1) advocacy; (2) assisting in the sensitization process; and (3) exercising rights stipulated by other legislative principles.

Advocacy

Many parents of handicapped students and the handicapped students themselves welcome the requirements of least restrictive placement as the most satisfactory method of providing educational services; others are bitterly opposed to the concept. Opinions fall at every interval from extremely positive to extremely negative. Generally, the reasons stated for positive endorsement include (1) having the opportunity to be in a more "normalizing" environment (2) having the stigma of special class placement removed (3) and having the opportunity to develop relationships with nonhandicapped peers. Negative reactions are often attributed to the feeling that the student will receive less individual attention in the regular class, will experience social exclusion, and will be teased by the nonhandicapped. Also the placement might be "less protective," thus creating greater safety hazards, like physically handicapped students losing their balance and falling, or an emotionally disturbed student being more dangerous to himself and others. The most adamant objectors to least restrictive policies are likely to be parents who presently have severely and profoundly handicapped children residing in institutions. Many of these parents placed their children in residential institutions years ago upon the advice of professionals. They may have agonized over the situation at the time, but they have come to the conclusion that it is in the child's best interest. These parents may have had minimal contact with their child (in the past, many institutions encouraged families to cut the ties) and developed a "new" life for themselves that would have to be substantially modified to accommodate the severely or profoundly retarded child. Further, many of these parents are acutely aware of the fact that their community and public schools may still have only minimal services for their child. For these reasons a significant number of parents across the country are strongly fighting the implementation of their state's deinstitutionalization plan. They are powerful lobbyists, and will probably be influential in defining the process of movement from more to less restriction for their institutionalized children.

Thus a major implication of the least restrictive requirements is the advocacy role it demands of many consumers. When it is your own handicapped child whose placement is to be reexamined, vested interest can reach its highest levels. Many parents of handicapped children have learned the lessons of the right-to-education movement; when they banded together and exerted pressure for a humane cause, the resulting litigation and legislation provided mandates for the direction of education for handicapped students. Public school and higher education officials are likely to hear more and more from consumers regarding their opinions of least restrictive implementation.

Parent advocacy groups in one state are training other parents to meet with their handicapped child's regular (mainstream) teacher at the beginning of the school year and ask in a frank and up-front manner: "What did you learn in college about how to teach my visually impaired (learning disabled, mentally retarded, etc.) child?" They are also being trained to report unsatisfactory answers to parent advocacy groups and school officials. Although this strategy may sound antagonistic, that is not its purpose. Parents generally want what is best for their child; parents of handicapped children are no exception. Many of these parents know that some systems have approached the implementation of the least restrictive requirements in a haphazard manner. What parents would want their child caught in the "crunch"? In another strategy used in parent advocacy, parents present their views on least restrictive placement to the board of education with recommendations they request the board to consider in regard to implementation. One recommendation might be for an ad hoc advisory committee composed of parents, teachers (regular and special), special services personnel, a state department representative, a handicapped student, and a nonhandicapped student be established to work with school officials on the development of a system for building-level implementation.

Many parents of nonhandicapped students have mixed opinions about the movement of handicapped students into less restrictive settings. One effective information sharing strategy is to devote a PTA program to the topic. After a presentation outlining the "facts" associated with least restrictive placement, a panel comprised of parents of both handicapped and nonhandicapped students could present their reactions and concerns. The audience would then be divided into small groups for further and more individual discussion. If themes keep surfacing in the small group discussions, priority concerns could be established and a committee could be appointed to prepare a written statement of the concerns. The statement could be used in the development of system and school-building plans.

Some school systems discourage the expression of parental opinion on the basis that parents can be "trouble-makers." However, parents have a tremendous amount at stake in the implementation of least restrictive placement. Capitalizing on their advocacy interest and potential can be a positive force for developing realistic, child-centered educational policies.

Assisting in the Sensitization Process

Many regular educators have had extremely limited exposure to handicapped individuals and as a result are uncomfortable around handicapped persons, who are perceived as more "different" than they really are. For example, when one student teacher was introduced to an eighth grade EMR student, she talked very loud (as if the student had a hearing impairment), used exaggerated lip movements, chose vocabulary associated with elementary grades, and generally gave the impression through bodily gestures of being very anxious. Although it might seem ridiculous, this teacher had always "heard" about retarded people and in her mind had imagined significant deviance from the "normal" population. After their initial encounter, the eighth grade EMR student probably thought the teacher was far "stranger" than vice versa.

There are also teachers who have not yet developed sensitivities to human differences, like the teacher who calls the learning disabled student with significant coordination problems "Bungle Bum" in physical education class, or the one who announces to the class, "Susie, it's time for you to go to the EMR room." Often the teachers do not mean to be cruel or to embarrass the student; they simply do not stop to think.

Sometimes there are problems related to sensitivity with peers. The physically handicapped child is called "spasette," and the retarded student is teased unmercifully if he cannot read the grade-level textbooks. These situations are likely to occur, particularly in the initial stages of implementation. The important point is that handicapped students need to be encouraged to let their parents know if the teacher or the nonhandicapped students are creating embarrassment for them in the classroom. Further, if the teacher is sensitive to the special needs of the handicapped student, he can have informal conferences with the child to discuss peer reactions. The teacher has many opportunities to observe peer interactions and can formulate a fairly accurate opinion of how the nonhandicapped students perceive the handicapped student.

Insensitive encounters should, of course, be eliminated, if possible. The starting point is for the parents, the teacher, and the student to discuss openly the problem. The school counselor might also be helpful in this area. In unfortunate situations, students and parents may seethe and harbor a grudge about a situation that could be changed if only it were constructively brought to the attention of educational personnel. If a sensitive educational environment is to be developed, consumers have a responsibility to provide evidence of problem situations. In turn, educators have a responsibility to work with the parents, handicapped students, and nonhandicapped students to create a more positive classroom environment of acceptance and respect for differences. Strategies in this regard are discussed by Gearheart and Weishahn[11] and Turnbull and Schulz.[12]

Exercising Rights Stipulated by the Other Legislative Principles

Providing an appropriate educational program to a handicapped student in the least restrictive setting requires adherence to the other major legislative principles: zero reject, classification, individualized education, procedural due process, and parent participation. There are specific implications for consumers in regard to each principle, which we discuss in the respective chapters. For the moment, let it suffice to say that least restrictive requirements are indivisible from the other legislative principles. Consumers need to be involved in every step of the process in order to increase the possibility that the requirements of least restrictive placement will be appropriately implemented.

NOTES

1. 343 F. Supp. 279,311 (E.D. Pa. 1972)
2. State ex ref. Warren v. Nussbaum, 64 Wisc. 2d 314, 219 N.W. 2d 577 (1974).
3. Panitch v. State of Wis., 390 F. Supp. 611, 614 (D. Wis. 1974).
4. Lora v. Bd. of Ed. of City of N.Y., #75–Civ. 919 (E.D. N.Y. filed June 11, 1975).
5. Stewart v. Phillips, Civ. Act. No. 70–1199–F (D. Mass., filed Sept. 14, 1970).
6. Civ. Act. No. DC–75–31–S (N.D. Miss., filed April 25, 1975).
7. No. 77–0341–ACW (N.D. Cal. Filed, 1976).
8. James Paul, Ann P. Turnbull, and William Cruickshank, *Mainstreaming: A Practical Guide* (Syracuse, New York: Syracuse University Press, 1977).
9. *Ibid*.
10. H.R. Turnbull and Ann P. Turnbull, ''The implications of the right-to-

education movement for institutions of higher education," *Education and Training of the Mentally Retarded* 12 (1977): 286-295.

11. Bill R. Gearheart and Mel W. Weishahn, *The handicapped child in the regular class*, St. Louis, Missouri: The C. V. Mosby Company, 1976.

12. Ann P. Turnbull and Jane B. Schulz, *Mainstreaming Handicapped Students: A guide for the classroom teacher*, Boston: Allyn and Bacon, 1978.

1978 Supplement

n. 4. Lora v. New York Board of Education,   F. Supp.   , 46 U.S.L.W. 2683 (1978), has been decided on the merits (see Chapter 5, n. 10), but the court did not reach the issue of "least restrictive placement."

n. 6. Mattie T. v. Holladay,   F. Supp.   , has been decided on the merits (see Chapter 3, n. 48, and Chapter 9, n. 25), and the court has ordered the placement of handicapped children with nonhandicapped children when not inappropriate for the handicapped children, as required by Sec. 504 regulations.

n. 7. Case filed Feb. 15, 1977; no decision on merits. See also N.J. Association for Retarded Citizens v. Department of Human Services (No. C-2473-76, N.J. Super. Ct., Hunterdon Cty., filed March 16, 1977), Frisch v. Board of Trustees of Jefferson County School Districts (D. Mont., Butte Div., filed Nov. 1978), and Egan v. School Administrative District 57 (No. CV-77-2835D, D. Me., filed Feb. 13, 1978), and Barbara C. v. Moritz (C2-77-887, E. Div., S.D., Ohio, filed Nov. 17, 1977), all challenging local education agencies' failure to provide community-based programs for institutionalized handicapped students. See, further, Pickett v. Prince Georges County Board of Education (No. 77-1883, D. Md., filed Nov. 11, 1977), in which the plaintiff dismissed his case voluntarily after the County Board of Education placed him in a public school program after he claimed that homebound instruction of only three hours a week violated his P.L. 94–142 rights to an appropriate placement.

7

Procedural Due Process

CONSTITUTIONAL FOUNDATIONS

The essence of fairness is procedural due process—the right of a citizen to protest before a government takes action with respect to him. In the case of the handicapped child, that means having the right to protest actions of the state education agency (SEA) or the local education agency (LEA). For those who pioneered the right-to-education doctrine, the procedures for implementing the right were as crucial as the right itself. Without a means of challenging the multitude of discriminatory practices that the schools had habitually followed, the children would have found that their right to be included in an educational program and to be treated nondiscriminatorily (to receive a free appropriate education) would have a hollow ring. Procedural due process—the right to protest—is a necessary educational ingredient in every phase of the handicapped child's education.

It also was seen as a constitutional requisite under the requirements of the Fifth and Fourteenth Amendments that no person shall be deprived of life, liberty, or property without due process of law. In terms of the education of handicapped children, this means that no handicapped child can be deprived of an education (the means for acquiring property, "life," and "liberty," in the sense of self development) without exercising his right to protest what happens to him.

The success of the right-to-education interests reaffirmed a belief widely held by lawyers—namely, that fair procedures will tend to produce acceptable, correct, and fair results. Due process took many forms in the right-to-education cases.

COURT DECISIONS

Notification

A person who is adversely affected by the action or inaction of a SEA or LEA is helpless to protect himself from the agency or to protest the decision unless he has adequate prior notice of what the agency proposes to do and for what reasons. The notion of *prior notice* clearly applies when a handicapped child is actually involved with an agency—when he has applied for admission to a program; has been placed or refused placement; has or has not been identified as handicapped; or has or has not been evaluated as handicapped. All of these actions can occur only after the child comes to the school's attention.

However, many handicapped children have been totally excluded from the schools, and often parents (or guardians) have been unaware of their child's right to an education. In the earliest right-to-education cases, *Pennsylvania Association for Retarded Children (PARC)* v. *Pennsylvania*[1] and *Mills* v. *D.C. Board of Education*,[2] an initial issue for due process consideration was parental ignorance of a child's right to an education. In response, *PARC* ordered local school boards to conduct door-to-door canvasses and directed the Department of Public Education and other state agencies serving children to comb their records for names of handicapped school-aged persons. *Mills* ordered the D.C. Board of Education to locate all handicapped children and advise them of their right to an education. In addition, *Mills* required that a notice be published in D.C. newspapers stating that all children, regardless of their handicap, have a right to publicly supported appropriate education. The notice informed parents of procedures for enrolling children in appropriate educational programs. *Mills* also required the school board to arrange for presentation of information on local radio and television stations.

Notice of the right to an education is related not only to the notion of fairness, but also to the principle of *zero-reject*—the idea that all handicapped children have the right to a free appropriate public education, *without regard to the nature or severity of their handicaps*. It is one thing to notify a child or his parents of legal rights; it is quite another to deal fairly with the child once he is enrolled in the public schools. Procedural due process speaks to both issues.

Evaluation and Placement

After the handicapped children were located, schools were required to evaluate them and place them in appropriate educational programs. The first detailed set of requirements for placing a child or changing his placement was provided in *PARC*, but these requirements applied only to the evaluation and placement of mentally retarded children. *Mills* extended basically the same procedure to all handicapped children. Later cases included the same procedural requirements.[3] The cases are unanimous in requiring three basic procedural safeguards.

First, the child's parent or guardian must be notified in writing. There are special provisions, not specified in the orders, for parents who cannot read English or who cannot read at all. The notice must describe the action the school proposes to take, the reasons for it (including references to the results of any tests or reports on which the action is based), and available alternative educational opportunities.[4] The right to a hearing prior to educational evaluation or placement includes the right to a conference before the school evaluates or places a child.[5] It is logical for a conference to precede formal notice of proposed action or inaction because the development of a child's individualized education program in the requisite conference also becomes, at the least, the basis for the child's placement.

In a natural extention of the principle of notice prior to placement, notice must be given prior to reassignment as well[6] since both the initial placement and any subsequent placement affects the child's right to an appropriate education. The notice must inform the parent of the reasons for the proposed action and of his right to object to the proposed action, to receive a hearing on his objection, and to obtain free medical, psychological, and education evaluations.[7]

One of the purposes of written notice is to give actual notice—to inform the parent of the proposed action—and it is doubtful that actual notice can be conveyed without a detailed explanation of what the school proposes to do and why. A statement of proposed action is meaningless unless the action is fairly described, unless the details of the action are clearly set forth. Likewise, a statement of proposed action is meaningless unless the reasons for the proposed action are fully described. The formality of notification is constitutionally insufficient; it is the reality of the notice—the *details of proposed action and the reasons* therefor— that is constitutionally required.

Second, if a parent requests a hearing, it must be conducted by a hearing officer independent of the local school authorities, at a time and place convenient to the parent. The hearing must be held within a specified period after the parent requests it, and is generally closed to the public unless the parent requests otherwise.[8]

Procedural due process not only allows a potentially adversely affected person to protest proposed governmental action; it also furnishes him with a forum where he can present his objections and have them heard and ruled on by a disinterested party. The parent is not just entitled to a hearing; he has a *meaningful* right to have the hearing before an impartial tribunal and at a time and place convenient to him. Justice delayed is justice denied, and the right to a reasonably prompt hearing is a prerequisite to any procedural safeguard. And because the hearing may involve evidence that divulges highly personal aspects of a child's or his family's life (e.g., whether he is emotionally disturbed or why he is physically disabled), the notion of a *right to privacy* permits hearings to be closed to the public unless the parent does not object to open hearings.

Third, the hearing must be conducted according to due process procedures. The parent must be informed that he has the right to be represented at the hearing by counsel, to present evidence and testimony, to confront and cross-examine witnesses, to examine school records before the hearing, to be furnished with a transcript of the hearing if he wishes to appeal the decision of the hearing officer, and to receive a written statement of the findings of fact and conclusions of law.[9] Under the *Cuyahoga* decision, he also has the right to be assured that the evidence he presents will come before the hearing officer,[10] that it will be considered by the officer, and that no evidence *not* offered by him or the school will be considered.

The results of a hearing significantly affect a child's right to an appropriate education and thereby affect his explicitly guaranteed constitutional rights of liberty and property as well. Sometimes (although not necessarily), due process hearings take on the aspects of an adversarial hearing. However, the hearing is governed by rules of procedure that offer each party in the hearing equal opportunity to present his "case." In a proceeding of such importance, an absence of legal counsel makes a mockery of the concept of fairness and due process; parents must be made aware of their right to counsel.

The right to present evidence and examine and cross-examine witnesses is the foundation of the right to be heard. Moreover, the right to call expert witnesses speaks directly to the issue that is often the very reason for the hearing—namely, the evaluation and placement of the handicapped child. Access to school records is part and parcel of the right to examine and cross-examine witnesses.

The right to appeal, to a record of the hearing, and to a statement of the hearing officer's decisions and reasons are indispensable in assuring a parent that arbitrariness will not govern the hearing and its results; that is, the hearing will have both the appearance *and* the reality of fairness.

Periodic Reevaluation

Another important requirement from the cases is that student assignments must be reevaluated periodically. *PARC* required automatic biennial reevaluation of any educational assignment other than to regular class; annual reevaluation was available at the request of the child's parent. Prior to each reevaluation, there was to be full notice and opportunity for a due-process hearing. *Mills* also required periodic reevaluation of the child's status. Without mandatory periodic reevaluation and notice thereof to the child's parent, the opportunity for protest (i.e., the opportunity for due process) might be effectively lost, since it is unlikely that schools would encourage parents to exercise their due process rights. Some parents, having been put off by their first hearing—not having achieved a decision they wanted, or having "learned" not to challenge the professionals—would not continue to assert their child's rights without the enforced reevaluation.

Misuse of Disciplinary Procedures

In the past, some disciplinary procedures were misused to exclude handicapped children from the public school. Subsequent court decisions have prohibited the application of those procedures in such a way as to exclude handicapped children from education. *Mills* directly addressed the problem of misused disciplinary procedures by setting out in detail the procedural safeguards to be used in any disciplinary proceeding.[11]

Mills required that the District of Columbia schools "shall not suspend a child from the public schools for disciplinary reasons for any period in excess of two days without affording him a hearing pursuant to the [due process] provision . . . and without providing for his education during the period of any such suspension."[12] The provisions for notice and hearing in disciplinary cases were much like those that apply to placement, transfer, or exclusion. The essential elements were *notice* to the parent of the action to be taken and the *reasons* for it, and the procedural *rights* of the parent, including the right to an evaluation and to examine the school records.

Classification Criteria

A different type of concern for the procedures used in placing children within the school system was shown in the cases challenging the use of various evaluation and testing materials and procedures for purposes of determining intelligence and student tracking. At issue was the validity of the criteria used in evaluation and placement—the alleged linguistic and cultural bias of the materials. In the leading cases where classification was an issue, procedural due process became an essential element to safeguard the child against discriminatory classification.[13]

Expunction or Correction of Records

Mills provided for the expunction from or correction of records of any handicapped children with regard to past expulsions, suspensions, or exclusions, through either academic classifications or disciplinary actions, that violated their rights. If a child is incorrectly placed in a program for the mentally retarded, his records can be examined and, if found in error, they must be corrected.[14] Only then can the effects of an incorrect record be ameliorated.

It is not surprising that the case-law requirements of due process are reflected, almost in perfect mirror image, in the applicable federal statutes.

FEDERAL LEGISLATION

P.L. 94—142

In order to receive the formula grant authorized by P.L. 94–142 for the education of handicapped children, the SEA and each public agency must give assurances to the Federal Office of Education that they have adopted appropriate due process procedures [Sec. 612(5)(A) applicable to the SEA; and Sec. 614(a)(7) applicable to the LEA and IEU, and Sec. 615, applicable to all three]. The requirement of *procedural safeguards* is consistent with the intent of P.L. 94–142 to assure that the rights of handicapped children and their parents and guardians are protected [Sec. 601(c)]. The due process guarantees must include, but need not be limited to, the following elements [Sec. 615].

Access to Records. A child's parents or guardians must have an opportunity to examine all relevant records relating to the child's identification, evaluation, or placement and the provision of a free appropriate public education for him.

Evaluation. The parents are entitled to an independent (non-agency) educational evaluation of their child. Sec. 121a.500 defines evaluation as "procedures used to determine whether a child is handicapped and the nature and extent of the special education and related services that the child needs." This refers to procedures used selectively with an individual child and does not include basic tests administered to or procedures used with all children in a school, grade, or class. Sec. 121a.503 defines who may make an independent evaluation—namely, a qualified examiner not employed by the public agency responsible for educating the child. A qualified person is one who has met certification, licensing, registration, or other such requirements of the SEA in the area in which he provides special education or related services [Sec. 121a.12].

Sec. 121a.503 also provides that public agencies must, upon request, give parents information about where they may have independent educational evaluations made. Under some circumstances, the independent evaluation must be made at public expense; the public agency either pays for the full cost of the evaluation or insures that the evaluation is otherwise provided to the parent without cost to him. A parent has the right to an independent evaluation at public expense if the hearing officer requests one for use in a due process hearing or if the parent disagrees with the evaluation made by the public agency. However, if in a due process hearing that it initiates, the agency can prove that its evaluation was appropriate, the parent may be required to pay for the new evaluation. When a parent obtains an independent evaluation at his own expense, the agency must take it into consideration as a basis for providing the child with an appropriate education or as evidence in a due process hearing, or both [Sec. 121a.503].

The parent's consent must be obtained for preplacement evaluation and for the child's initial placement in a special education program [Sec. 121a.504(b)]. Consent, in this context and in all others, means that (a) the parent has been fully informed in his native language, or in another suitable manner of communication, of all information relevant to the activity (e.g., evaluation) for which consent was sought; (b) the parent understands and agrees in writing that the activity may be carried out; (c) the consent describes the activity and lists the records (if any) that will be released and to whom; and (d) the parent understands that he gives his consent voluntarily and may revoke it at any time.

If a parent refuses to consent when his consent is required, the parties must first attempt to resolve the conflict by complying with any applicable state law. If there is none, then the agency initiates a due process hearing. Should the hearing officer rule in favor of the agency, the parent's refusal will be overruled and the agency may evaluate or place the child, notifying the parents of its actions so that they may appeal [Sec. 121a.504 and .510 through .513].

Surrogate Parents. Sec. 615 and Sec. 121a.514 require the SEA to insure that the rights of a child are protected if his parents are unknown or unavailable or if he is a ward of the state. (The child's rights are not the responsibility of the SEA when his parents are simply uncooperative or unresponsive.) The SEA may comply with this requirement by assigning a parent surrogate. There are other ways, but Sec. 615 and Sec. 121a.514 mention only this one. If the SEA goes the route of parent surrogates, it must devise methods for determining whether a child needs a surrogate and then for assigning one to him. The regulations give no guidance on the methods; they do, however, set out the criteria for selecting a surrogate—primarily, there should be no conflict of interest and the individual should have the skill to represent the child. A superintendent or other employee of an institution in which a child resides may not serve as a surrogate for him. If there is a disagreement about who the surrogate will be, the conflict may be resolved by a due process hearing. The regulations also make it clear that a person paid by a public agency solely for the purpose of being a surrogate does not thereby become an agency employee. The surrogate may represent the child in matters affecting his identification, evaluation, and placement, and his right to a free appropriate public education.

Notice. The agency must give prior written notice to the parent, guardian, or surrogate whenever it proposes to initiate or change, or refuses to initiate or change, the child's identification, evaluation, or placement and the provision of a free appropriate public education to him [Sec. 615(b)(1)(C) and (D)]. Sec. 121a.505 requires the notice to contain:

(1) A full explanation of all the procedural safeguards available to the parents . . . ;

(2) A description of the action proposed or refused by the agency, an explanation of why the agency proposes or refuses to take the action, and a description of any options the agency considered and the reasons why those options were rejected;

(3) A description of each evaluation procedure, test, record, or report the agency uses as a basis for the proposal or refusal; and;

(4) A description of any other factors which are relevant to the agency's proposal or refusal.

It also requires that the notice be:

(1) Written in language understandable to the general public, and

(2) Provided in the native language of the parent or other mode of communication used by the parent, unless it is clearly not feasible to do so.

If the native language or other mode of communication of the parent is not a written language, the SEA or LEA must take steps to insure:

(1) That the notice is translated orally or by other means to the parent in his or her native language or other mode of communication;

(2) That the parent understands the content of the notice; and

(3) That there is written evidence that the requirements (of oral translation and parent understanding) have been met.

Complaints and Due Process Hearings. The agency must give the parents, guardian, or surrogate an opportunity to present complaints relating to any matter concerning the child's identification, evaluation, or placement, or his right to a free appropriate public education [Sec. 615(b)(1)(E)]. If the parents or guardian file a complaint with an agency, they are entitled to an opportunity for an impartial hearing conducted by the agency, as determined by state law or the SEA. The agency must inform the parents about any available low-cost or free legal aid in the geographical area [Sec. 121a.506].

The right to a due process hearing is not limited to consumers. Under Sec. 121a.504 and Sec. 121a.506, an agency may also initiate a due process hearing on its proposal or refusal to initiate or change the identification, evaluation, or placement of a handicapped child, or the free appropriate public education provided to him.

Unless the parties agree to an extension, the hearing must be held and a final decision reached within forty-five days after the hearing is requested, and a copy of the decision must be mailed to the parties. (The hearing officer may extend this deadline.) The time and place of the hearing and each review involving oral argument must be reasonably convenient to the parents and child.

Each agency must keep a list of the hearing officers and their qualifications. The hearing may not be conducted by an employee of the agency involved in education or caring for the child [Sec. 615(b)(2)]. Sec. 121a.507 prohibits a due process hearing from being conducted by any person having a personal or professional interest that might conflict with his objectivity in the hearing. A person who otherwise qualifies to conduct a hearing is *not* considered an employee of the agency solely because he is paid by the agency to serve as a hearing officer.

At the initial hearing and on appeal, each party has the right to be accompanied and advised by an attorney and by other experts (persons with special knowledge or training with respect to the problems of handicapped children); to present evidence and confront, examine, cross-examine and compel the attendance of witnesses; to make written and oral argument; to receive a written or electronic verbatim record of the hearing; and to receive a written account of findings of fact. No evidence may be introduced by any party unless it was disclosed at least five days before the hearing. The parents must have the opportunity to have their child present and to have the hearing open to the public [Sec. 615(d) and Sec. 121a.508]. The decision must be sent to the state advisory panel established under Sec. 613(a)(12).

Unless a party appeals from the initial hearing or begins a court action after the appeal, the decision of the initial hearing is final [Sec. 615(e)]. If the hearing is conducted by an LEA, an aggrieved party may appeal to the SEA, which is required to conduct an impartial review of the hearing, reach a decision, and send a copy of the decision to the parties within thirty days. The hearing officer on appeal must make an independent decision after reviewing the matter [Sec. 615(c)].

Persons who are aggrieved by the findings and decision in the initial hearing but who do not have the right to appeal to the SEA (the act and proposed regulations do not say who these people may be) and persons who are aggrieved by the findings and decision on appeal (that is, any party in the appeal) may file a civil action in either a state court or a federal district court. (For the purposes of the federal suit, the jurisdictional rules about dollar amounts in controversy do not apply.) The court, whether state or federal, is to receive the records of the administrative proceedings, hear additional evidence if offered, and, on the basis of the preponderance of the evidence, grant appropriate relief [Sec. 615(e)(2) and (4)].

During the initial hearing or appeal, the child remains in his current educational placement unless the SEA or LEA and his parents or guardian agree otherwise. If he is applying for initial admission to school, he will be placed in the public school program, if his parents or guardian agree, until all the hearings (including appeals) have been completed [Sec. 615(e)(3)]. The agency may of course use its normal procedures for dealing with children who are endangering themselves or others.

The right of the parents or guardian to have a hearing with respect to the provision of a free appropriate public education for a child is quite broadly stated. In the view of Senator Williams, one of the principal sponsors of the act, the right to file allows them to question important matters related to the child's individualized education program. The definition of "free appropriate public education" includes special education and related services provided at public expense, under public supervision and direction, without charge, or within the SEA's standards, as well as an appropriate preschool, elementary, or secondary school education in the state provided in conformity with an individualized education plan [Sec. 602(18)]. Senator Williams also contends that a parent or guardian may present a complaint allleging that an SEA or LEA has refused to provide services to which a child may be entitled—a complaint of equal protection or substantive due process—or that it has erroneously classified him—a complaint of substantive due process (*Cong. Rec.*, Sen., Nov. 19, 1975, pp. S20432–133).

Sec. 504

The Sec. 504 regulation (Sec. 84.36) provides that an SEA or LEA may satisfy Sec. 504 due process requirements by complying with the procedural safeguards of Sec. 615 of P.L. 94–142. The alternative, and minimum, requirement for the SEA and LEA are to furnish notice, to make the child's records accessible, to guarantee an impartial hearing, to afford the right to counsel, and to assure an impartial review.

IMPLICATIONS FOR PUBLIC SCHOOLS

Practically everything a school might do concerning a handicapped child's education can be "tested" or challenged in a due process hearing. To have established this much is to have recognized that the implications of due process hearings for schools are massive. It is important for schools and consumers to understand why recent cases and current federal legislation are so concerned with due process; if they understand the reason, they will more readily accept its use.

Due process is an indispensable technique for fairness: a fair process of governing people (in this case, a fair way of dealing with handicapped children in the public schools) is more likely to produce fair and acceptable results than an unfair process. The due process hearing requirement is the vehicle by which the law puts the principle of fairness into effect.

Due process in the public education of handicapped children also underscores the notion that those children are not to be treated any differently than employees of the schools they attend and nonhandicapped children. The states have seen fit, for various reasons, to guarantee teachers and nonhandicapped students due process rights with respect to their employment and education in the public schools. The right-to-education cases and legislation simply carry forward that notion of fairness and extend it to handicapped children, emphasizing their essential equality, at law, with those who serve them and with their nonhandicapped peers.

Due process hearings can also highlight the contrast between the noble ideal and the primitive reality, showing the alarming gap that exists between the rights that are legally granted and the rights that are in fact available to handicapped children.[15]

Major implications of the due process for the public school include: (1) due process' relationship to the function of education; (2) the application of due process and its "uses"; (3) due process as a new forum; (4) other benefits of a due process hearing; (5) the logistics of due process hearings; and (6) central reporting of due process results.

The Relationship of Due Process to the Function of Education

The function of a public school system is to educate all children, creating opportunities for them to receive a free public education regardless of their handicaps. The zero-reject principle (education for all handicapped children) demands no less. But the principles of nondiscriminatory evaluation, appropriate and individualized education, and least-restrictive placement demand that the public school system educate handicapped children appropriately by taking their handicaps into account, not so that they may be excluded from a public education but so that they receive a meaningful education.

To aid in accomplishing both objectives, the cases and federal legislation have given schools and consumers a way to "test" whether a handicapped child, is in fact, receiving an appropriate education: the due process hearing. The hearing is a forum for determining whether the child is receiving an appropriate education, for focusing on the child's needs, and for providing school officials with information on whether they are accomplishing what they are required to accomplish.

In brief, due process is a technique for accountability, a means of assuring that the educational system will do or become able to do what it is designed and required to do.[16] It provides school administrators and consumers with information on whether the LEAs are doing what they can and must do, and enables educators and consumers to correct illegal or legally inadequate practices. Moreover, it is a technique for child-centered education. (For a more detailed discussion see "Implications for Consumers," page 189).[17] Due process harmonizes the separate but similar interests of educators and consumers: both are concerned about actual compliance with legal requirements and due process allows them to act on their concerns.

Recent federal legislation has also attempted to redress the balance of power between the previously powerful school officials and the previously powerless consumers. It reflects a new principle in the education of the handicapped child—''shared decision-making.'' The due process hearing can be a tool for advancing this principle if both school administrators and consumers see it as a vehicle for accomplishing mutually consistent goals (appropriate education of handicapped children). Under this view, the due process hearing becomes a forum in which both parties can take a non-adversarial approach to a common interest, appropriate education. If the two parties treat the due process hearing as an adversarial confrontation, it is highly unlikely that due process will demonstrably contribute to the advancement of shared interests. Hearings will not always be ''friendly,'' but the potential for shared decision-making through due process is there.

Application of Due Process and Its Uses

P.L. 94–142 is a carefully constructed procedural approach to the free appropriate public education of handicapped children. It provides procedures to be followed in advance of school actions that may affect a handicapped child. The planning, full service (dates-certain, ages-certain), and child census requirements are intended to support the zero-reject policy. Nondiscriminatory testing procedures, requirements for an individualized educational program, and the ''least restrictive alternative placement'' mandate are couched in procedural terms and are designed to furnish appropriate education and safeguard against functional exclusion. The provisions on parent access to records, public notice and public hearing on SEA and LEA plans, and the creation of advisory panels made up of representatives of handicapped children are intended to carry out the principle of shared decision making (participatory democracy).

All of these procedures tell SEAs and LEAs what they must do or may not do; due process assures that they will comply or be asked why they have not. If a school fails to carry out the procedures, another procedure—a due process hearing—can correct the situation. In short, although other sections of P.L. 94–142 provide ''in-put'' safeguards, the due process section provides ''output'' safeguards. The other sections are concerned with what the schools must do to guarantee free appropriate public education to a handicapped child; the due process safeguards deal with what consumers can do if schools fall short in complying with the other requirements of the act.

Of course, due process rights can also be exercised by an LEA if consumers object to LEA action or withhold their consent to an LEA evaluation of their children. From this viewpoint, due process safeguards speak to what can be done when educators believe that the parents have failed in meeting their obligations to their children. Everyone involved in the educational process needs to understand this use of due process, because the procedures shape the substance of the legislation.[18]

Due Process as a New Forum[19]

The traditional forums for debating legal and educational policies concerning the education of handicapped children have been the classrooms, the courts, and the legislatures. The due process hearing is one more place for educators and representatives of the handicapped to have their say. It allows educators to demonstrate what their needs are and to develop the evidence that will convince policymakers and funding sources that their needs are indeed real and immediate. It allows them to defend their professional judgments and gain support when they make the "right" decision concerning a child's educational needs, particularly when objections or questions have been raised by the child's parents. It also allows them to resolve problems in such a way that later litigation against them, particularly on grounds of professional negligence, is held to a minimum. A favorable due process ruling does not exactly create a situation of res judicata (a final decision on a particular point of law in the same factual context, which prevents later litigation), but it is at least highly persuasive evidence if the educators are later sued on the same issue. It enables them to defend on the grounds of "good faith"—having been fully justified in their course of conduct because the decision of the due process hearing required them to follow that course.

Some commentators have suggested that the due process hearing may not bring forward all the relevant facts when decisions are made concerning a child's classification, and they may be correct.[20] Why is that so? Granted, a due process hearing may be friendly or adversarial, but in either case there is nothing to prevent all the relevant facts from being presented and explored. Indeed, a skillfully conducted due process hearing is more likely to develop those facts than not. Other commentators have said that the due process hearing provides consumers with a golden opportunity to challenge educators' domain and their authority.[21] They argue that due process makes educators practice "defensive" education, which undermines their professional judgments and status. Such criticisms are invalid because, as pointed out earlier, the due process procedure can do distinguished service for both educators and the representatives of handicapped children; it provides both with an opportunity to have their say on mutual and divergent interests.

Other Benefits of Due Process

The due process forum not only helps all parties achieve mutual goals and enables educators to indicate why they can or cannot do as they are asked; it also has "process" functions. It facilitates the process of educating handicapped children in many ways.[22] For example, it legitimatizes educational decisions, and can legitimatize the process by which those decisions are reached. It is a process for assessing the school's needs as well as the child's. It provides consumers and educators with feedback on whether their interests are mutually consistent. When consumers are backed by expert witnesses, the due process hearing enables them to achieve at least temporary parity with educators, thus advancing the principles of shared decision making and providing all parties with an opportunity to address the child's needs. By increasing the potential for communication between educators and consumers, due process offers the possibility of decreasing the misunderstandings that exist now or that might develop in the future. In addition, due process will serve to increase the competence and impartiality of the decision-making process, to make long-range planning more accurate, and to boost public confidence in the public schools.

The Logistics of Due Process Hearings

There are some real problems in administering the due process requirements. For instance, who will develop the list of "surrogate parents" and what process will they follow? What will qualify a person to serve as a surrogate parent, and who decides on the criteria? Shared decision making on such issues should assure that the list of surrogate parents consists of legally and functionally qualified persons. With representatives of the SEA or LEA and state or local consumer groups suggesting criteria and proposing qualified persons, the surrogates will be legally independent of the SEA and LEA and will be able to carry out the responsibilities assigned to them.

And what about the costs? With so few dollars available (even from federal sources) to enable the schools to provide a free appropriate public education to handicapped children, where will the money be found to pay for independent evaluations, hearing transcripts, counsel fees, the wages of hearing officers and surrogate parents, or the expense of appeals? It is an unhappy fact that funds for the education of all children are short. Of the meagre dollars available to SEAs and LEAs for all purposes, the funds for educating handicapped children are particularly scarce. Due process can play an important role in guiding additional local and state funds to the right areas. It functions as a check on potentially illegal or legally inadequate school practices, and its costs should be planned for and treated on the same basis as other "overhead" costs, such as salaries, equipment, personnel development, and administrative expense. The handicapped child, short-changed for many years, surely deserves to receive the full benefit of one of his most important safeguards—the due process hearing.

Other issues surround the hearings: when will they occur; where; and how often? What effect will after-school hearings have on matters like personnel assignments and regulations, union or teacher association contracts governing the terms of teacher employment, the availability of all interested parties and their counsel and witnesses, and convenience to hearing examiners? If the hearing is held during the day, what about release time and teacher substitutes or aides? And what about compensatory pay if they are held in the evening? School days are often arranged to accommodate a host of other "nonclass" events of significantly less importance than a due process hearing; rearrangements of the school days, flexibility for teacher workdays and release time, and regularly set hearing dates can all contribute to reducing the personnel "costs" of the hearings.

Another potential problem is the selection of suitable hearing officers. It is crucial that they be impartial as well as qualified in other respects. The regulations only set minimum standards, requiring that the officer not be an employee of the SEA or LEA involved in educating or caring for the child and eliminating persons who have personal or professional conflicts of interest. There are several good rules of thumb for selecting hearing officers who are likely to be unbiased: (1) the SEA or LEA should ask consumer organizations to nominate persons as hearing officers; (2) the SEA and LEA should give those organizations the rights to approve or object to persons selected as hearing officers; (3) hearing officers should be professionally unaffiliated with the agency involved in the due process hearing or with a consumer agency (for example, school employees from one LEA should not serve as officers for LEA-level hearings although they may preside in hearings involving state or local mental health services or institutions in other jurisdictions); and (4) hearing officers should not reside or work in the jurisdiction involved in the hearing. These rules are designed to assure that, in general, the list of hearing officers will be prepared in such a way as to eliminate the more obvious objections to an officer's impartiality. Some other procedures that might be even better would involve the SEA and consumer organizations with the state or local bar association's young lawyers' section as a source for names of lawyers who would serve. They might also hire labor arbitrators or other persons experienced in hearing procedures; enlist the services of faculty in community colleges, technical institutes, and institutions of higher education; or seek out locally distinguished citizens to "ride circuit" and hear cases in jurisdictions where they do not have professional or personal interests.

There is no substitute for well-trained hearing officers. When they are thoroughly schooled on the procedures to be followed in the hearings, the substance of case law, the statutes and regulations, the nature and organization of the LEA involved in the hearing, the general characteristics of various handicapping conditions, and the general abilities of educators to respond to those disabilities, they will be likely to make more informed and more correct (less reversible or objectionable) decisions with less deliberaton. It may well be that interdisciplinary training of hearing officers (by "school" and "legal" experts) will become necessary.

Because hearing officers usually have other obligations, the problem of when to hold hearings and how to keep a backlog of cases from developing requires careful attention from the SEAs and LEAs. The techniques of judicial administration that help process cases rapidly through the trial courts may be useful to the SEAs and LEAs. Regularly scheduled hearing dates, pre-hearing conferences between parties and the hearing officer, easy access to school records and evaluations by LEA and consumer expert witnesses before hearings, pre-hearing stipulations of facts and issues of law, flexibility in granting a limited number of postponements, and the willingness of the parties to use affidavits in lieu of live testimony can all contribute to regularized, efficient hearings.

Central Reporting of Due Process Hearing Results

It is rare, as a matter of state law, for SEAs to require LEAs to report the frequency of, the reasons for, and results of due process hearings. Yet, such a requirement is set out in the regulations under P.L. 94–142 and should have great value to the SEAs and LEAs. Requiring the LEAs to report to the state advisory panel [Sec. 615 (d) (4)] provides the SEAs with a data bank that should enable them to make more informed judgments in areas like whether to require LEAs to consolidate applications for funds under Part B of the Education of the Handicapped Act, whether LEAs are complying with individualized educational plans, when and why technical assistance is appropriate, where more hearing officers are needed, and whether existing hearing officers are adequately trained. The increased information flow will enable the SEAs to help schools implement the rights of handicapped children and to better monitor school compliance or noncompliance with applicable laws. Central reporting of due process hearings should also help the SEAs in their annual requests for additional federal and state funds.

IMPLICATIONS FOR HIGHER EDUCATION

Colleges and universities with schools or departments of education (especially departments of special education) can also play a useful role in implementing the judicial and legislative requirements of procedural due process. This role consists of three components: (1) training; (2) service; and (3) research.

Training

In their traditional role as trainers of future teachers, resource consultants, school administrators, and educational policy makers, colleges and universities should recognize the significance of the due process hearing and the increasingly important part it will play in the professional lives of their students. By focusing on the judicial and legislative requirements of procedural due process and its uses in courses on school law, school administration, special education administration, organizational theory and behavior, school psychology, and parent training (to name but a few of the courses that might appropriately include due process in addition to the usual course content), they can introduce students to the importance of due process considerations. For example, in courses on school or special education administration future administrators could learn how to avoid unnecessary due process hearings, what the procedures of a due process hearing are, how to behave when faced with a request for a hearing, how to participate in or conduct one, and how to prepare the record of the case for appeals. Courses in school psychology should present the due process issues as they relate to the school psychologist's record keeping, testing and evaluation procedures, and documentation of evaluation results and recommendations. They should also learn about their role as an expert witness. Courses in parent training or parent counseling should concentrate on how to make parents aware of their due process rights and how, when, and why to exercise them. Preservice training in the relevance of due process to future professionals will not only prepare them to carry out their future responsibilities more effectively, but also make the due process hearing a more effective device for accomplishing its diverse goals.

Many colleges and universities provide inservice training programs as well as preservice education. If they teach their inservice students about the aspects of due process that are covered in their preservice training, they can make an additional positive contribution. For many inservice students, due process carries negative connotations only; they see the objections, problems, and criticisms, and few are aware of the positive aspects of due process. The unfamiliar (due process for handicapped students) is often frightening simply because it is unknown; by instructing inservice students on due process, colleges and universities can change attitudes, making inservice students more effective professionals, and thus making it more likely that due process will serve its purposes.

A potentially useful role for colleges and universities is the training of future hearing officers. The training of hearing officers is sometimes done—and done well—by the SEA. But it has also been done poorly in some cases: the attitudes of SEA employees may not be as impartial as those of college and university faculty members. The psychological set or negative attitude that they may convey in training can undermine any of the good work they do. Moreover, SEA employees may not have the requisite expertise (such as a law professor's legal knowledge) to make their training as helpful as it could be. Interdisciplinary training of hearing officers by schools of education and law is one of the unique contributions that colleges and universities can make.

Colleges and universities also can work through their schools of education and law (in conjunction with SEAs and state or local bar association representatives) to prepare guidelines for the use of LEAs, consumer groups, hearing officers, and courts. When college and university faculty consult with consumer groups about the education of handicapped children, they have an ideal opportunity to discuss due process and its many facets. Many consumers (particularly parents of handicapped children) need and want training in child development and child management; they also need and want information about their children's educational rights, including their rights to procedural safeguards. Adding due process to parent training and consultation efforts can significantly enhance the parents' effectiveness with regard to the schools and would allow them to contribute to making due process meaningful for all concerned.

Services

Colleges and universities have traditionally furnished educational services to state and local educational agencies, and they will continue to do so. With the advent of right-to-education cases and federal legislation requiring handicapped children to be educated, however, the nature of those services has changed and will continue to change. Faculty members have begun to serve as expert witnesses in right-to-education cases; they have also begun to make the independent evaluations of handicapped children that Sec. 615 entitles parents to have. Finally, they have started to serve as hearing officers for the SEAs and LEAs. Two of these new roles—expert witness and hearing officer—provide faculty with actual experience that will benefit their inservice and preservice students who will one day work in similar capacities.

Research

There are promising areas of research—made possible by centralized reporting of due process results—that faculty members can investigate. What is the effect on the nature and result of a due process hearing when the parents are represented by counsel and produce testimony of expert witnesses? Is the hearing more adversarial than it would be otherwise? Is the result more likely to be in favor of the parents? If the legal result favors the parents, does the school then take informal sanctions against the child? Why did the parents exercise their due process rights? The answers to these questions should provide valuable information for teacher preparation, inservice or parent training, and other aspects of college or university training and service.

IMPLICATIONS FOR CONSUMERS

Through due process, consumers may: (1) assure effective education for handicapped children; (2) hold school systems accountable; (3) help school systems improve themselves; (4) effect changes in education other than through more traditional routes, such as case law, legislation, and regulations; and (5) assert the worth of handicapped children.

The focus of the due process hearing is whether the school system did, refused to do, or failed to do something that affects the child's identification, evaluation, placement, or right to a free appropriate public education. Because the hearing focuses on the child and gives him a means for testing whether his rights have been satisfied by the SEA or LEA, it forces the SEA or LEA to become child-centered. The central question is whether the system has served the child by satisfying his legal claims, not whether the child has fitted into the system (a system-centered approach). The premise of the due process right is that a child-centered school system is more likely to assure effective education for handicapped children than a system-centered one.

Accountability

The right to a due process hearing is analogous to the right to carry a "big stick": give the consumer the right to protect himself, tell him he has four sticks to use (identification, evaluation, placement, and free appropriate public education), and let him wield the sticks (ask for a due process hearing) whenever he believes his rights are not satisfied. The result will be that the SEA or LEA will become more accountable to the parent. Accountability—making the schools account to the consumers for what they do or fail to do for handicapped children—is one of the foundations of the right-to-education movement, and no technique is more effective in accomplishing accountability than the power to protest the action or inaction of an SEA or LEA. It enables the consumer to demand that the school system justify its actions or inactions.

Consumers will find that the *threat* of a due process hearing can often be as effective in securing accountability as a hearing itself. This is particularly true if the SEA or LEA already has been found wanting with respect to certain aspects of a free appropriate public education for handicapped children and one of those aspects is at issue in the due process hearing that they threaten to bring. In short, nothing succeeds like success, and the use of precedent by consumers will tend to achieve accountability without the necessity of a hearing itself.

To achieve successful precedents, or to prevail in a particular case, a consumer will want to be well prepared for the hearing. He will, for example, want to attend other due process hearings (if open to him) so that he will have a sense of what occurs, who does and says what, and how the proceedings are conducted. He should learn the rules of procedure so he can present his case without stumbling over potentially hazardous technicalities. He will need to gather all of his facts and know what the applicable law is. (In this respect, he may find the advice of many a good lawyer helpful: "When you have the facts, argue the facts, when you have the law, argue the law, and when you have neither, scream like hell!") Of course, before going to the hearing he should examine the school's records on the handicapped child and the SEA and LEA application for funds under Part B so he will be able to make a match between his child's needs and the plans of the SEA or LEA. In short, he will want to be prepared to offer a solution or remedy to the hearing officer. He will need to line up his witnesses, including expert witnesses, and, if possible, he should interview the SEA's or LEA's expert witnesses or at least see their written reports. In the hearing itself, he should "make a record" for potential use on appeal by attempting to introduce all relevant evidence, make proper objections to the SEA's or LEA's evidence and arguments, and argue and rely on every legal theory available to him (including all that arise under federal and state constitutional provisions, federal and state law, and federal, state, and local regulations, paying particular attention to the remedies available under both Sec. 504 and P.L. 94–142). And, of course, he should know in advance what the facts and legal theories are that the SEA or LEA will rely on. He should also be prepared to deal with possible "negotiations" or "settlements"—he will have to identify which issues and remedies he is willing to compromise on and which he is not.

Obviously the hearing requires research and knowledge that may not be within every consumer's reach, for one reason or another. The advice and assistance of legal counsel may tend to make the hearing more adversarial, but the assistance of counsel can be immeasurably helpful to the consumer because the SEA or LEA is more experienced in due process hearings than most consumers, comes well prepared, has the assistance of counsel in preparation of its "case," and may indeed have counsel present at the hearing.

Improvement of School Systems

Consumers speak to each other; in the due process hearings (as well as in other legally required forums such as the development of IEPs, participation on SEA advisory panels and through access to school records and plans) they speak to SEAs and LEAs. The hearings allow them to work with the SEAs and LEAs to reach the common goal of improving services to handicapped children. If both parties approach hearings as a forum for making a match between the handicapped child's needs and the school's capabilities, they will help the system improve itself and thus better serve the handicapped child.

The risk in consumers treating the due process hearing as a "friendly" forum, however, is that the SEA or LEA may not see the hearing in the same way. If the consumer assumes too quickly that his nonadversarial posture will be reciprocated by the SEA or LEA, he may lull himself into a false sense of security and not take every possible advantage of the hearing. The consumer must be prepared to do battle, if necessary.

Consumers have the power to affect school systems and improve the services schools provide to the handicapped children through shared information and effective use of due process hearings to point up school strengths and weaknesses. By sharing information with each other about the results of local due process hearings parents can in turn help SEAs understand where they believe improvements can be made. They can also be effective at the local level through consumer organizations that use shared information as an informal ''discovery'' technique (a way of learning what SEAs and LEAs are doing or not doing to comply with the applicable laws). The result of this discovery process may be to show state-level consumer organizations what legislative, regulatory, or other changes are necessary (and even whether litigation is necessary) to achieve improved services for handicapped children. Reporting LEA due process hearing results to the state advisory panel seems destined to increase the consumer organizations' powers to communicate and engage in discovery.

Redress of Grievances

If the right-to-education movement has proven anything to date, it is that the recent legal advances have been a long time coming and, as spectacularly successful as they have been, they are but the first steps of the many that still need to be taken. These first steps—achieving the right to an education—require implementation and monitoring, roles that consumer organizations are particularly apt in doing. The due process hearing is designed not only to accomplish accountability, but also to assist consumers in their new roles of assisting in the implementation of rights and monitoring school compliance with those rights. The due process hearing is perhaps more successful as a forum for this purpose than the traditional forums—the courts and legislatures.[23] The due process hearing is relatively inexpensive and does not take as long to bring about change as regular litigation and legislation. Unlike the traditional forums of courts and legislatures, it is a forum in which the schools and the consumers are more at ease with each other and more attuned to their specific needs and capabilities. It is sort of an ''in-house'' or ''neighborhood'' forum for compliance with laws and for a change of systems, and as such it offers the advantages of a more tailor-made remedy than courts or legislatures can offer.

One of the criticisms of the cases and legislation is that the lawmakers in those forums tend to be unfamiliar with the problems of the LEAs and impose requirements that are either not applicable to the LEAs or cannot be met by them. The due process hearing is not likely to fall under this criticism. However, because the parties are familiar with each other and with the local issues, and because locally administered law has the potential to be too "personal"—the law may be administered according to the relative power of the parties, rather than according to the letter and spirit of the law—the due process hearing may not be as effective as case law or legislation in assuring compliance by LEAs with the rights of handicapped children. Consumers must be on their guard against personalized administration of the law: it can work to their advantage, but it can work to their disadvantage as well.

Asserting the Worth of the Handicapped Child

There is nothing quite as pleasurable for a parent as his feelings when he is able to address a representative of an SEA or LEA and say, "I no longer need your charity, I have my rights and they are . . ." The due process hearing enables the consumer to change his posture from one of supplicant to one of strength. It is a place in which he can assert not only his rights but also his worth as an individual.[24] The body politic has said to the handicapped child that it sees him as having worth equal to the majority of school-served children—the nonhandicapped.

NOTES

1. 334 F. Supp. 1257 (E.D. Pa 1971) and 343 F. Supp. 279 (E.D. Pa. 1972).

2. 348 F. Supp. 866 (D.D.C. 1972).

3. *See*, e.g., LeBanks v. Spears, 60 F.R.D. 135 (E.D. La. 1973), Quadalupe Org. v. Tempe Elem. School Dist., Civ. No. 71-435 (D. Ariz. 1972), and Larry P. v. Riles, 343 F. Supp. 1306, *aff'd* 502 F.2d 963 (9th Cir. 1974).

4. Doe v. Kenny, No. H-76-199 (D. Conn. 1976).

5. Cuyahoga Ass'n. for Retarded Children and Citizens v. Essex, No. C74-587 (N.D. Ohio, 1976).

6. Doe v. Kenny, *supra* n. 4.

7. Mills v. Bd., *supra* n. 2, Cuyahoga Ass'n. v. Essex, *supra* n. 5, and Doe v. Kenny, *supra* n. 4.

8. LeBanks v. Spears, *supra* n. 3, Mills v. Bd., *supra* n. 2; contra, PARC v. Pa., *supra* n. 1.

9. Cuyahoga Ass'n. v. Essex, *supra* n. 5.

10. *Id.*

11. Mills v. Bd., *supra* n. 2.

12. *Id.* at 882-3.

13. Diana v. State Bd. of Educ., C-70-37 F.R.P. (N.D. Cal. 1970, 1973), LeBanks v. Spears, *supra* n. 3, and Larry P. v. Riles, *supra* n. 3.

14. Mills v. Bd., *supra* n. 2.

15. Roos, P. Reaction Comment. In M. Kindred et al. (Eds.), *The Mentally Retarded Citizen and the Law*. New York: The Free Press, 1976.

16. Abeson, A. et al. Due Process of Law: Background and Intent. In F. Weintraub et al. (Eds.), *Public Policy and the Education of Exceptional Children*. Reston, Va.: Council for Exceptional Children, 1976, and Turnbull, H. Accountability: An Overview of the Impact of Litigation on Professionals. In F. Weintraub et al. (Eds.), *Public Policy and the Education of Exceptional Children*. Reston, Va.: Council for Exceptional Children, 1976.

17. Kirp, Buss, & Kuriloff, *Legal Reforms of Special Education: Empirical Studies and Procedural Reforms*, 62 Cal. L. Rev. 40 (1974), and Turnbull, H. *Legal Aspects of Educating the Developmentally Disabled*. Topeka: National Organization on Legal Problems of Education, 1975.

18. Turnbull, H., *supra* n. 17.

19. Gilhool, T. The Right to Community Services. In M. Kindred et al. (Eds.), *The Mentally Retarded Citizen and the Law*. New York: The Free Press, 1976; and A. Abeson, et al. Due Process of Law: Background and Intent. In F. Weintraub et al. (Eds.), *Public Policy and the Education of Exceptional Children*. Reston, Va.: Council for Exceptional Children, 1976.

20. N. Hobbs (Ed.). *Issues in the Classification of Children* (2 vols.) San Francisco: Jossey-Bass, 1975.

21. *Id.*

22. Sorgen, M. Labelling and Classification. In M. Kindred et al. (Eds.), *The Mentally Retarded Citizen and the Law*. New York: The Free Press, 1976, and A. Abeson et al. Due Process of Law: Background and Intent. In F. Weintraub et al. (Eds.), *Public Policy and the Education of Exceptional Children*. Reston, Va.: Council for Exceptional Children, 1976; and T. Gilhool, The Right to Community Services. In M. Kindred et al. (Eds.), *The Mentally Retarded Citizen and the Law*. New York: The Free Press, 1976.

23. Full Educational Opportunities for Handicapped Individuals (An Awareness Paper prepared for The White House Conference on Handicapped Individuals). In J. Jordan (Ed.), *Exceptional Children Education at the Bicentennial: A Parade of Progress*. Reston, Va.: Council for Exceptional Children, 1976.

24. Gilhool, T. The Right to Community Services. In M. Kindred et al. (Eds.), *The Mentally Retarded Citizen and the Law*. New York: The Free Press, 1976.

1978 Supplement

n. 8. The local school board and employees of the state board are not impartial hearing officers under P.L. 94–142, Compochiaro v. Califano (Cir. No. H-78-64, D. Conn., May 18, 1978).

n. 11. The application of school discipline codes to handicapped children poses one of the more difficult issues arising out of P.L. 94–142. Does the federal law mean that a local education agency may not suspend or expel handicapped children who violate student conduct regulations? If the effect or purpose of the suspension or expulsion is to change a student's placement (rather than doing so by IEP and placement decisions), the school may be enjoined from suspending or expelling the student until the placement decision is made in the ordinary course of complying with P.L. 94–142, Stuart v. Nappi, 433 F. Supp. 1235 (D. Conn., 1978), decision on order granting preliminary injunction. *Accord*, Howard S. v. Friendswood Independent School District, 454 F. Supp. 634 (S.D. Tex., 1978). Where the suspension or expulsion has resulted in a child being denied free appropriate public education as guaranteed by P.L. 94–142, two school districts have entered into consent agreements providing for the child to be readmitted or given compensatory education (in a community college) at the school's expense, Donnie R. v. Wood (No. 77-1360, D.S.C., consent decree entered Aug. 22, 1977) and Lopez v. Salida School District (C.A. No. C-73078, Dist. Ct., Denver Cty., Colo., Jan. 20, 1978). Finally, emotionally disturbed children are claiming that they must be treated in the same way as mentally retarded children in due process hearings on issues of discipline, J. v. Klein (No. 77-2257, E.D. Pa., filed June 28, 1977).

On access to records under P.L. 94–142, see *Mattie T. v. Holladay*, discussed in Chapter 9 at p. 216-7.

8

Parent Participation and Shared Decision Making

Participatory democracy is a phrase that describes shared decision making in the schools or in other public agencies. It refers to the legal right or political opportunity of those affected by a public agency's decisions to participate in making those decisions. It is a long-standing tenet of government in this country, but it has not always been in good standing; too often it has been given little more than lip-service. But as this chapter will show, P.L. 94–142—like the cases—has started to make inroads on unilateral decision making in the schools.

CONSTITUTIONAL FOUNDATIONS

Although the constitutional foundations for parent participation in the education of handicapped children are not well articulated by the courts—probably because they involve the children's rights instead of the parents'—they nevertheless exist and can be identified and explained. At the core of the constitutional principles is the common law doctrine that parents have a duty to support their children and a corollary right to their children's services and earnings for as long as the children have the legal status of minors. Under common law and even by today's statutes these rights and interests mean that parents may control their children in various ways.

For example, parents are empowered to consent (on the minor's behalf) to medical treatment for the minor and, more recently, to educational diagnosis and evaluation. The compulsory school-attendance laws usually make the parents criminally liable if they do not require their child to attend the public schools. Also, state statutes make parents criminally liable for failing to support their minor children. The reason for these and similar laws is that a minor is presumed incapable, because of his age, of acting on his own behalf except in limited ways, as granted by statute or as recently recognized under the constitutional "privacy interest" by the courts. Parents, then, have rights that they exercise on behalf of their child; in many instances, the child's right to have an education is exercised by his parents.

The child's right to procedural due process can be exercised by him or by his parents; his rights to a proper evaluation and appropriate classification can be enforced by his parents; and his right to be included in school can also be enforced by his parents. Thus, the child's rights to procedural and substantive due process and to equal protection are enforceable by his parents acting in their representative capacity (acting on the child's behalf). The courts explicitly recognize the parent's power to exercise their child's constitutional rights on his behalf, with regard to compulsory school attendance,[1] zero reject and child census procedures,[2] tuition-expense grants,[3] and procedural due process[4] (particularly the right to notice and to a hearing concerning school decisions[5]).

The cases clearly have made an indirect but nevertheless damning criticism of the schools by recognizing that children have rights of their own and their parents have rights in a representative capacity: they have said that schools have been making unilateral decisions about handicapped children's education but that, in the future, those decisions must be shared with the parents and other representatives of handicapped children.

FEDERAL LEGISLATION

P.L. 94–142

P.L. 94–142 declares that the act is intended to "assure that the rights of handicapped children and their parents or guardians are protected" [Sec. 601(c)]. It carries out its policy in the following ways (in addition to those already mentioned in connection with classification, evaluation, individual education programs, and procedural due process).

Notice, Consultation, and Hearings. P.L. 94–142 requires SEAs to give assurances to HEW that, in carrying out the act's requirements to provide a free appropriate public education, the state will establish procedures for consultation with persons involved in or concerned with the education of handicapped children, including the handicapped individuals and their parents or guardians [Sec. 612(7) and Sec. 121a.137]. P.L. 94–142 also requires SEAs to establish procedures for making the state plan available to the public and to the parents [Sec. 121a.234]; for having public hearings [Sec. 121a.280] for giving adequate notice of those hearings; and for allowing the general public to comment on proposed policies, programs, and procedures required by Sec. 612 or Sec. 613 before they are adopted [Sec. 612(7) and Sec. 121a.280].

As is more fully discussed in the implications section of this chapter, the regulations require SEAs to give public notice of policy hearings, to provide an opportunity for public participation and public comment, to review the public comments before adopting the annual plan, and to publish and make the plan generally available [Secs. 121a.281–.284]. In addition, the act requires LEAs to give assurances that, in giving full educational opportunities to all handicapped children, they will provide for the participation and consultation of the parents or guardians of the children [Sec. 614(a) (1) (C) (iii) and Sec. 121a.226].

Advisory Panels. The Commissioner of Education must establish a fifteen-member national committee on handicapped children to advise him concerning the administration of P.L. 94–142 and to recommend improvements in the administration and operation of the act [Sec. 604]. At least eight of the fifteen members must be persons affiliated with educational, training, or research programs for the handicapped. Although it is not required that the federal panel be composed of representatives of handicapped children, it may include some.

Similarly, the act requires SEAs to create an advisory panel whose members are to be appointed by the governor or other official authorized to make such appointments. The panel should be composed of individuals involved in or concerned with the education of handicapped children, including at least one representative of handicapped individuals, teachers of handicapped children, parents of such children, state and local educational officials, and administrators of programs for handicapped children [Sec. 613(a) (12) and Sec. 121a.651]. The panel is to advise the SEAs on the unmet needs of handicapped students, make public comment on the annual plan and on pertinent state rules or regulations to be issued by the SEA, and assist the state in developing and reporting whatever data and evaluations the Commissioner might require.

Access to System Records. The act requires that certain information about school programs for the handicapped children and about the children themselves be treated as public information, available to all, including parents of the handicapped children. An LEA must give assurances that its application for federal funds and all documents related to the application are available to parents, guardians, and other members of the general public. This includes information that is necessary for an SEA to perform its evaluation duties and information relating to the educational achievement of handicapped children in programs financed under the act [Sec. 614(a) (3) and (4)]. Likewise, before submitting an amendment to the state plan, an SEA must give at least thirty days' prior notice of the amendment to parents, guardians, and other members of the general public

[Sec. 612 (2) (E)]. These regulations are discussed in detail in the implications section of this chapter.

Protection of Student Records. P.L. 94–142 also provides for the confidentiality of student records and access to those records by parents or guardians [Secs. 617(c) and 612(2)(D)]. Both the SEAs and LEAs will be subject to action by the Secretary of HEW, in accordance with the so-called "Buckley-Pell Amendment" [Sec. 438, General Education Provisions Act, as amended by P.L. 93–380, Sec. 513] that assures the confidentiality of any personally identifiable data, information, and records collected or maintained by the commissioner, an SEA, or any LEA. Sec. 438 of the General Education Provisions Act requires recipients of federal education grants to give parents, guardians, and, in some cases, pupils access to their own public school records. Parents must be given an opportunity for a hearing to challenge the content of the records, and certain parts of the records cannot be released without parental consent. The confidentiality regulations [Sec. 121a.550-.576] are final, and were published in the February 27, 1976, *Federal Register* (pp. 8604-8610). They are incorporated in the P.L. 94–142 regulations, which are discussed in detail in the implications section of this chapter.

Sec. 504

The only requirement under Sec. 504 regulations is that LEAs must annually try to identify and locate every qualified handicapped person in the school district who is not receiving a public education and notify those persons and their parents or guardians of the school's duty to provide them with a free education [Sec. 84.32].

IMPLICATIONS FOR PUBLIC SCHOOLS

Like the due process requirements, the requirements of parent participation (participatory democracy) in educational decision making and parental access to educational records affects the balance of power among professionals and consumers. They bring consumers more into the forefront as informed decision-makers, and thus equalize a relationship that traditionally has often been one of superiority (professionals) speaking to inferiority (consumers). Implications of parent participation for public schools will be discussed in terms of: (1) providing information to consumers; and (2) consumer involvement in decision making.

Providing Information to Consumers

A major implication of the parent participation regulations is that both LEAs and SEAs have new responsibilities for providing educational information to consumers. For example, an SEA must provide notice to parents of handicapped students (in the parent's native language) that personally identifiable information (including the name of the child, his parents, and other family members; his address; any personal identifier like a social security number or student number; or any list of personal characteristics or other information that would make it possible to identify the child [Sec. 121a.500]) is on file. Further, it must explain the type of information it plans to collect and how it plans to use the information. An SEA might for example collect information on the number of children with a particular handicapping condition, or it might seek data for a description of the educational achievement of a group of handicapped children.

In addition, parents must be provided with a summary of policies and procedures to be used by "participating agencies" (*any* agency or institution that collects, maintains, and uses or provides information) for storing information, releasing it to third parties, or destroying it, as well as the agency's plan for protecting personally identifiable information. An SEA must publicly announce, through the newspapers or some other appropriate media, any child identification and evaluation activities it plans [Sec. 121a.561]. Thus, the SEA has responsibility for developing policies for access to system records and protection of student records to be followed by all participating agencies. Representatives from LEAs may wish to request an opportunity to participate in the SEA's development of these policies.

Parents and their representatives have the right to inspect personally identifiable information in their child's records within forty-five days, maximum, after requesting to inspect the records. If the record includes information on more than one child, parents are only entitled to see or be informed about the portion relating to their child [Sec. 121a.564]. The agency may presume that the parent has access rights unless it is advised otherwise in cases of guardianship, separation, and divorce. Parents may request an explanation or interpretation of the information and must be provided with copies if failure to provide copies would result in their being unable to inspect or review the information [Sec. 121a.562]. A fee for copies may be charged, unless the fee would prevent a parent from having access to the record [Sec. 121a.566]. Upon request, parents must also be provided with a list of the types and locations of information collected and used by the agency [Sec. 121a.565]. The school must keep a record of access [Sec. 121a.563].

These requirements for parental access to records represent a radical change from traditional educational practices. In countless situations, the specific results of evaluations administered to handicapped children have been withheld from the parents. For example, parents have typically been informed that their child has been evaluated as mentally retarded without ever being allowed to see the child's actual IQ score. Professionals have justified their refusal to release test scores on the basis that parents would not understand the meaning of such data. This reasoning has also served as an excuse to exclude parents from sharing in the process of educational planning.

Another practice has been for educators to write subjective notes in the records, such as, "Johnny's problems stem from the unfavorable home environment. His parents appear to be totally unconcerned about his personal and educational needs. He is a troublemaker and has limited potential." Comments like these have been entered in permanent records with little regard for the value judgments involved or for the validity of the actual data the opinion was based on. In the past, records with such subjective comments were often circulated among a wide group of educators and potential employers (but not the parents) and undoubtedly became a noose around the necks of the handicapped students involved.

One of the inherent problems of traditional practices was the lack of accountability of the professionals who compiled the records. Under the new legislative requirements, educators must develop skills for objective and accurate record-keeping. They will be held accountable by the parents who will now not only read the records, but also request an interpretation of the data. Educators will thus be encouraged to make only factual comments based on facts supported by educational data in their files. Before writing any information in the records, educators will have to ask themselves if they would be willing to discuss the comments face-to-face with the students' parents or have it reported in a due process hearing or in a courtroom. Any record may possibly wind up being interpreted in one of these situations.

There are further requirements for the protection of student records. After reading the records and having them appropriately interpreted, parents may request that the participating agency amend the information. The agency must consider the request and give an affirmative or negative response within a reasonable time period. If the agency disagrees with the request, they must inform the parents of their right to a hearing to protest this decision [Secs. 121a.567–570]. Thus, parents not only have rights to access of student records; they also have rights to informally or formally challenge the contents of student records. This underscores again the necessity for educators to recognize the importance of their responsibilities for maintaining accurate student records and developing skills in documenting educational progress.

The regulations safeguarding the confidentiality of student information set forth clear implementation guidelines for public schools. First, there must be one official appointed at each participating agency to assume overall responsibility for insuring that personally identifiable information remains confidential [Sec. 121-a.572(b)]. This person might be the director of special education, the director of special services, or some other administrator who has concomitant responsibility for the implementation of P.L. 94–142 and Sec. 504. All persons who participate in the collection or use of confidential information must receive training related to the state's policies and procedures on the confidentiality of personally identifiable information [Sec. 121a.572(c)]. The administrator responsible for this area would be the likely person to provide the necessary inservice training to faculty members.

Written copies of state and local policies regarding confidentiality should be distributed at inservice sessions to minimize the possibility of misunderstanding. The participating agency must also maintain an updated roster of persons (and their positions) employed by the agency who have access to personally identifiable information. This list is to be available for public inspection [Sec. 121a.572(d)]. When such clear documentation exists, the random circulation of confidential information among unauthorized persons can be eliminated.

Public agencies must obtain parental consent before releasing personally identifiable information to anyone other than the agency officials authorized to collect and use the information, unless otherwise authorized to do so under the "Buckley-Pell Amendment" in the federal Family Educational Rights and Privacy Act. The SEA must establish policies and procedures to be followed when a parent refuses to give consent. [Sec. 121a.571]. (The policies and procedures would probably include the initiation of a due process hearing.)

Public agencies must notify parents when personally identifiable information that had been collected and maintained is no longer needed for educational services; upon the request of the parents, the information must be destroyed. Permanent information that can be kept without regard to time limitations includes a student's name, address, phone number, grades, attendance record, classes attended, grade level completed, and year completed [Sec. 121a.573]. Public agency officials should advise parents that their child's records may be needed for such purposes as securing social security benefits or qualifying for certain income tax deductions. In addition, the safeguards for maintaining confidentiality of records should be fully explained to parents before they make a decision about having the records destroyed.

In their annual program plans, SEAs are required to specify policies and procedures to assure the rights of children as well as the rights of their parents. Consideration should be given to the age of the child and the type or severity of disability [Sec. 121a.574]. The Family Educational Rights and Privacy Act requires the rights of parents pertaining to educational records to be transferred to the student at age eighteen. This requirement has major implications for schools serving handicapped students in the eighteen to twenty-one age range.

Consumer Involvement in Decision Making

Two major avenues for consumer involvement in educational decision making are consumer participation at public hearings and consumer membership on advisory panels. However, P.L. 94–142 and Sec. 504 require SEAs and other public agencies to extend opportunities for educational decision making to consumers in other ways, including membership on the IEP committee, rights related to due process, and providing access to student records. (These requirements have already been individually discussed.)

SEAs have the responsibility of holding public hearings prior to the adoption of the annual program plan [Sec. 121a.280]. The requirements specify that notice must be provided in the newspaper (or some other media) with enough advance time to allow a reasonable opportunity for consumer participation. The notice must provide the following information: the purpose and scope of the annual program plan; the availability of the plan; the date, time, and location of each hearing; procedures for submitting written comments on the plan; and the timetable for developing and submitting the final plan [Sec. 121a.281]. The plan must be available for comment at least thirty days after the public notice. Furthermore, SEAs are required to conduct the public hearings at times and locations that will give interested persons the opportunity to attend [Sec. 121a.282 and .120]. In order to meet this last requirement SEAs will probably have to hold regional public hearings to insure that interested persons are not denied the opportunity to attend because of lengthy traveling distances.

The purpose of the public hearings is to inform consumers and to solicit their comments and opinions. It is insufficient for an SEA to merely provide information; nor may it ignore the comments made by interested parties. SEAs are required to review and consider all public comments, and make necessary modifications in the plan. If consumers object to a portion of the annual plan at a public hearing, and their objection is a valid one, SEAs should make changes immediately rather than risk direct confrontation in the implementation phase of the plan [Sec. 121a.283]. SEAs may wish to tape-record all comments made at public hearings for review purposes.

After the SEAs have made necessary modifications in their plans based on public comments, the plans are submitted to the Commissioner of Education for approval. When approval has been obtained, each SEA must provide notice of the approval in the newspaper or other media, including a list of the locations where copies of the plan are available for examination by any interested person [Sec. 121a.284].

LEAs also have a responsibility for insuring consumer participation in the development of their applications for P.L. 94–142 funds. The requirements state that such an application must include procedures for providing parents and guardians of handicapped students with the opportunity to participate in the development of the application [Sec. 121a.226]. Additionally, the application and all documents related to it are to be made available to parents and the general public. Specific implementation guidelines for involving consumers in educational decisions are not included in the requirements for LEAs. LEAs would be well advised, however, to follow the public hearing procedures outlined for the SEA.

Another strategy for obtaining consumer involvement in decision making is to establish an advisory panel composed of professionals and consumers. As pointed out earlier in this chapter, SEAs are required to create such panels [Sec. 121a.650]. The panel is required to have professional and consumer membership, including at least one handicapped individual and one parent of a handicapped child [Sec. 121a.651]. The panel is charged with responsibility for advising the SEA of unmet needs of handicapped students, commenting publicly on the annual program plan and the rules and regulations related to the education of handicapped students, and assisting the SEA in developing and reporting necessary information to the Commissioner of Education [Sec. 121a.652]. The panel must develop a report of their activities and suggestions, and the report must be made available to the public. Official minutes of the panel meetings, notice of upcoming panel meetings, and the agenda of the meetings must also be publicly announced. Finally, panel meetings must be open to the public [Sec. 121a.653]. Thus, the panel requirements not only insure consumer membership, but also insure that consumers not represented on the panel will be informed of the operation of the panel. Providing consumers with information enables them to assume an active role in agreeing or disagreeing with panel decisions. It extends to them the opportunity to share in educational decisions.

Again, LEAs are not required by the regulations to develop such advisory panels at the local level, but it is likely that many SEAs will require the establishment of such LEA panels in the state plan. Sec. 121a.226 does require LEAs to provide for parent participation in developing its long-range, full-service goals under Sec. 121a.222. In order to comply with all the other regulations of P.L. 94–142 and Sec. 504, advisory panels are, in reality, essential. Involving consumers in educational decision making at the point of policy development and review can substantially contribute to meeting both the letter and spirit of the law.

IMPLICATIONS FOR HIGHER EDUCATION

The regulations for participatory democracy do not merely extend the rights of shared educational decision making to parents of handicapped children; these rights are also extended to professionals interested in the educational development of handicapped students. Rights to participatory democracy can be exercised by college and university faculty members as well as by consumers. Implications for higher education in regard to participatory democracy include: (1) participation in hearings and on advisory panels; (2) training; and (3) research.

Participation: Hearings and Advisory Panels

Faculty members from various college and university departments who are advocates of handicapped individuals and teach courses related to handicapping conditions should be encouraged to participate in reviewing LEA and SEA annual plans. They should study the plans in advance, attend public meetings, and make recommendations that they believe will enhance effective implementation. When advisory panels are established to help develop plans or to monitor practices, faculty members might also actively seek a seat on the panel.

There are reciprocal pay-offs for faculty members and educational agencies as a result of collaborative efforts. Faculty members have expertise to offer based on knowledge of the professional literature and their own academic study of issues related to the educational programming of handicapped students. They also stand to gain a great deal from involvement in public hearings and advisory panels, such as firsthand understanding of the legislative requirements and the educational realities that must be dealt with in order to implement those requirements in a successful manner. The experience should enhance both the relevance of their training and their research efforts.

Training

Meaningful participatory democracy requires consumers and professionals to assume an active advocacy posture. Students who are trained in active advocacy are more likely to get involved in advocacy in their later professional endeavors than students who are not systematically trained in the role of an advocate. The implication is that all students enrolled in programs related to the education of handicapped students (e.g., special education, regular education, administration, school psychology, counseling, physical therapy, and speech) need to have an understanding of participatory democracy requirements, and they need experiential training for participating in public hearings. Students should be taught the types of information to seek at public hearings and how to make a meaningful response to the information they obtain. Relevant training might include student involvement in actual public hearings.

Institutions of higher education might also take an active role in teaching consumers their rights and responsibilities as related to participatory democracy. In addition to information on the legislation, training sessions could include simulated hearing situations where consumers could experience raising concerns and making comments. Some consumers might also benefit from assertiveness training for clearly and forcefully expressing their point of view at public hearings.

Research

Participatory democracy issues that warrant careful examination include methods for effectively planning and conducting public hearings, the nature of concerns expressed at public hearings, the persons likely to attend public hearings, the roles and responsibilities of advisory committees, the influence an advisory committee has on the development of policy, methods for effectively implementing access to system records, and methods for insuring the confidentiality of student records and access to those records by the student's parents. Participatory democracy is a new concept for public agencies, and empirical research data are needed to help develop guidelines for the most fruitful way to proceed with implementation.

IMPLICATIONS FOR CONSUMERS

The legislative principle of parent participation has obvious implications for consumers. The purpose underlying this principle is the creation of a new partnership between consumers and professionals. This is to be accomplished by requiring that consumers be given adequate information for making informed decisions and that procedures be developed to insure consumer participation in the educational process. The major implications have strong similarity to the implications of parent participation for the public schools, and include: (1) access to information, and (2) consumer involvement in decision making.

Access to Information

As discussed previously in this chapter, legislative requirements specify that consumers (parents) have access to and interpretation of the following information:

1. SEA records compiled on handicapped students;
2. SEA policies and procedures in regard to system and student records;
3. the handicapped child's educational records;
4. a list of the types and location of information collected on the child; and
5. advance notice of any plan to release personally identifiable information on a handicapped student to a third party (parental consent must be obtained prior to the release of records).

Access to such information allows consumers to hold educators accountable for their decisions and actions. For example, a parent may read his handicapped child's entire record, request an interpretation of any of the information therein, and challenge the content of the records by requesting that they be amended. This parental right and responsibility provides a system of checks and balances for the professionals who compile the records. It also insures the parents' right to full and complete information on their child. No longer do professionals represent a privileged few entitled to personally identifiable information on handicapped students. Parents are now entitled to information concerning the full results of evaluations, documentation of student progress, and behavioral observations. No educationally relevant data is to be withheld from them.

Public agencies must inform parents of their rights to information access. Consumer groups at local and state levels, like the Association for Retarded Citizens and the Association for Children with Learning Disabilities, might join with SEAs and LEAs to inform parents of their participatory rights under P.L. 94–142 and Sec. 504. Consumer groups might also hold meetings to explain the legislative requirements and offer training sessions on understanding the types of information that can be damaging to handicapped students, the distinction between data-based information and subjective comments, the types of interpretative questions they can ask about their child's records, and the kinds of amendments to the records they might propose. Reviews of simulated student records and role-playing parent conferences with educators might be useful training strategies. These training sessions could be jointly conducted by parents and professionals, but one professional who should definitely be involved in planning and implementation is the official appointed by each LEA to assume overall responsibility for insuring that personally identifiable information remains confidential (P.L. 94–142 requires the appointment of such an official). It cannot be assumed that all parents have the self-confidence and skill to be effective advocates for their children. Training parents to exercise their rights and responsibilities is a necessary step towards full implementation of P.L. 94–142 and Sec. 504.

Consumer Involvement in Decision Making

Attendance at public hearings on SEA annual program plans and LEA applications for P.L. 94–142 funds, and membership on advisory panels at state and local levels have been identified as mechanisms for consumer involvement in educational decisions. The success of the mechanisms will largely depend on the willingness of consumers to become actively involved.

Consumer groups might try sharing responsibility with public agencies for such tasks as advertising public hearings and encouraging parents to attend. Practical considerations like transportation problems or child care prevent some parents from participating in hearings. Consumer groups might help to arrange carpools and babysitting services to eliminate these obstacles. They can also monitor the final revision of SEA annual program plans to insure that consumer comments made at public hearings are given appropriate consideration.

Consumer groups should see that consumers have membership on any advisory panels. They should also take advantage of the opportunity to review official minutes, to have access to meeting notices, and to attend the panel meetings. When important matters are to be discussed by the advisory panel, consumers should actively and openly express their opinions for the consideration of panel members. They might contact individual panel members, circulate petitions, or organize a delegation to attend the meeting and present their concerns. The important point is that consumers must seize the opportunity to have input into educational decisions. Parents organized into advocacy groups that speak collectively for a substantial number of people have far more clout and are more likely to influence policy decisions.

Parent participation in educational decisions results in parent accountability. If parents advocate particular policies or procedures, they have a responsibility to suggest policies or procedures that are soundly based. When parents share in the planning, implementation, and monitoring of any system, they must be willing to be accountable for their choices.

There are many other ways consumers are involved in educational decision making. The opportunity to be a member of the IEP committee, the availability of due process rights, and access to system and student records assure parents of meaningful participation in the education of their handicapped child. If parents have extensive rights under P.L. 94–142 and Sec. 504, they have awesome responsibilities as well. All parents will not have the interest, energy, or time to fully carry out these rights and responsibilities. Parent participation is more likely if they can be assured that they are respected members of the educational team, if logistical obstacles can be minimized (evening meetings for working parents, special transportation arrangements), and if their educational concerns are addressed in the parents' order of priority rather than the professional's. The effective implementation of the principles and regulations related to parent participation requires new skills and sensitivity on the part of professionals and parents alike.

NOTES

1. Pennsylvania Association for Retarded Children v. Pennsylvania, 334 F. Supp. 1257 (E.D. Pa. 1971) and 343 F. Supp. 279 (E.D. Pa. 1972) (hereinafter cited as PARC); Mills v. Board of Education of Dist. of Columbia, 348 F. Supp. 866 (D.D.C. 1972) (hereinafter cited as Mills); and Maryland Association for Retarded Citizens v. Maryland, Equity No. 100/182 77676 (Cir. Ct., Baltimore City, filed May 3, 1974) (hereinafter cited as MARC).

2. Mills, *supra*, n. 1.

3. PARC, Mills, and MARC, *supra*, n. 1.

4. *Id.*

5. Killiany v. Vaul, No. 76–3220 (Pa. C. P., Delaware Cty., filed Mar. 15, 1976) and Stewart v. Phillips, Civ. Act. No. 70–1199–F (D. Mass., filed Sept. 14, 1970).

1978 Supplement

On parent access to records, see discussion of *Mattie T.* v. *Holladay*, Ch. 9 at pp. 216-7.

SECTION III:

TECHNIQUES FOR IMPLEMENTING THE SIX PRINCIPLES

9

Case Law Techniques

Litigation has been a major, and, indeed, was the original, source for establishing the educational rights of handicapped children. Were it not for the landmark decisions (e.g., *PARC, Mills, LeBanks, Larry P.,* and *Diana*), it is doubtful if subsequent litigation would have had such widespread success, if the "second-generation" litigation (defining "appropriate" education) would have had any useful precedents, or if state and federal legislation would have been enacted, much less mirror the case law so closely.

Court decisions and orders are not self-executing; they demand compliance by the parties involved, but they cannot assure or guarantee it. Court orders in the right-to-education movement are only effective if the defendants (school authorities) are willing or able to carry them out. When, as it sometimes happens, the defendants are neither willing nor able, the plaintiffs are compelled to return to court and seek additional relief. The alternative types of relief they usually seek described in the sections that follow.

CONTEMPT CITATIONS

In *Mills,* the court required the defendants to provide handicapped children with an appropriate or suitable education.[1] Three years later, their "victory" having proven shallow because the defendants were unwilling or unable to comply,[2] the plaintiffs filed a motion to enforce the court's earlier order. The court granted the motion and found the superintendent, the board of education, and the director of the department of human resources to be in contempt of court for failing to make appropriate placements and to notify the court of problems that prevented them from complying with the court's order. The court chose not to impose any penalties because funds had been made available to appropriately place some of the handicapped children.[3]

A similar contempt citation was issued in *Rainey v. Tennessee*.[4] In 1974 a consent decree was entered that obligated the defendants to provide appropriate programs for handicapped children. Two years later, the plaintiffs petitioned the court for a contempt citation and alleged that the defendants had not complied with the consent decree and were in continuing violation of the state's 1972 Mandatory Education Law for Handicapped Children and Youth. Two years after the plaintiffs filed the petition, the court found the defendants to be in violation of the consent decree and issued a contempt order, rejecting the defense that they should not be held in contempt because they did not have sufficient funds to comply with the order. The defendants were ordered to submit an implementation plan by March 1977, and to put the plan into effect by July 1977.

The New York City School Board was held in contempt in *ASPIRA of New York, Inc.* v. *Board*[5] for failing steadily and repeatedly to exercise their power and authority to make the board's employees proceed promptly and in good faith to accomplish the tasks commanded by a consent decree (providing a broad program of bilingual education in New York City schools). The court found that there had been clear and convincing proof that the board, though not wilfully flaunting the consent decree, had not been reasonably diligent and energetic in attempting to accomplish what the decree ordered. They had failed to marshall their own resources, assert their "high" authority, and demand the results needed from subordinate agencies in order to accomplish the terms of the decree. They had allowed deadlines to pass without volunteering explanations, and had tolerated long periods of nonperformance, inadequate performance and outright defiance from community school boards. Furthermore, they had tolerated slipshod procedures, failed to enlist or order the placement of needed and available personnel, had displayed a sense of nonurgency that bordered on indifference.

Contempt citations have also been sought in *Allen* v. *McDonough*[6] for the failure of the Boston school board to provide educational plans for special st students and to review students' placement in special classes within a specified period of time. The citations have not yet been ruled on.

COURT-APPOINTED MASTERS

Although a contempt order is an indication of the failure or unwillingness (or both) of the defendants to comply with court orders, its initial effect in both *Mills* and *Rainey* was to hold the individual defendants and the school systems potentially liable to the court through the imposition of civil or a criminal fine. It is not intended to assure that the court's orders will be carried out—it only holds out the threat of punishment to those who fail to carry them out. Thus, it is of limited value for accomplishing the education of handicapped children.

In both *Mills* and *Rainey,* however, the contempt order was accompanied by orders that the defendants must report to the court on the identification of other children needing services and how they will provide those services, and file with the court a plan for the implementation of its orders. Like the original orders, the ones accompanying the contempt order in *Mills* required the defendants to make extensive changes in the way they provided special education services. And, as could perhaps have been predicted from the defendants's reaction to the 1972 orders,[7] the defendants once again failed to adequately comply. Thus, a scant two months after finding the defendants in contempt, the court appointed a special master to oversee the implementation of its order that the defendants furnish a suitable education to handicapped children.

A master is an agent of the court, appointed to accomplish certain court-assigned tasks to ensure that the defendants carry out the court's orders. In *Mills,* the court assigned the master extensive duties: (1) investigate and evaluate the appropriateness of special education programs in the public schools, institutions operated by the D.C. department of human resources, and alternative educational services furnished outside the school system; (2) review the defendants' child-census and tuition-subsidy programs to determine if they are adequate; (3) report on the status of procedures and programs formulated to carry out the court's order by the school board, the department of human resources, and the D.C. government; (4) review the defendants' procedures for estimating the budgets, justifying special education needs, identifying budgetary shortages, and obtaining supplemental funding to make up deficits; (5) help the defendants prepare a plan to implement the court's orders; and (6) file periodic interim reports, file a final report with the court, and make recommendations to the court. The court did not grant the master power to give directions or orders to the school board or to supervise its operations; it did, however, order the board to pay the master for his services.

OTHER JUDICIAL REMEDIES

There are judicial remedies other than contempt citations and masters. Indeed, courts have extensive power to enforce their decrees. For example, they may order a defendant school to regularly file its plans for implementing a court decree or state statute with the court.[8] They may retain jurisdiction over a case in order to monitor the school's implementation of the court's order,[9] set dates by which certain of the orders must be carried out,[10] award attorneys' fees to the prevailing parties,[11] and assign actual or punitive damages, or both.[12]

FINANCIAL REALLOCATION AND WITHHOLDING OF FUNDS

One of the earliest defenses in the right-to-education suits, which has fared least well with the courts, is the defendants' contention that they do not have sufficient funds to provide an appropriate education to all handicapped children. In *Mills*, the court made short shrift of this argument, stating (in now well-known dicta) that the absence of funds is no defense of a failure to provide constitutional rights (equal educational opportunities) to handicapped students, and that the burden of inadequate funds may not fall more heavily on handicapped pupils than on nonhandicapped ones.[13] In *MARC*, the Maryland Circuit Court also gave little heed to the defense claims of financial difficulty when it ordered the defendants to take appropriate action to request additional funds from the state legislature.[14]

It is one thing to say that defendants must be equitable in the use of funds or that they should request more from their funding sources; it is altogether another to step into the budget process. Indeed, throughout the right-to-education cases, the courts have been extremely reluctant to interfere in any way with the financing of public education.[15]

The *Mills* court hesitated to appoint a master because it recognized that his compensation would drain off funds that would otherwise be available to educate handicapped children.[16] When it finally did appoint a master, it ordered only that he review the school board's budget process. Further evidence of judicial reluctance to interfere with the traditional legislative function of taxation and appropriation is shown in *Rainey*,[17] where, in response to the defendants' claim that they could not comply with the consent decree because they had insufficient funds, the court ordered them to submit an implementation plan by March 1977 and to put it into effect by July. Voicing a threat it had the power to enforce, the court said, "From and after that date, the defendants shall be enjoined from expending money for the operation of a public school system in this state unless the plan to be submitted is incorporated into the operation of the department of education and fully pursued to implement the consent decree." It is unlikely that the court's threat will ever be carried out, not only because the defendants will probably make a plan and incorporate it into their operation, but also because most courts are extremely reluctant to dive into legislative matters.

A similar result is sought in *Killiany* v. *Vaul*.[18] The issue there is whether the state commissioner of education will enforce the provisions of a state law that permits him to withhold state funds from a local school district if it does not comply with the education laws. The commissioner has issued a "show cause" order requiring the local school district to show him why he should not withhold educational funds (approximately $12 million), since the district did not comply with the state law requirement that the parents of a handicapped pupil are entitled to see the school's records on the child in a due process hearing. The significant difference between *Mills* and *Rainey* and this case is the agent seeking to impose financial sanctions. In the former cases, it is the court that would interfere with a legislative decision; in the latter, it is the commissioner who would enforce a legislatively granted power to withhold funds.

FEDERAL ABSTENTION, MOOTNESS, DORMANCY, AND VOLUNTARY DISMISSALS

Not every case reaches the stage at which judicial remedies become necessary; indeed, there are several avenues "out" of litigation and enforcement of court orders. One way out is through the use of the doctrine of "federal abstention." When a right-to-education suit is filed in a federal court (on the grounds that the defendants are violating the equal protection and due process guarantees of the Fifth and Fourteenth Amendments) this doctrine permits the court to rule that the case, although involving "federal" claims, should be tried first in state courts because it also involves "state" issues (like the violation of state law) that may dispose of the case and make it unnecessary for the federal constitutional issues to be tried. It is not uncommon for federal courts to dodge right-to-education cases on this ground[19] and to remit the plaintiffs to state courts. Defendants favor the abstention doctrine because it enables them to try their cases in forums traditionally less hostile to school systems and less inclined to find constitutional violations.

The federal trial court's power to abstain is discretionary. It may choose to abstain or not, and, if its order of abstention or nonabstention is appealed, the appellate court will inquire only whether the trial court abused its discretion. In *Frederick L.* v. *Thomas*,[20] the plaintiffs alleged that the Philadelphia school district did not provide learning disabled students with a minimally appropriate education; did not test all students in order to identify those who are learning disabled; and, instead, placed primary reliance on teacher referrals to school psychologists. The trial court held that the referral method was inadequate for identifying learning disabled students and ordered the district to submit a plan for identifying all learning disabled students in the district.

Responding to the defendants' claim that the trial court should have abstained because the case raised a constitutional claim of functional exclusion (see Chapters 3 and 5) and an accompanying claim based on state law—which the defendants argued was ambiguous and should have been resolved by a state court before the federal court ruled on it—the appellate court found that the trial court had not abused its discretion and was not required to abstain. It said that (1) the state statutes were not wholly ambiguous, (2) the defendant's abstention motion was not filed until more than a year after the plaintiffs had filed their complaint, and (3) ordering abstention now would mean that many members of the plaintiff's "class" (the case was a class-action suit) would go through school without obtaining the education they claim they are entitled to under state law and the federal constitution.

If a federal court does not wiggle out on abstention grounds, it sometimes may avoid the issues on the ground of "mootness". Indeed, state courts also may defer or escape trying a case on that ground. Typically, a case is "moot" (and thus need not be tried) if state legislation or state agency regulations provide a sufficient answer to the claims that the plaintiffs have raised in their lawsuit. For example, a classic right-to-education case was brought in Michigan in a federal district court in 1972. After the case was filed, the state legislature enacted a right-to-education law, and, after that law was enacted, the defendant school officials successfully persuaded the court to dismiss the case because it was "moot"—the legislation ostensibly satisfied the plaintiffs' requests for relief.[21]

Some cases do not become moot; they simply become dormant or inactive. For example, in both North Carolina[22] and North Dakota,[23] federal right-to-education cases filed in 1972 are still awaiting a final disposition, largely because the state legislatures have enacted "mandatory" legislation and the plaintiffs and court are waiting to determine what effect, if any, the legislation will have on the plaintiffs' claims. In both cases, the legislation has set a future date (in North Carolina the date is 1982, and in North Dakota it is 1980) for full implementation. The future date gives the plaintiffs the opportunity to resist any motion the defendants might make to dismiss the case, but it also gives the defendants temporary freedom from judicial intervention.

It is possible for plaintiffs to dismiss their cases voluntarily—on their own motion. Apparently the only case in which they have taken a voluntary dismissal, however, is the Colorado right-to-education suit.[24]

ACCESS TO STUDENT RECORDS IN CLASS-ACTION SUITS

In *Mattie T.* v. *Holladay*,[25] a class-action suit that challenged classification practices, exclusion from mainstream programs, inadequacy of special education programs (functional exclusion), and absence of compliance with due process safeguards, the plaintiffs sought access to the records of individual members of the class bringing the suit. Although the plaintiffs stipulated that names and other information that would allow the students to be personally identified could be deleted, the defendant school districts declined to release the records, claiming that they were to be treated confidentially under the provisions of the Family Educational Rights and Privacy Act of 1972 (20 U.S.C. Sec. 1232g). (See Chapters 7 and 8.) The court granted the plaintiffs' request, holding that their request allowed personally identifying information to be deleted, and that the plaintiffs did not have the burden of notifying the students or their parents that the records were being subpoenaed. The decision opens up wide avenues of discovery for plaintiffs in class-action suits.

NOTES

1. 348 F. Supp. 866 (D.C.C. 1972).

2. Kirp, Buss, & Kuriloff, Legal Reform of Special Education: Empirical Studies and Procedural Proposals, 62 CAL. L. REV. 44 (1974).

3. *Mills, supra* n. 1, orders filed Mar. 27, 1975 and Apr. 22, 1975.

4. No. A–3100 (Chancery Ct., Davidson Cty., Tenn., order filed Jan. 21, 1976).

5. 423 F. Supp. 647 (S.D. N.Y. 1976).

6 . No. 14948 (Super. Ct., Suffolk Cty., Mass., motions filed Oct. 27, 1976 and Feb. 14, 1977).

7. *Supra* n. 2.

8. Allen v. McDonough, *supra* n. 6; Frederick L. v. Thomas, 408 F. Supp. 832, aff'd._____F.2d_____, 46 U.S. L.W. 2008 (July 5, 1977) (3rd Cir. 1977); and Panitch v. Wisconsin, Civ. Act. No. 72–L–461 (D. Wis., order filed Feb. 21, 1974) and 390 F. Supp. 611 (D. Wis. 1974) on other aspects of case.

9. Panitch v. Wisconsin, *supra* n. 8.

10. Frederick L. v. Thomas, *supra* n. 8 and Panitch v. Wisconsin, *supra* n. 8.

11. ASPIRA of New York, Inc. v. Board of Education of New York City, 423 F. Supp. 647 (S.D. N.Y. 1976); *contra* LeBanks v. Spears, 417 F. Supp. 169 (E.D. La. 1976).

12. On issue of actual damages, *see* Cloud v. Minneapolis Public School, No. 87399 (Dist. Ct., Hennepin Cty., Minn., filed Mar. 29, 1976); Dembrowski v. Knox Community School Corp., Civ. Act. No. 74–210 (Starke Cir. Ct., Indiana, filed May 15, 1974); Marcombe v. Dept. of Ed., No. 73–102 (M.D. La., filed Oct. 31, 1973); and Stewart v. Phillips, Civ. Act. No. 70–1199–F (D. Mass., filed Sept. 14, 1970). For cases seeking punitive damages, *see* Cloud and Marcombe, *supra.*

13. 348 F. Supp. 866, 876 (D.C.C. 1972).

14. Equity No. 100/182/77676 (Cir. Ct., Baltimore Cty., May 4, 1974).

15. Rodriguez v. San Antonio, 411 U.S. 1 (1973) may be explained partially on the basis that the Supreme Court was more worried about becoming embroiled in school-financing issues and related matters of taxation for public services than with dealing with the difficult constitutional issues the case posed.

16. Mills, *supra* n. 1, orders of March 27, 1975 and April 22, 1975.

17. *Supra* n. 4, order of Jan 26, 1977.

18. No. 76–3220 (Com. Pleas Ct., Delaware Cty., Pa., filed Mar. 15, 1976).

19. Reid v. Bd. of Ed. of City of N.Y., 13 Ed. Dept. Rep._____, No. 8742 (Comm'r. of Educ. of St. of N.Y., Nov. 26, 1973), federal abstention order, 453 F.2d 238 (2d Cir. 1971); Rhode Island Society for Autistic Children, Inc. v. Rhode Island Board of Regents for Education of State of Rhode Island, Civ. Act. No. 5081 (D.R.I., stipulations signed Sept. 19, 1975); Silva v. Bd. of Ed., Civ. No. 73–3779, (D. Hawaii, filed Apr. 12, 1973); Tidewater S.A.C., Inc. v. Virginia, Civ. No. 426–72–N (E.D.Va., filed Dec. 26, 1972); Wilcox v. Carter, Civ. Act. No. 73–41–CIV (M.D. Fla., July 10, 1973).

20. Frederick L. v. Thomas, *supra* n. 8.

21. Harrison v. Michigan, Civ. Act. No. 38357 (E. D. Mich., 1972); Florida A.R.C. v. State Board of Education, Civ. Act. No. 730250–CIV–NCR (S.D. Fla., 1973); and Radley v. Missouri, Civ. Act. No. 73–C–556(3), E.D. Mo., Nov. 11, 1973).

22. North Carolina Ass'n. for Retarded Children v. North Carolina, Civ. No. 3050 (E.D. N.C., filed May 18, 1972).

23. North Dakota Ass'n. for Retarded Children v. Peterson (D.N.D., filed Nov. 1972).

24. Colorado Ass'n. for Retarded Children v. Colorado, Civ. Act. No. C–4620 (D. Colo., 1976).

25. Mattie T. v. Holladay, Civ. Act. No. DC–75–31–S (N.D. Miss., filed Apr. 25, 1975).

1978 Supplement

n. 4. See Chapter 6   for discussion of August 7, 1978, order implementing "least restrictive setting" rules. The appeals court reversed the trial court's order enjoining the state from spending any money for education of any children in the state if handicapped children were not receiving special education services by July 1, 1977, holding the remedy excessive and causing more damage than it cures.

n. 6. The court has awarded counsel fees of $30,000 to the plaintiffs' attorneys, offered the defendants an opportunity to purge themselves of contempt, found they failed to do so, ordered additional compensatory programs for children denied education who are entitled to it under state law, and appointed a master to evaluate the compensatory programs. Order of April 13, 1977, September 27, 1977, and April, 1978.

n. 7. See also Allen v. McDonough, *supra*, n. 6.

n. 8. Paintch v. Wisconsin, 371 F. Supp. 935, 390 F. Supp. 611 (E.D. Wis., 1974), 444 F. Supp. 320, 76 F.R.D. 608 (E.D. Wis., 1977), *per curiam* order, April 18, 1978, finding state's policies denied plaintiff publicly supported free education, awarding counsel fees for plaintiffs' attorneys, but denying appointment of special master.

n. 11. See Allen v. McDonough, *supra*, n. 6, and Paintch v. Wisconsin, *supra*, n. 8.

n. 12. The "negligence" or "malpractice" cases are increasing in number and significance. In Hoffman v. Board of Education of City of New York, 410 N.Y.S. 2d 99 (1978), a state appellate court

(continued on page 279)

10

Statutory Techniques

The donkey chasing a carrot while running from a possible beating with a stick is a familiar image, and it is an appropriate one in the case of P.L. 94–142 because Congress seeks to achieve the education of handicapped children by similar approaches. To enforce the six principles of the law—zero reject, nondiscriminatory evaluation, individualized appropriate education, placement in the least restrictive setting, protection of rights through due process, and parent participation in school decisions—Congress holds out the promise of federal funds to SEAs and LEAs while requiring certain behaviors under threat of withdrawal of federal funds.

On closer examination, however, the image is somewhat misleading, for it suggests that Congressional altruism is tinged with more than a bit of cynicism. In fact, Congress legislates the establishment of effective special education programs and demands normal fiscal accountability for them. It is helpful to look at P.L. 94–142 in this light: Congress puts money where the problems are; it seeks ways to require that programs for handicapped children be accountable to the Congress and to the intended beneficiaries of P.L. 94–142; it imposes normal requirements of fiscal accountability to insure that the federal funds are in fact used as they were intended to be used; and it empowers the appropriate federal officials and agencies to review, correct, and impose sanctions on noncomplying recipients.

PUTTING MONEY WHERE THE PROBLEMS ARE

There are more than eight million handicapped children in the United States whose special education needs are not being fully met [Sec. 601(b)(1) and (2)]. Having concluded that it is proper to see that all of those children have a free appropriate public education available to them [Sec. 601(c)], it was logical for Congress to attempt to solve the national problem through already existing state and local governmental mechanisms. It is through the use of those mechanisms, and not by establishing separate and distinct federally-operated programs of public education, that Congress has traditionally sought to respond to educational needs. Congress' initial step was to provide money for state and local school programs; the second was to insure that the public agencies spend the money on the children it was intended for; and the third was to insure that the money was shared between local and state agencies (that is, between the agencies most directly responsible for educating handicapped children and the agencies with overall supervision and some direct responsibility). The techniques were authorization of expenditures, appropriation of funds, and pass-through requirements.

A Bit of History

Before describing the principal techniques for putting federal funds where they are most needed, it is appropriate to recite some of the facts Congress was responding to.

In very general terms, financing for the education of handicapped children is the stepchild of public school financing. Many handicapped children were without programs because funds had not been appropriated; others were fortunate enough to be admitted to a program (although some of their handicapped peers were not), but they were often inadequately funded programs. The use of labels by special educators and others involved in serving handicapped children put them into categories—a convenient practice for serving those children and receiving appropriations for them, but of no use to the handicapped children not labeled and categorized. In many school districts, handicapped children were not sought out through child census or child-identification programs and were therefore excluded from school planning, programming, and appropriations. Because of the lack of free public programs, parents were frequently forced into starting private school programs or buying into existing private programs. In either case, they were required to make tuition payments that parents of nonhandicapped children did not have to make, and in some cases the programs were located far from the parents' homes or in residential institutions. Some states did decide to help defray the tuition for private schooling, but they often did not appropriate sufficient funds to meet the needs of all affected parents. Unhappily, not all state institutions for handicapped children provided them with an education; centers for the mentally retarded and hospitals for the mentally ill were notoriously deficient in school programs, especially when compared to state schools for the deaf or blind. State governments were often organized in a way that prevented institutional school programs from being supervised by public school authorities. Departments of public instruction lacked jurisdiction over departments of social services or human resources, and they did not have the authority or the will to supervise other departments' education of handicapped children.

Authorization and Appropriation

Congress has authorized the expenditure of federal funds for handicapped children, ages three to twenty-one, inclusive, for a five-year period covering the fiscal years beginning October 1, 1977 (FY 1977–78), and ending September 30, 1982 (FY 1981–82) [Sec. 611]. The authorized funds will be allocated to the states through the SEAs, and to local agencies through the LEAs and IEUs in each state. Each SEA must have its application for funds approved by the Bureau for Education of the Handicapped (BEH); the LEAs and IEUs must have their applications approved by the SEAs [Secs. 612, 613, and 614]. All authorizations for state and local appropriations are keyed to a formula. In the case of an LEA, the allocation is based on the number of handicapped children in the state, aged three through twenty-one, who are receiving special education and related services, multiplied by:

—5 percent of the average per-pupil expenditure in the public elementary and secondary schools for the fiscal year beginning October 1, 1977, and ending September 30, 1978 (estimated funds available, $378 million);
—10 percent of the same expenditure for the next fiscal year (1978–79) (estimated funds available, $775 million);
—20 percent of the same expenditure for the next fiscal year (1979–80) (estimated funds available, $1.2 billion);
—30 percent of the same expenditure for the next fiscal year (1980–81) (estimated funds available, $2.32 billion); and
—40 percent of the same expenditure for the last fiscal year (1981–82) (estimated funds available, $3.16 billion).

The *basis of the authorization* is the number of handicapped children in all states; the *basis of the allocation* to each state is the number of handicapped children in that state in proportion to the number in the United States; and the *amount of the allocation* to each state is a percentage of the average per-pupil expenditure for handicapped children receiving special education and related services in all public elementary and secondary schools in the United States [Sec. 121a.701].

The following formula is used to compute the average per-pupil expenditure:

The aggregate expenditures (without regard to source) for all LEAs in the United States (including the District of Columbia) are determined for the second fiscal year prior to the one the computation is being done for. If satisfactory data for that year are not available, suitable data for the most recent preceding fiscal year may be used. That figure, along with any direct expenditures by the state for the operation of the LEAs (without regard to their source), must be divided by the aggregate number of children in average daily attendance who were provided with free public education by the LEAs during that fiscal year [Sec. 121a.701(c)]. The 12 and 2 percent ceilings, as well as the exclusions (handicapped children funded under Sec. 121, ESEA), apply—they are not to be taken into consideration [Sec. 121a.701].

There is also a "hold-harmless" clause guaranteeing that, despite the above provisions, no state will receive a lesser amount than it received for fiscal year 1976–77 under Part B, Assistance for Education of All Handicapped Children, of Part X, Education and Training of the Handicapped, in the Education of the Handicapped Act [Sec. 611(a)(1) and Sec. 121a.704].

Pass-Through

Having devised a way to get money to the states, Congress had to make it trickle down to where the problems and the handicapped children are—the LEAs. It accomplished this by requiring that the funds "pass through" the SEA to the LEAs. No more than 50 percent of the funds may be retained by the SEA in fiscal year 1977–78, and no more than 25 percent may be retained in the fiscal years beginning 1978–79 and ending 1981–82. What is not retained by the SEA must be passed through to the LEAs. The SEA may, if it wants, pass through more than the statutory minimum [Sec. 611(b)(1) and (c)(1) and Sec. 121a.705 and .706].

To determine how much each LEA and IEU is entitled to receive from the SEA, Congress used a simple formula based on the proportionate population of each LEA and IEU to its SEA population. The funds are allocated in the same ratio to the total amount available for pass-through that the number of handicapped children (aged three through twenty-one) receiving special education and related services in the LEA or IEU bears to the total number of handicapped children in all LEAs and IEUs applying for funds [Sec. 611(d) and Sec. 121a.707]. If an SEA determines that an LEA is adequately providing a free appropriate education to all of the handicapped children in its jurisdiction by using state and local funds otherwise available to it, the SEA may reallocate all or part of the funds the LEA would have received under the pass-through provisions. The allocation must be made to other LEAs that are not adequately providing such an education [Sec. 121a.708].

Who are the Handicapped; "Average Expenditures"

The LEA and IEU entitlement depends on the number of handicapped children in the state who receive special education and related services. This number is defined as the average number of children receiving those services on October 1 and February 1 of the fiscal year preceding the fiscal year for which the determination is being made [Sec. 611(a)(3) and Sec. 121a.751]. LEA entitlement also depends on the average per-pupil expenditure in public elementary and secondary schools of the United States (defined above). Thus, the population of handicapped children is always computed at least one year in arrears, and the cost of educating them is always computed at least two years in arrears.

Ceiling

In determining the LEA allotment, the following children may not be counted: the number of handicapped children in excess of the 12 percent limitation and handicapped children counted under Sec. 121 of the Elementary and Secondary Education Act of 1965 (so-called "Head Start handicapped children") [Sec. 611(a)(5) and Sec. 121a.702].

Limitation on "Allowable" Administrative Costs

SEAs are limited in how they may use funds not passed through. They may not use more than 5 percent of the funds or $200,000, whichever is greater, for administrative costs related to Sec. 612 (state eligibility) and Sec. 613 (state plans) [Sec. 611(b)(2) and (c)(2) and Sec. 121a.620 and .621]. The funds available to the SEA for administration may be spent only for the following "allowable costs" [Sec. 121a.621]:

1. Administration of the annual program plan and for planning at the State level, including planning, or assisting in the planning, of programs or projects for the education of handicapped children;
2. Approval, supervision, monitoring, and evaluation of the effectiveness of local programs and projects for the education of handicapped children;
3. Technical assistance to local educational agencies with respect to the requirements of this part;
4. Leadership services for the program supervision and management of special education activities for the handicapped; and
5. Other State leadership activities and consultative services.

The SEA must use the remainder of the funds (those not allocated to "allowable costs" of administration of P.L. 94–142) to provide support and direct services for the benefit of handicapped children in accordance with the service priorities [Sec. 611(b)(2)(B) and (c)(2)(iii)]. Sec. 121a.370 defines support and direct services as follows:

1. "Direct services" provided to a handicapped child directly by the State, by contract, or through other arrangements.
2. "Support services" include implementing the comprehensive system of personnel development, recruitment and training of hearing officers and surrogate parents, and public information activities relating to a free appropriate public education for handicapped children.

In the fiscal years beginning in 1978, the amount spent by SEAs from Part B funds not passed through for support or direct services must be matched, "on a program basis," with state funds for the provisions of support or direct services for the fiscal year involved. The matching funds may not be federal funds [Sec. 611(c)(2)(B) and Sec. 121a.371]. "Program basis" refers to the major programs such as personnel development and training hearing officers.

Disentitled LEAs

No LEA may receive funds if it is entitled to less than $7,500 in any fiscal year, if it has not submitted an application that meets the requirements of Sec. 614 (SEA applications), if it is unable or unwilling to establish programs of free appropriate education, if it is unwilling to consolidate with another LEA, or if it has one or more handicapped children who can best be served by a state or regional center specially designed to meet their needs [Sec. 611(c)(4) and Sec. 121a.360]. If an LEA has no right to funds, the SEA must use the funds the LEA would otherwise receive to assure a free appropriate education to the handicapped children in the LEA's jurisdiction [Sec. 121a.360].

Funds for Territories and Bureau of Indian Affairs Programs

Congress has also provided for federal funds to Guam, American Samoa, the Virgin Islands, the trust territory of the Pacific Islands [Sec. 611(c)], and the Bureau of Indian Affairs in the Department of the Interior [Sec. 611(f)].

Ratable Reductions

If Congress does not appropriate enough funds for the states to receive what they are authorized to receive, there will be a ratable reduction in the amount each state receives [Sec. 611(g)(1)]. By the same token, there will be a ratable reduction of funds available to LEAs [Sec. 611(g)(2) and Sec. 121a.703].

Early Childhood Incentive Grants

Sec. 121m. of the regulations makes it clear that the early-childhood incentive grants authorized under Sec. 619 of the act may be used for children ages three through five who are counted as receiving special education and related services, or for children who were previously unserved. Equal dollars for each child are not required; the state has flexibility in determining the best or optimal use of the grant funds. Moreover, although early childhood education is effective for handicapped children between birth and age two, the regulations limit the use of the Sec. 619 funds to children ages three through five. A state may, however, use the funds it receives under Sec. 611 (entitlements and allocations to the states, with the SEA retaining some portion of the funds and passing through the other) for children from birth through twenty-one. A state may also receive Sec. 619 funds even though it is not serving every handicapped child in an age bracket. It must, however, be offering programs to those children, or be disqualified from receiving the funds.

Antidilution Provisions; Excess Costs

Recognizing that inclusion of handicapped children would be necessary but insufficient to help them, Congress set out to make sure that federal funds would not be diluted—that it would get the biggest bang for its buck. It required LEAs and IEUs to assure the SEAs that federal funds would be spent only for "excess costs" related to child identification, confidentiality of records, full-service goals (including personnel development, adherence to the service priorities, parent participation, and least restrictive placement). Congress also established a timetable for accomplishing the full-service goal, and implementing that goal [Sec. 614(a)(1) and Sec. 121a.182].

An LEA meets the excess-cost requirement if it spends a certain minimum amount of its *own* money on each handicapped child. This does not include costs of capital outlay or debt expenditure. The purpose of the excess-cost requirement is to insure that children served with Part B funds have at least the same average amount spent on them (from sources other than Part B funds) as on children in the school district as a whole.

The minimum amount that must be spent for educating handicapped children is computed under a formula. Any costs that exceed the amount determined by the formula are excess costs (they exceed the minimum). Only if an LEA can prove that it has spent the minimum may it use Part B funds to educate handicapped children.

The minimum average amount is computed as follows: (1) The LEA adds all of its expenditures from the prior year except capital outlay and debt service for elementary or secondary students (depending on whether the mimumum is being computed for an elementary or secondary handicapped child); (2) The following sums are then subtracted from that amount: (a) amounts spent from Part B funds and Title I and Title VII of ESEA (1965); and (b) amounts from state and local funds spent for programs for handicapped children, programs to meet the special educational needs of educationally deprived children, and programs of bilingual education. (3) The resulting amount is divided by the average number of students enrolled in the LEA's elementary or secondary programs in the preceding year (depending on whether the minimum is being computed for an elementary or secondary child). The following example of an elementary school computation comes from the comments on the regulation [Sec. 121a.184]:

> a. First, the local educational agency must determine its total amount of expenditures for elementary school students from all sources—local, State and Federal (including Part B)—in the preceding school year. Only capital outlay and debt service are excluded.
> *Example:* A local educational agency spent the following amounts last year for elementary school students (including its handicapped elementary school students):

> (1) From local tax funds $2,750,000
> (2) From State funds 7,000,000
> (3) From Federal funds 750,000
>   _____
>   10,500,000

> Of this total, $500,000 was for capital outlay and debt service relating to the education of elementary school students. This must be subtracted from total expenditures:

> $10,500,000
>   −500,000
> Total expenditures for elementary school students (less capital outlay and
>   debt service) 10,000,000
> b. Next, the local educational agency must subtract amounts spent for:
> (1) Programs for handicapped children;
> (2) Programs to meet the special educational needs of educationally deprived children; and
> (3) Programs of bilingual education for children with limited English-speaking ability.
> These are funds which the local educational agency actually spent, not funds received last year but carried over for the current school year.
> *Example:* The local educational agency spent the following amounts for elementary school students last year:

> (1) From funds under Title I of the Elementary and Secondary Education
>   Act of 1965 .... $300,000
> (2) From a special State program for educationally deprived children 200,000
> (3) From a grant under Part B 200,000
> (4) From State funds for the education of handicapped children 500,000
> (5) From a locally-funded program for handicapped children 250,000

(6) From a grant for a bilingual education program under Title VII of the
Elementary and Secondary Education Act of 1965.................... 150,000

Total 1,600,000

(A local educational agency would also include any other funds it spent from Federal, State, or local sources for the three basic purposes: handicapped children, educationally deprived children, and bilingual education for children with limited English-speaking ability.)

This amount is subtracted from the local educational agency's total expenditure for elementary school students computed above:

$$\begin{array}{r} \$10,000,000 \\ -1,600,000 \\ \hline 8,400,000 \end{array}$$

c. The local educational agency next must divide by the average number of students enrolled in the elementary schools of the agency last year (including its handicapped students).

Example: Last year, an average of 7,000 students were enrolled in the agency's elementary schools. This must be divided into the amount computed under the above paragraph:

$$\frac{\$8,400,000}{7,000 \text{ students}} = \$1,200/\text{student}$$

This figure is in the minimum amount the local educational agency must spend (on the average) for the education of each of its handicapped students. Funds under Part B may be used only for costs over and above this minimum. In this example, if the local educational agency has 100 handicapped elementary school students, it must keep records adequate to show that it has spent at least $120,000 for the education of those students (100 students times $1,200/student), not including capital outlay and debt service.

This $120,000 may come from any funds except funds under Part B, subject to any legal requirements that govern the use of those other funds.

If the local educational agency has handicapped secondary school students, it must do the same computation for them. However, the amounts used in the computation would be those the local educational agency spent last year for the education of secondary school students, rather than for elementary school students.

The basic intent of the excess-cost provision is to insure that SEAs and LEAs provide the same support for handicapped children as for all other children, and that Part B funds are used to supplement the state and local commitment. The regulations stipulate that SEAs and LEAs may not use Part B funds to pay *all* of the special education and related services given to a handicapped child [Sec. 121a.186]. However, the excess-cost requirement does not prevent an LEA from using Part B funds to pay for all of the costs directly attributable to the education of a handicapped child in any of the age ranges three through five and eighteen through twenty-one if no local or state funds are available for nonhandicapped children in that age range. However, the LEA must comply with the nonsupplanting and other requirements of this part in providing the education and services.

In another step to prevent dilution, Congress required LEAs to give satisfactory assurances to the SEAs that federal funds received under P.L. 94–142 will be used to pay only the excess costs directly attributable to the education of handicapped children, to supplement, and increase the amount of state and local funds expended for the education of handicapped children, and to provide services in program areas that are comparable to services provided to other handicapped children in the LEA [Sec. 614(a)(2)(C) and Sec. 121a.229–.231]. (The exact meaning of the comparability requirement has not yet been made clear by regulation.) Congress also stipulated that LEAs required by state law to carry out a program for educating handicapped children are entitled to receive pass-through payments for use in carrying out that program, but pass-through funds may not be used to reduce state and local expenditures for the program below the level of such expenditures in the preceding fiscal year. In effect, LEAs must maintain their effort in order to qualify for P.L. 94–142 funds [Sec. 614(f)].

Another antidilution provision prohibits SEAs from using federal funds to match other federal funds [Sec. 611(c)(2)(B) and (c)(4)(B)]. In a sense, too, the requirement that private schooling be paid for by the LEA is also an antidilution requirement.

Consolidated Applications

Some LEAs may not be eligible for P.L. 94–142 funds because they do not generate $7,500 annually, because their application is not approvable, or because they are unable to establish and maintain programs of sufficient size and scope to affectively meet the educational needs of handicapped children. To maintain control of these LEAs, Congress authorized SEAs to require consolidated LEA applications and to allocate funds to LEAs submitting a consolidated application [Sec. 614(c) and Sec. 121a.190–.192]. This provision clearly prevents LEAs from escaping the provisions of the act.

SEA Direct Services

An SEA may provide direct services to handicapped children, thus displacing an LEA's authority, if the LEA does not seek Part B funds, submits an unapprovable application, or if the SEA determines that the LEA is unable or unwilling to establish and maintain a free appropriate public education. If the LEA is unable or unwilling to be consolidated with another LEA in order to meet those requirements, or has one or more handicapped children who can best be served by a regional or state center, the SEA can also provide direct services [Sec. 614(d) and Sec. 121a.360]. In such instances, the SEA may use payments that would have gone to the LEA and may provide appropriate services at locations it considers appropriate (including regional or state centers), subject to the general requirements of the act, including least-restrictive placement. An LEA that is able but unwilling to comply with P.L. 94—142 would, of course, be subject to the sanctions of that act. Moreover, it would be in violation of Sec. 504.

Through all of these measures, Congress has attempted to put its money where the problems are —in the local schools. It has authorized funds, provided for their allocation, required that they be shared by state and local agencies, mandated that they be spent for "excess costs" and not used in any manner that would dilute their intended effect, and closed the door to LEAs attempting to escape the requirements of the act. Having done this much, Congress turned to the problem of making the recipients' programs effective and accountable.

EFFECTIVE SPECIAL EDUCATION

Congress' intent to provide a free appropriate public education to all handicapped children [Sec. 601(c) and Sec. 602(18)] is accomplished through six techniques that are intended to enhance the effectiveness of SEA and LEA programs: (1) BEH assistance and involvement in state and local programs; (2) state and local program conformity with other federal legislation affecting the handicapped; (3) state and local program effectiveness; (4) state and local program accountability; (5) limitations on administrative costs to be charged against P.L. 94–142 funds; and (6) sanctions. Although it will be organizationally convenient to discuss each technique separately, they are inseparable from each other as a means of accomplishing the Congressional intent.

BEH Assistance and Involvement in State and Local Programs

Recognizing that it was appropriate for the federal government to assist, assess, and assure the effectiveness of state and local agency programs for educating handicapped children [Sec. 601(c)], Congress created the Bureau for the Education of the Handicapped. It was designated as the principal agency in the Office of Education for administering and carrying out programs and projects to train teachers of the handicapped and to conduct research in education and training [Sec. 603 (a)]. To advance BEH's role in P.L. 94–142 programs, Congress required the Commissioner to assist the states in implementing P.L. 94–142 by providing short-term training programs and institutes if necessary, disseminating information, and making sure that each state certified the number of children included in its child-count [Sec. 617(a)(1)]. The Commissioner was also authorized to issue regulations for SEA financial reports [Sec. 617(a)(2)], for the implementation of P.L. 94–142 [Sec. 617(b)], and to assure the confidentiality of information received from SEAs and LEAs [Sec. 617(c)]. He can also hire personnel to help him execute his duties [Sec. 617(d)]. Congress provided for evaluation of SEA and LEA programs by requiring the Commissioner to measure and evaluate the impact of P.L. 94–142 programs and the effectiveness of SEA efforts to furnish a free appropriate public education to handicapped children [Sec. 618(a)]. The Commissioner has the right to conduct studies, investigations, and evaluations to assure the effective implementation of P.L. 94–142 [Sec. 618(b)], and to report those evaluations to Congress [Sec. 618(d)].

Congress empowered the Commissioner to authorize the use of Part B funds by SEAs and LEAs for acquiring equipment and constructing necessary facilities if he determines that a program for education of the handicapped (including P.L. 94–142 programs) will be improved by the use of federal funds for those purposes [Sec. 605].

In addition, Congress created the National Advisory Committee on Handicapped Children to review the administration and operation of programs authorized by Congress under Title X (Education and Training of the Handicapped) and to make recommendations to the Commissioner concerning them [Sec. 604(a)].

Conformity with Other Federal Programs

Approaching the implementation of P.L. 94–142 on several fronts, Congress required SEAs to make plans for the proper use of Part B funds [Sec. 613(a)(1)] containing programs and procedures to assure that SEAs, LEAs, and other political subdivisions (such as cities, counties, and special districts) use federal funds in a manner consistent with the goal of establishing a free appropriate education for handicapped children [Sec. 613(a)(2)]. Congress referred to funds received under Sec. 121, ESEA; Sec. 305(b)(8), ESEA; and Sec. 122(a)(4)(B), Vocational Education Act. Each of these laws specifically authorizes federal assistance for the education of handicapped children.

In an effort to make the education of handicapped people meaningful by providing them with job opportunities after they leave school, Congress ordered the Secretary of HEW to make sure that each recipient of P.L. 94–142 funds make "positive efforts" to employ and advance in employment qualified handicapped individuals in programs assisted by P.L. 94–142 funds [Sec. 606]. This requirement is consistent with other federal legislation prohibiting employment discrimination against otherwise handicapped individuals [Secs. 101, 501, 503, and 504, Rehabilitation Act Amendments].

In order to make public school practices conform with the requirements of federal architectural barrier legislation (P.L. 90–480), the Commissioner of BEH may make grants to SEAs and LEAs for alterations to existing buildings and equipment "in the same manner and to the same extent" as authorized by P.L. 90–480 [Sec. 607].

Program Effectiveness

Although the regulations presented in the first two sections will contribute to the free appropriate education of handicapped children, nothing can accomplish that goal better than making SEA and LEA programs effective. Unless those programs deliver effective special education services to handicapped children, federal, state, and local funds will not have been wisely spent—the hopes of consumers and educators will be crushed, discriminatory practices illegally foisted upon the handicapped will not be fully redressed, and the notion that handicapped children are not worth the investment of substantial amounts of time, money, and energy will not be dispelled.

To insure program effectiveness, Congress first required special education programs to be appropriate to the child and individualized for full benefit. Second, it required public school personnel to become more competent in educating and training handicapped children through personnel development programs [Sec. 613(a)(3) and Sec. 614(a)(1)(C)(i) and Sec. 121.380-.387]. Third, it limited the number of children who may be counted as handicapped for P.L. 94–142 purposes—the "exclusion" and "ceiling." Fourth, it extended P.L. 94–142 to private programs and established single-agency responsibility. Finally, it required both BEH and SEAs to create procedures for at least annual evaluation of the effectiveness of state and local programs. [Sec. 613(a)(11)].

Program Accountability

Program accountability is another means of helping special education do the job it is designed to do. The techniques for accomplishing this end are multifaceted. Among them are requirements for single-agency responsibility, SEA preemption, LEA consolidation, public notice of LEA and SEA programs, parental access to records, and requirements that SEAs and LEAs provide information or assurances to BEH or to the SEA, as appropriate [Secs. 613(a)(7), 614(a)(3), 617, and 618]. Program accountability is also advanced by the creation of advisory panels [Secs. 604 and 613(a)(12) and Sec. 121a.650], the establishment of timetables for the implementation of the act, and the formulation of full-service goals. The provisions for program evaluation are also a means of producing program accountability.

Limitations on Administrative Costs

By limiting the amount of administrative costs that can be charged against P.L. 94–142 funds by SEAs or LEAs [Sec. 611(b)(2), (c)(2), and (e)(3)], and by other techniques designed to put the money where the problems are, Congress clearly intends for programs for the handicapped to be made as effective as possible as well as accountable for how they operate.

Sanctions

It might become necessary to apply stronger measures to recipients of P.L. 94–142 funds if they do not comply with the requirements of the act. Accordingly, Congress provided four types of sanctions.

In spite of provisions dealing with exclusion, ceiling, and nondiscriminatory classification of students children might still be erroneously classified as eligible so that the LEA could count them for receipt of federal funds. Obviously, the LEA should not receive federal funds for such children. Congress required the state plan to contain policies and procedures for seeking to recover federal funds available under Part B of the Act that are allocated for incorrectly classified children [Sec. 613(a)(5) and Sec. 121a.141].

An SEA may impose other sanctions against troublesome LEAs. It may refuse to approve an LEA application that does not meet the requirements of Sec. 614(a), setting out the contents of the LEA application, including child-census, confidentiality, full-serviced goals, and related assurances [Sec. 614(b)(1) and Sec. 121a.193]. If, after reasonable notice and opportunity for a hearing, an SEA determines that an LEA has failed to comply with any requirement set forth in an SEA-approved application, the SEA must take one of two steps: (1) withhold payments to the agency until satisfied that the default has been cured; or (2) take the determination into account in reviewing any later application the LEA or IEU might make. It might even take both steps. In any event, the noncomplying agency must give public notice that it is subject to sanction [Sec. 614(b)(2)(A) and (B) and Sec. 121a.194].

The SEA is not alone in imposing sanctions on LEAs; the Commissioner of Education may also invoke sanctions against them. If, after providing reasonable notice and an opportunity to be heard, the Commissioner finds that an SEA or LEA has failed to comply substantially with any provision of Sec. 612 (SEA eligibility) or Sec. 613 (state plan), or has failed to comply with any provision of Part B of the Act or with any requirements set forth in an SEA-approved application from an LEA he must withhold any further payments to the state and he may stop further payments to the state of handicapped education funds under his jurisdiction granted pursuant to Sec. 121 and Sec. 305(b), ESEA, and Sec. 122, Vocational Education Act. The Commissioner may limit the withholding of federal funds to specific programs or projects under the state plan [Sec. 613], or portions of the state plan that are affected by the noncompliance. Under P.L. 94–142, he may also order SEAs not to make further payments to noncomplying LEAs. He may continue to withhold funds until the noncompliance is ended. A noncomplying SEA or LEA must give public notice of the sanction [Sec. 616(a)]. [Secs.

121.580–.593 govern Office of Education sanction procedures].

After exhausting all statutory appeals any aggrieved party in a due process hearing has the right to bring a civil action in a state or United States district court concerning the identification, evaluation, or educational placement of a child, or the provision of a free appropriate public education to a child [Sec. 615(e)(2)].

FISCAL ACCOUNTABILITY

Another way to accomplish the major principles of the act is to require fiscal accountability of SEAs and LEAs. The act imposes fiscal accountability in a variety of ways. It requires the state plan to set forth policies and procedures to assure that federal funds are spent according to the provisions of the act [Sec. 613(a)(1) and Sec. 121a.112]. In order to trace the expenditures and determine if the funds have been spent in accordance with the act, Sections 613(a)(6), (9), and (10) require public control of federal funds, prohibit commingling or supplanting by the state [Sec. 121a.145], and require the state to impose fiscal control [Sec. 121a.142] and fund accounting procedures. Sec. 614(a)(2) requires LEAs to give assurances of public control of funds [Sec. 121a.228]. The requirement of fiscal control by the state also applies to the LEAs [Sec. 613(a)(10)].

1978 Supplement

A federal district court has held that an individual does not have authority under P.L. 94–142 to file a court suit that seeks to require the U.S. Commissioner of Education to withhold funds from a noncomplying LEA, Campochiaro v. Califano, Civ. No. H-78-64 (D. Conn., May 18, 1978).

Final regulations provide that states may not use federal funds for special education services formerly provided through state funds. But, if a state "provides clear and convincing evidence that all handicapped children have available to them a free appropriate education," the state may request that the U.S. Office of Education (OE) "waive in part" the non-supplanting provision.

Claiming that most of their school districts are in full compliance, Massachusetts asked OE if "waiver in part" could mean waiving the non-supplanting restriction on a district-by-district basis. Compliance evaluation would be conducted by the State Education Agency.

BEH replied on June 29, 1978, that "waiver in part" means that OE may waive part, not all, of the non-supplanting requirement. "In part" cannot refer to partial compliance with the full service goal.

BEH added that there may be the possibility of individual school districts who are in full compliance with P.L. 94–142 applying for a non-supplanting waiver from the federal government. In such cases, BEH will visit the school district to determine compliance.

SECTION IV:

FREE APPROPRIATE PUBLIC EDUCATION AND THE AMERICAN VALUE SYSTEM

11

Objections to P.L. 94—142 and Answers to Them

A person with even the most casual knowledge about P.L. 94–142 can recognize that it makes revolutionary changes in the education of handicapped children and in the relationships between the individuals and interest groups involved in educating them. No law as complex and innovative as P.L. 94–142 can escape severe criticisms. They are already numerous; some may prove to be justified, some may prove to be more justified than others, some may be unjustified, and others are unjustifiable. They come from sources like the "regular" education constituency, administrators, and teacher associations and unions. They are based on educational, moral, and ethical grounds, but they can all be answered more or less satisfactorily.

This chapter lists the most common objections and some of the answers to them. Because we have already discussed the history of the act, its implications, and some methods of implementation, we will be concise in stating the objections and answers although more complete statements could be made.

Objection 1: Congress requires compliance but it does not appropriate sufficient funds. He who regulates should appropriate. **Answer:** The education of handicapped children is an obligation that each state has assumed for itself in its constitution or mandatory education laws; it is not an obligation that the federal government initially or traditionally has undertaken. The federal government seeks to help the states comply with their own self-imposed responsibilities. Its "presence" is designed to underwrite some, but not all, of the costs of special education that state and local governments have inadequately funded in the past.

Objection 2: It is too expensive to educate handicapped children. Public education cannot stretch its dollars any further. **Answer:** Although it may cost more to educate handicapped children, the states have a constitutional duty to do so. Federal funds help state and local educational agencies comply with that duty. Perhaps the costs of educating handicapped children will require additional tax levies, but reallocation of present state and local educational funds can be made. Funds spent on the far more costly task of maintaining a handicapped person in an institution during his school-age years and afterwards can be reduced and diverted to educating him; the long-term cost of maintaining a handicapped person at public expense is far greater thant the short-term cost of educating him as a child.

Objection 3: Granted, it is cheaper in the long run to educate a handicapped person than to have the state pay for his lifetime care, but state and local educational agencies look only to their own funds and really have little concern about the wider fiscal benefits of educating a handicapped person. **Answer:** Short-sightedness is common among all agencies of government, but it is not forgiveable. P.L. 94–142 addresses the wider concerns through provisions allowing SEAs to use funds not passed through to LEAs for service contracts with state and private agencies, requiring state and local agencies (other than educational ones) to educate handicapped children in their care or custody, and providing increased levels of federal funds.

Objection 4: The law requires funding of "related services" not usually thought of as "special education" services. **Answer:** The "related services" are essential to the appropriate education of a handicapped child; without them special education is an inadequate education.

Objection 5: Requiring the SEAs and LEAs to provide "related services" to handicapped children will encourage them to create their own capacities to furnish those services, in spite of the fact that other agencies (like mental health, social services, or human resources) already have the necessary capacities. The resulting interagency competition will dilute already inadequate state fiscal and personnel resources. **Answer:** Through the state plan and single-agency responsibility SEAs can orchestrate the efforts of different agencies so that they cooperate rather than compete.

Objection 6: The law tips the scales of state-federal relationships so drastically toward the federal that state and local discretion in the education of handicapped children is all but eliminated. This represents an intolerable intrusion on the concepts of federalism and state and local autonomy in education. **Answer:** P.L. 94–142 is a formula-grant act that does not require the states to participate. Moreover, state and local autonomy has permitted the states to fail in their legal duties to educate handicapped children. Were it not for such massive failure, federal regulations governing the use of federal funds would be unnecessary. The federal government must correct violations of citizens' Fifth and Fourteenth Amendment rights and, to that end, can legislate even without appropriating funds.

Objection 7: The requirement for single-agency responsibility runs against the grain of the Tenth Amendment, which provides that states retain powers not specifically delegated by the United States Constitution to the federal government. **Answer:** As a condition for allocating federal funds to states that seek them, the federal government constitutionally may require administrative convenience through the single-agency device. Moreover, the single-agency requirement will seal service gaps that excluded handicapped children from a free appropriate education.

Objection 8: The law represents an unwarranted shift in educational philosophy, requiring individualized education when, as a rule, mass education has been acceptable. **Answer:** There is no shift in philosophy, only an extension of the accepted philosophies of education. Individualized education is necessary if handicapped children are to be adequately educated; that is, if public policy is to be accomplished.

Objection 9: The law omits the gifted child, whose educational needs are clearly exceptional. **Answer:** Gifted children have not been subjected to the same discrimination and violation of their constitutional rights as handicapped children. Federal programs already provide funds for their education. And, like the nonhandicapped child, they have been receiving at least a minimum level of education.

Objection 10: The law also does not require early childhood education (ages birth through three). **Answer:** The federal law reflects the educational practices and requirements of most states by not requiring early childhood education. However, funds are made available for early childhood education if the states wish to undertake it. The federal "presence" is designed to assist states in doing better what they already have undertaken to do.

Objection 11: P.L. 94–142 creates a special law for special (handicapped) people, thus contradicting one of its own principles—the integration of all students. Its concepts are internally inconsistent. **Answer:** If handicapped people are to be included in the benefits of a public education, integration through least-restrictive appropriate placement and equal opportunities (the same as extended to nonhandicapped students) are a must. The long-standing and severe discrimination against the handicapped justifies remedial legislation that redistributes public benefits in compliance with federal and state constitutional requirements and laws. Both integration and preferential treatment of the handicapped is justified in light of past wrongs and within the principles of distributive justice.

Objection 12: P.L. 94–142 places unwarranted emphasis on handicapped children by putting an inordinate amount of public resources behind their education. More to the point, it says that handicapped students are entitled to more of society's benefits than other children, thereby misconstruing the contribution—the "return"—that handicapped children will make to society. **Answer:** The issue of competing equities—who is to be inconvenienced so that the needs of handicapped students may be met, and to what degree they are to be inconvenienced—is at the heart of all legislation that advances the interests of any minority group, whether the group is characterized by race, sex, handicap, or some other trait. The answers have not yet been generally articulated, but in the case of P.L. 94–142 they can be easily set forth. The act corrects massive past discrimination; it redresses the balance of fiscal equities only slightly by providing a limited portion of the additional costs of educating handicapped children; it requires only that LEAs spend the same amount on handicapped children as on nonhandicapped ones; it cures the imbalance of educational equities by enabling many handicapped persons to make substantial contributions to society through the requirement that they be given equal educational opportunities; and it institutionalizes values that the majority hold dear (see Chapter 12). It is not likely to overbalance the competition for equities or put the handicapped in a position of significant advantage.

Objection 13: Leaving aside the issue of competing equities, the law grants special rights to the handicapped, like the right to an IEP and individualized appropriate education. **Answer:** Although nonhandicapped students do not have the same legal claims as the handicapped, they are generally receiving a far more appropriate education. The act extends to the handicapped the soundest current educational principles, including least-restrictive appropriate placement, individualized programming, and procedural safeguards. It may, and indeed should, set the stage for nonhandicapped students to receive those same benefits. It can help special educators to make important contributions to the education of all children.

Objection 14: P.L. 94–142 sets a policy that is simply disagreeable. Handicapped children really should not be educated; they should be placed in institutions or in special schools with their own kind. **Answer:** Besides the fact that the states have a legal obligation to educate handicapped children and have violated the state and federal constitutional rights of those children, it is definitely in the public interest to educate them outside institutions whenever possible. Only with education can the handicapped contribute to society rather than be dependent on it. All the evidence shows that they can learn if appropriately trained, and appropriate training usually occurs outside of institutions.

Objection 15: P.L. 94–142 imposes such an administrative burden that it will divert educators from their proper role—educating handicapped children. Bureaucrats will devise coping behaviors resulting in mere paper compliance with the law. **Answer:** Although it may seem that more paperwork is required, only *better* paperwork is called for, and SEAs and LEAs may charge some administrative costs against Part B funds. Some educators may indeed take approaches that undermine or diminish childrens' rights under the law, but it is by no means true that this reaction will be universal. The required personnel development programs for preservice and inservice personnel and federal and state technical assistance should make the administrative "costs" more manageable. Educators' time should be increasingly available for the actual education and handicapped students.

Objection 16: The state will simply certify to the federal government that the public agencies have complied with P.L. 94–142 when, in fact, they have not. **Answer:** P.L. 94–142 is full of accountability devices that consumers and the BEH may invoke if they believe that noncompliance exists. The act's sanctions should be strong enough to induce the states to comply.

Objection 17: To avoid certifying that something is true when it is not, the state will try to reduce their responsibilities under the act. They will lower their program standards to a level at which they will become relatively meaningless for handicapped children. **Answer:** An appropriate education entails not only compliance with state standards but also the avoidance of functional exclusion. Handicapped children may invoke the procedural safeguards, including their right to sue in federal or state courts, to insure that they are not denied an appropriate education even though their educational program may comply with state standards.

Objection 18: In an effort to make compliance easier, educators will write IEPs that call for easily obtainable goals and objectives. This will also reduce personal liability, in spite of the fact that the regulations make it clear that the child's inability to meet IEP goals and objectives will not make educators personally liable. **Answer:** Although educators may seek to minimize IEP goals and objectives, parents and other participants at IEP conferences can see to it that the IEP is realistic.

Objection 19: A child's failure to achieve the goals and objectives set for him by the IEP does not make the educators liable. The IEP is really not a technique for holding educators accountable. **Answer:** There are procedural safeguards in the act that allow parents to raise the issue of the school's failure to write an IEP, and courts may hold the schools as well as individual educators liable for failing to write an IEP. The claim of such a case would be that the schools and educators failed to perform a statutory duty owed to the child, not that they or the child failed to perform as the IEP required.

Objection 20: The procedural safeguards of P.L. 94–142 are inconsistent with procedural safeguards under the laws of many states. P.L. 94–142 creates confusion and conflicts with some state laws. **Answer:** P.L. 94–142 is a federal law that rightly seeks uniformity in its application and interpretation; for this reason, it is appropriate to include a single set of procedural safeguards. Although the safeguards in P.L. 94–142 may differ slightly, or even conflict in some respects with state laws, they reflect the basic provisions of case law and of state law to a surprisingly accurate degree. The differences or conflicts are minimal.

Objection 21: The costs of complying with the procedural safeguards are high, and may require that funds be diverted from the education of handicapped children to pay for the safeguards. **Answer:** The safeguards are integral parts of the legislation; without them, there would be no way to make the schools accountable or to enable them to do their jobs properly. The safeguards do require administration, time, and personnel, but they are indispensable to the statutory guarantee of a free appropriate education. Compliance with child census, nondiscriminatory evaluation, IEP, and other provisions are means of forestalling due process hearings. In states where similar safeguards have been in the law for several years, the number of cases has been well below educators' fearful expectations and not all were decided against the schools. Educators are far from defenseless in due process hearings.

Objection 22: P.L. 94–142 requires the schools to answer to too many masters; there is an excess of "enforcers." **Answer:** Although both the Bureau for Education of the Handicapped and the Office for Civil Rights have enforcement powers (as do hearing officers and courts), the principles of *res judicata* (the same matter has been adjudicated before) and the *stare decisis* (the precedent for this case has been set by an earlier case with similar facts involving the same issue of law) can prevent duplication of enforcement. For that matter, educators' compliance is the best guarantee against sanctions.

Objection 23: P.L. 94–142 creates potential liability for school systems and educators; both "institutional" and personal liability are likely. Educators may start to practice "defensive education," just as some physicians practice "defensive medicine" and some mental health professionals practice "defensive treatment." **Answer:** P.L. 94–142 may encourage the practice of defensive education, but it is more likely to require and enable educators to do what they have been trained to do, and should have been doing all the time—giving each handicapped child a free appropriate public education. The act takes the best practices of special education and writes them into the law, thereby both requiring and enabling educators to practice as professional standards require. Moreover, the requirements for IEPs, nondiscriminatory testing, and parent participation should actually forestall lawsuits against educators if they comply with those requirements. The due process hearing itself can protect educators against later liability if they comply with the orders of hearing officers.

Objection 24: P.L. 94–142 is a lawyer's dream, creating a multitude of potential lawsuits against educators and schools. **Answer:** It is undoubtedly true that litigation will be necessary to enforce P.L. 94–142 and to define or refine the rights of handicapped children under it. However, litigation can also show school systems how to carry out their obligations and give them desirable political clout in dealing with state and local funding sources. Moreover, the duties and the potential liabilities litigation creates exist independently of P.L. 94–142; they are based on federal and state constitutional claims and state mandatory-education laws.

Objection 25: The deadlines of P.L. 94–142 cannot be met; the law requires too much too soon. **Answer:** Many state mandatory education laws have earlier deadlines for zero-reject and other goals, and all state constitutions (and Sec. 504) call for immediate enforcement of the rights of handicapped children to a free appropriate education. Indeed, P.L. 94–142 gives schools lead time that other laws do not.

Objection 26: The requirement of least-restrictive appropriate placement guarantees some form of educational integration, but it does not and cannot guarantee social integration or a change in attitudes about the handicapped. **Answer:** Not only can school integration lead to social integration (to the extent that any student chooses to make friends of any other student, handicapped or not), but it can also have long-term social integration effects. It can positively influence the attitudes the nonhandicapped hold towards the handicapped.

Objection 27: The requirement for nondiscriminatory evaluation cannot always be satisfied, and the requirement institutionalizes the undesirable practice of classifying and labelling children. **Answer:** The nondiscriminatory evaluation techniques found to be effective with handicapped children in some minority populations can be adapted for use with handicapped children in other minority populations. Moreover, classification itself is not entirely invidious; it does have educational benefits. The nondiscriminatory testing requirement attempts to encourage fairness in evaluation procedures and assumes, with justification, that fair procedures will yield acceptable results.

Objection 28: The requirement for parental consent to initial evaluation and nondiscriminatory testing may prevent school psychologists from testing a child, and thereby deny the child the educational opportunities he needs. **Answer:** The school may invoke due process hearings if the parents refuse to consent to an initial evaluation. The requirement for fair testing procedures does not prevent testing; it requires testing to be accurately and appropriately performed. If anything, it will result in greater accuracy in tests and a better basis for judgments by school personnel.

Objection 29: Realizing that a child who is designated handicapped has substantial rights, schools may be reluctant to classify a child as handicapped and might instead treat him as nonhandicapped, perhaps to his detriment. **Answer:** Although this may occur, at least the child would not suffer the stigma of being labeled "handicapped." The child's parents may, of course, invoke a due process hearing if the school refuses to identify or evaluate their child, or if it refuses to grant him an appropriate education.

Objection 30: The practice described in Objection 29 would leave the "hardest cases" in special education and remove the "best" children from programs for the handicapped. **Answer:** If this occurs, it may prove to be consistent with the principle of least-restrictive appropriate placement, thus making special education programs and classes truly special. This reflects the service priorities Congress set forth for the expenditure of Part B funds. Also, some handicapped children are not so different from nonhandicapped children in the way they learn, the rate at which they learn, or the methods they need to be taught with, that they should be left out of the mainstream.

Objection 31: Teachers are inadequately prepared to implement the law; this is especially so of "regular" teachers. **Answer:** SEAs have the responsibility and available federal funds to carry out preservice and inservice personnel development programs.

Objection 32: Although SEAs have the authority for personnel development, the law does not make any demands on colleges or universities that engage in teacher training. It does not require them to change their preservice curriculum to enable future regular and special educators to carry out provisions of the law like least-restrictive placement. **Answer:** Congress could extend the regulations to colleges and universities receiving federal funds, but it chose not to impose requirements on them, singling out the SEAs as the agency responsible for state-wide implementation. The SEAs may contract with colleges and universities for preservice and inservice training.

Objection 33: The law requires too much of the schools, which must cope with severe personnel shortages in some school programs, an abundance of personnel in others, and inadequately trained personnel throughout. **Answer:** The personnel-development mandate should ease those immediate concerns, and the requirements for long-range planning (full-service goals), child census, and the ability of SEAs to contract with colleges and universities will also help schools with implementation. The act simply requires schools to do what they were supposed to be doing all along.

Objection 34: Personnel problems are serious enough in metropolitan areas, but they are extreme in rural areas. In fact, rural school systems will have a very hard time complying with the law. **Answer:** In addition to the provisions of P.L. 94–142 just mentioned in reply to Objection 33, the act provides for consolidated grant applications, which should be especially appropriate for rural areas. The act also provides for direct services by the SEAs, and optional purchase of services from private agencies, colleges, and universities.

Objection 35: P.L. 94–142 creates unequal services for handicapped children by setting priorities for some but not for others. **Answer:** The first-priority children are entitled to the first priority on the use of Part B funds because they must be included in a school program; equal protection and zero reject demand no less. The second-priority children are entitled to the second priority because the inadequate education they receive amounts to functional exclusion and may be tantamount to no education at all. Those handicapped children not in the first or second priorities do not have the same needs as other handicapped children; school systems are already serving them better than the children in the first two priorities.

Objection 36: P.L. 94–142 creates artificial ceilings for the classification of handicapped children for Part B funding purposes. For example, some school systems will typically have more learning disabled children than 2 percent of all their children. **Answer:** The ceilings place reasonable limits, based on available data, on the responsibility of the federal government to fund state and local programs. Open-ended funding would be disastrous. At present, a school may serve more than the number of children covered by the federal ceilings by using its own funds. The ceilings force the school systems to adhere to the priorities by counting only the most needy children as eligible for Part B funds.

Objection 37: The foregoing criticisms all make the point that P.L. 94–142 goes too far in regulating and falls short in appropriating. It is true that more money is needed to educate handicapped children, and P.L. 94–142 does not provide enough. For example, it does not include children ages birth through two in mandatory programs, does not establish a right to compensatory education for children denied their rights to education when they were of school age, and sets low ceilings on federal funding. **Answer:** The rights to preschool and compensatory education are not generally granted by state constitutions or laws, and one purpose of the federal law is to be generally consistent with state laws. The federal ''presence'' is designed to assist the states to comply with *self-imposed* laws. Without the ceilings there would be an unlimited—and unrealistic—federal obligation. P.L. 94–142 is a remarkable beginning, one of the most important federal education laws ever enacted. It builds on case law, sets forth rights and techniques for securing these rights, commits the federal government to the education of handicapped children, moves them into the mainstream of the schools and gives them a means of joining the mainstream of society.

Objection 38: The law itself may be sufficient, but the regulations do not sufficiently implement it. Specifically, the child-census procedures, the IEP regulations, and the evaluation and monitoring requirements are all inadequately addressed in the regulations. **Answer:** The regulations are the first attempt at implementing P.L. 94–142 and they were designed to strike balances between over- and under-regulation. If they are found to be insufficient, they can be strengthened later.

Objection 39: P.L. 94–142 does not create in-school advocacy systems, despite ample evidence that child advocacy with school systems is necessary for the implementation of children's rights. **Answer:** Although it does not create a single formal advocacy system within the schools, P.L. 94–142 does offer many techniques for monitoring, like the procedural safeguards, parent participation, and administrative sanctions.

Objection 40: Whether P.L. 94–142 goes too far or not far enough in creating rights for handicapped children is beside the point. What is important is whether the law overpromises and underperforms, creates unintended consequences (negative reactions to handicapped children), or acts as a proper vehicle for interpreting and applying educational principles. **Answer:** P.L. 94–142 is based on court decisions and congressionally gathered data that prove that handicapped children have suffered long-standing and severe discrimination in the public schools. It promises them a redress of their grievances and follows up that promise with Part B funds, accountability techniques, and the requirement of sound educational principles. Of course there will be negative reaction to any act that regulates, especially if it affects the traditionally sacrosanct practices of state and local schools. P.L. 94–142, however, can positively shape attitudes about handicapped children, show the schools how to perform duties they must perform as a matter of state law, provide financial support to the schools, and make important contributions to the education of nonhandicapped children. The educational practices that it mandates are sound and have been sound for a long time. If, for some reason, they *are* found to be unsound after careful research and review, they can be deleted from the law, but there is no present reason to change them.

Objection 41: The "bottom line" is not P.L. 94–142 or the cases; it is the values they enforce. Simply stated, the act and the cases do not articulate the values of the majority. **Answer:** The objection is untrue, as the next chapter will demonstrate.

12

Underlying Beliefs and Values In
Right-To-Education Laws

No radical change of public policy occurs and is sustained unless there are generally accepted social and political beliefs to support the change. This is particularly true of the right-to-education movement, and although our beliefs and values may not have been well-articulated in the past, they do exist and can be put forward.

THE UNDERLYING BELIEFS:
A RIGHT-TO-EDUCATION CREDO

We believe that education makes a difference in a person's life. That was one of the foundations of *Brown* v. *Board of Education* and is supported by the six principles of P.L. 94–142.

We know and believe that handicapped children can profit from an education appropriate to their capacities; hence, P.L. 94–142 and the case law grant each handicapped child a right to a suitable education. In the case of P.L. 94–142, an affirmative duty to hire handicapped people is also imposed on the public schools.

We also believe in equity; that is, in equal educational opportunity. Thus P.L. 94–142 and the cases grant the right of education to all handicapped students.

We believe in the value of an education for all people—the universality of education. Accordingly, P.L. 94–142 and case law grant the right to an education to all handicapped students.

Most of us believe that governmental benefits should not be parcelled out on the basis of unalterable characteristics of the receipients. We believe that such a practice says something demeaning and invidious about the person who is denied benefits, and it places the government in the position of causing that person to feel and act inferior simply because he is different from those who are receiving the benefits. Our acceptance of this belief is seen in racial discrimination cases and in both criminal and civil law where a person is denied benefits because he is indigent, an alien, a member of one sex or the other, or handicapped. In the case of the handicapped, the right-to-education cases and P.L. 94–142 challenge the old distribution of governmental benefits (education) and attempt to redistribute them more equitably. They attack a system of distribution founded on the false premise that the handicapped are expendable and that the bulk of benefits in education should be given to the most meritorious (where merit was measured by intelligence or conformity to the nonhandicapped norm).

We believe in the essential sameness of all persons. Grounded in concepts of normalization, egalitarianism, and equal protection, this belief leads us to assert that the handicapped student is no less worthy of constitutional protection and statutory benefits than a nonhandicapped student. Although people may be classified, their rights to an education should not be denied because of a classification. The principle of free appropriate public education for *all* handicapped children illustrates this belief.

We also believe that the economic investment of furnishing a handicapped person with an education appropriate to his needs will yield long-term returns in the increased productivity and decreased dependency of that person. On humanitarian grounds we also point out that handicapped students have been seriously shortchanged in the competition for governmental benefits. Each principle of the right-to-education movement attests to this belief.

We believe that the ample evidence of longstanding state and local neglect of the educational claims of handicapped children will not be abated in the foreseeable future. We even believe that it will be permanent. For that reason, permanent federal funding and control is amply justified.

We believe that, because we choose who governs us, we have the right to ask our representatives to be accountable to us. To that end, P.L. 94–142 and the case law require several types of accountability.

We believe that people should treat each other fairly and decently and that government should deal fairly and decently with the governed. Alternatively stated, we believe that a fair process of governing will produce fair and acceptable results. Thus, P.L. 94–142 and the case law requiring that procedural safeguards be made available to handicapped students and their parents.

We believe that the best government is one we can influence or affect. We believe in participatory democracy in the education of children, and P.L. 94–142 may well be the high-water mark of participatory democracy in public education.

P.L. 94–142 translates our beliefs into public policy for the education of handicapped children, assigns legal rights that reflect our collective decency, and defines and refines our relationships to each other and among the government and the governed.

THE LAW, OUR BELIEFS, AND OUR VALUES

More often than not, our beliefs harmonize with our values. In this respect, and particularly in the right-to-education movement, the word "value" has a familiar meaning.

A value is something we, as individuals and as a society, highly prize and cherish; it is something we do not want to be without and we do not want others to be without. In a constitutional sense, a value is a "fundamental interest."[1] There are many such values, and the right-to-education movement reflects at least four of them.

One, we do not want to be without access to courts or other forums for the peaceful solution of our differences with others. Expressed in another way, we do not want to be without a way of being heard and heeded when we have disagreements with others. Access to the courts as an avenue for redress of grievances is constitutionally required and is provided in P.L. 94–142 and in the right-to-education cases through requirements for procedural due process.

Two, we do not want to be denied a right to participate in self-government. Thus, the right to vote is constitutionally protected and the right to participate in school (as a "government") is provided for in P.L. 94–142 and the case law under the concept of parental participation.

Three, we do not want to be without the opportunity to acquire property or fulfill ourselves. The principles of substantive due process guarantee us these opportunities as a matter of constitutional law, and P.L. 94–142 and the case law address them through the requirements of nondiscriminatory evaluation (protection from classifications that inevitably forestall or retard the opportunities of handicapped children to develop to their maximum potential) and least-restrictive appropriate placement (protection from programs that will have equally debilitating results).

Four, we do not want our unalterable traits, such as race, sex, ancestry, or place of birth, to be used as a basis for government distribution of benefits. Thus, P.L. 94–142 and the case law provide for free appropriate public educational opportunities for all handicapped students.

PUTTING OUR BELIEFS AND VALUES TO WORK: CONCEPTS INTO LAW[2]

It is remarkable to see how effectively P.L. 94–142 puts our beliefs and values to work for the education of handicapped children. The act shows how we develop our resources to allow our beliefs and values to flourish. This function is performed by the requirements for IEPs, personnel development, BEH technical assistance, parent involvement, full-service goals, timelines for educating handicapped children of certain ages, the child census, priorities for the use of funds, early intervention programs, and affirmative action in employing the handicapped.

P.L. 94–142 also shows how we allocate status to people as a reflection of our values and beliefs. We allocate power to handicapped children through such provisions as permanent funding of P.L. 94–142, service priorities, zero-reject principles, and least-restrictive placement requirements. We distribute power to their parents through participation in IEP conferences, procedural safeguards, membership on advisory panels, and participation in developing state and local plans. Finally, we allocate status to educators through requirements for personnel development, by legitimatizing the truly special functions of special education (through the service priorities), and by changing the roles of educators with respect to each other (through the principle of least-restrictive placement).

P.L. 94–142 changes not only the status or power of people involved in the right-to-education movement, but also the procedures by which power and status are allocated. That is the ultimate meaning of the procedural safeguards and parent participation provisions.

P.L. 94–142 changes more than the procedures; it changes the very rights that government distributes, the beneficiaries of those rights, and the methods of distributing them. It guarantees a free appropriate public education to *all* handicapped children, changes the nature of their education so that it will be appropriate to them, prefers some handicapped children over others (the service priorities), grants rights to parents of handicapped children, and demonstrates that federal funds are a means of enforcing those rights (by funding the excess costs of educating handicapped children, requiring the pass-through of funds, setting limits on administrative costs that may be charged against Part B funds, and making federal funding permanent).

THE PRICES WE PAY

P.L. 94–142 and the case law thus perfectly illustrate the unique role of law and lawmakers in changing existing institutions of society and building new ones. But the price has been dear and P.L. 94–142 and the case laws are not without their detractors. We have paid in the redistribution of governmental power over the education of handicapped children; the balance of power now clearly rests with the federal government and the principles and values of local autonomy in education have been diminished. We have legislated a change in the competition for equities and weighted the law in favor of handicapped children by requiring state and local educational agencies to make their own investments in the education of those children (by way of the excess-cost formula). We have given advocates for handicapped children a quantum increase in ammunition. The "first generation" issues—whether all handicapped children have a right to an appropriate education at public expense—are fading fast and will soon be replaced by "second generation" issues dealing with the specifics of the right to a free apropriate public education. As advocates select their ammunition to advance the claims of handicapped children in second-generation matters, they must be on their guard as to the forums they choose for their battlegrounds and the issues around which battle is joined lest the reaction to implementing the rights of handicapped children cause our underlying beliefs and values to be denied by those in the majority (the nonhandicapped) whose very beliefs, values, and attitudes are so crucial to the success of the law and the acceptance of handicapped children.

Advocates for handicapped children must continually articulate the beliefs and values that are the foundations for P.L. 94–142 and the case law, be willing and able to say that the educational rights of handicapped children should be made available to nonhandicapped children as well, and arouse the sympathetic imagination of nonhandicapped people so that *their* claims to better educational opportunities will be supported by and give support to the claims of handicapped children.

Zero reject and protection from functional exclusion, individualized appropriate education, nondiscriminatory and nonstigmatizing classification procedures and placement, rights to procedural safeguards, and the rights of participation are six principles that are supported by widely and deeply held beliefs and values. They have, however, more than that—they have a touch of justice, and no child, handicapped or nonhandicapped, has a monopoly on justice.

NOTES

1. Michelman, Frank I., "Foreword: On Protecting the Poor Through the Fourteenth Amendment," 83 *Harv. L. Rev.* 7 (1969).

2. See Gil, David G., *Unravelling Social Policy*. Cambridge, Massachusetts: Schenkman Publishing Company, 1977.

APPENDIX A: *Brown v. Board of Education*

OLIVER BROWN, et al., Appellants,

v.

BOARD OF EDUCATION OF TOPEKA, Shawnee County,
Kansas, et al. (No. 1.)

HARRY BRIGGS, Jr., et. al., Appellants,

v.

R. W. ELLIOTT et al. (No. 2.)

DOROTHY E. DAVIS et al., Appellants,

v.

COUNTY SCHOOL BOARD OF PRINCE EDWARD
COUNTY, Virginia, et al. (No. 4.)

FRANCIS B. GEBHART et al., Petitioners,

v.

ETHEL LOUISE BELTON et al. (No. 10.)
(347 US 483, 98 L ed 873, 74 S Ct 686, 38 ALR2d 1180)

Mr. Chief Justice Warren delivered the opinion of the Court.

These cases come to us from the States of Kansas, South Carolina, Virginia, and Delaware. They are premised on different facts and different local conditions, but a common legal question justifies their consideration together in this consolidated opinion.[1]

In each of the cases, minors of the Negro race, through their legal representatives, seek the aid of the courts in obtaining admission to the public schools of their community on a nonsegregated basis. In each instance, they had been denied admission to schools attended by white children under laws requiring or permitting segregation according to race. This segregation was alleged to deprive the plaintiffs of the equal protection of the laws under the Fourteenth Amendment. In each of the cases other than the Delaware case, a three-judge federal district court denied relief to the plaintiffs on the so-called "separate but equal" doctrine announced by this Court in Plessy v. Ferguson, 163 US 537, 41 L ed 256, 16 S Ct 1138. Under that doctrine, equality of treatment is accorded when the races are provided substantially equal facilities, even though these facilities be separate. In the Delaware case, the Supreme Court of Delaware adhered to that doctrine, but ordered that the plaintiffs be admitted to the white schools because of their superiority to the Negro schools.

The plaintiffs contend that segregated public schools are not "equal" and cannot be made "equal," and that hence they are deprived of the equal protection of the laws. Because of the obvious importance of the question presented, the Court took jurisdiction.[2] Argument was heard in the 1952 Term, and reargument was heard this Term on certain questions propounded by the Court.[3]

Reargument was largely devoted to the circumstances surrounding the adoption of the Fourteenth Amendment in 1868. It covered exhaustively consideration of the Amendment in Congress, ratification by the states, then existing practices in racial segregation, and the views of proponents and opponents of the Amendment. This discussion and our own investigation convince us that, although these sources cast some light, it is not enough to resolve the problem with which we are faced. At best, they are inconclusive. The most avid proponents of the post-War Amendments undoubtedly intended them to remove all legal distinctions among "all persons born or naturalized in the United States." Their opponents, just as certainly, were antagonistic to both the letter and the spirit of the Amendments and wished them to have the most limited effect. What others in Congress and the state legislatures had in mind cannot be determined with any degree of certainty.

An additional reason for the inconclusive nature of the Amendment's history, with respect to segregated schools, is the status of public education at that time.[4] In the South, the movement toward free common schools, supported by general taxation, had not yet taken hold. Education of white children was largely in the hands of private groups. Education of Negroes was almost nonexistent, and practically all of the race were illiterate. In fact, any education of Negroes was forbidden by law in some states. Today, in contrast, many Negroes have achieved outstanding success in the arts and sciences as well as in the business and professional world. It is true that public school education at the time of the Amendment had advanced further in the North, but the effect of the Amendment on Northern States was generally ignored in the congressional debates. Even in the North, the conditions of public education did not approximate those existing today. The curriculum was usually rudimentary; ungraded schools were common in rural areas; the school term was but three months a year in many states; and compulsory school attendance was virtually unknown. As a consequence, it is not surprising that there should be so little in the history of the Fourteenth Amendment relating to its intended effect on public education.

In the first cases in this Court construing the Fourteenth Amendment, decided shortly after its adoption, the Court interpreted it as proscribing all state-imposed discriminations against the Negro race.[5] The doctrine of "separate but equal" did not make its appearance in this Court until 1896 in the case of Plessy v. Ferguson (US) supra, involving not education but transportation.[6] American courts have since labored with the doctrine for over half a century. In this Court, there have been six cases involving the "separate but equal" doctrine in the field of public education.[7] In Cumming v. County Board of Education, 175 US 528, 44 L ed 262, 20 S Ct 197, and Gong Lum v. Rice, 275 US 78, L ed 172, 48 S Ct 91, the validity of the doctrine itself was not challenged.[8] In more recent cases, all on the graduate school level, inequality was found in that specific benefits enjoyed by white students were denied to Negro students of the same educational qualifications. Missouri ex rel. Gaines v. Canada, 305 US 337, 83 L ed 208, 59 S Ct 232; Sipuel v. University of Oklahoma, 332 US 631, 92 L ed 247, 68 S Ct 299; Sweatt v. Painter, 339 US 629, 94 L ed 1114, 70 S Ct 848; McLaurin v. Oklahoma State Regents, 339 US 637, 94 L ed 1149, 70 S Ct 851. In none of these cases was it necessary to reexamine the doctrine to grant relief to the Negro plaintiff. And in Sweatt v. Painter (US) supra, the Court expressly reserved decision on the question whether Plessy v. Ferguson should be held inapplicable to public education.

In the instant cases, that question is directly presented. Here, unlike Sweatt v. Painter, there are findings below that the Negro and white schools involved have been equalized, or are being equalized, with respect to buildings, curricula, qualifications and salaries of teachers, and other "tangible" factors.[9] Our decision, therefore, cannot turn on merely a comparison of these tangible factors in the Negro and white schools involved in each of the cases. We must look instead to the effect of segregation itself on public education.

In approaching this problem, we cannot turn the clock back to 1868 when the Amendment was adopted, or even to 1896 when Plessy v. Ferguson was written. We must consider public education in the light of its full development and its present place in American life throughout the Nation. Only in this way can it be determined if segregation in public schools deprives these plaintiffs of the equal protection of the laws.

Today, education is perhaps the most important function of state and local governments. Compulsory school attendance laws and the great expenditures for education both demonstrate our recognition of the importance of education to our democratic society. It is required in the performance of our most basic public responsibilities, even service in the armed forces. It is the very foundation of good citizenship. Today it is a principal instrument in awakening the child to cultural values, in preparing him for later professional training, and in helping him to adjust normally to his environment. In these days, it is doubtful that any child may reasonably be expected to succeed in life if he is denied the opportunity of an education. Such an opportunity, where the state has undertaken to provide it, is a right which must be made available to all in equal terms.

We come then to the question presented: Does segregation of children in public schools solely on the basis of race, even though the physical facilities and other "tangible" factors may be equal, deprive the children of the minority group of equal educational opportunities? We believe that it does.

In Sweatt v. Painter (US) supra, in finding that a segregated law school for Negroes could not provide them equal educational opportunities, this Court relied in large part on "those qualities which are incapable of objective measurement but which make for greatness in a law school." In McLaurin v. Oklahoma State Regents, 339 US 637, 94 L ed 1149, 70 S Ct 851, supra, the Court, in requiring that a Negro admitted to a white graduate school be treated like all other students, again resorted to intangible considerations: ". . . his ability to study, to engage in discussions and exchange views with other students, and, in general, to learn his profession." Such considerations apply with added force to children in grade and high schools. To separate them from others of similar age and qualifications solely because of their race generates a feeling of inferiority as to their status in the community that may affect their hearts and minds in a way unlikely ever to be undone. The effect of this separation on their educational opportunities was well stated by a finding in the Kansas case by a court which nevertheless felt compelled to rule against the Negro plaintiffs:

"Segregation of white and colored children in public schools has a detrimental effect upon the colored children. The impact is greater when it has the sanction of the law; for the policy of separating the races is usually interpreted as denoting the inferiority of the Negro group. A sense of inferiority affects the motivation of a child to learn. Segregation with the sanction of law, therefore, has a tendency to [retard] the educational and mental development of Negro children and to deprive them of some of the benefits they would receive in a racial [ly] integrated school system."[10]

Whatever may have been the extent of psychological knowledge at the time of Plessy v. Ferguson, this finding is amply supported by modern authority.[11] Any language in Plessy v. Ferguson contrary to this finding is rejected.

We conclude that in the field of public education the doctrine of "separate but equal" has no place. Separate educational facilities are inherently unequal. Therefore, we hold that the plaintiffs and others similarly situated for whom the actions have been brought are, by reason of the segregation complained of, deprived of the equal protection of the laws guaranteed by the Fourteenth Amendment. This disposition makes unnecessary any discussion whether such segregation also violates the Due Process Clause of the Fourteenth Amendment.[12]

Because these are class actions, because of the wide applicability of this decision, and because of the great variety of local conditions, the formulation of decrees in these cases presents problems of considerable complexity. On reargument, the consideration of appropriate relief was necessarily subordinated to the primary question—the constitutionality of segregation in public education. We have now announced that such segregation is a denial of the equal protection of the laws. In order that we may have the full assistance of the parties in formulating decrees, the cases will be restored to the docket, and the parties are requested to present further argument on Questions 4 and 5 previously propounded by the Court for the reargument this term.[13] The Attorney General of the United States is again invited to participate. The Attorneys General of the states requiring or permitting segregation in public education will also be permitted to appear as amici curiae upon request to do so by September 15, 1954, and submission of briefs by October 1, 1954.[14]

It is so ordered.

NOTES

1. In the Kansas case, Brown v. Board of Education, the plaintiffs are Negro children of elementary school age residing in Topeka. They brought this action in the United States District Court for the District of Kansas to enjoin enforcement of a Kansas statute which permits, but does not require, cities of more than 15,000 population to maintain separate school facilities for Negro and white students. Kan Gen Stat Sec. 72–1724 (1949). Pursuant to that authority, the Topeka Board of Education elected to establish segregated elementary schools. Other public schools in the community, however, are operated on a nonsegregated basis. The three-judge District Court, convened under 28 USC Secs. 2281 and 2284, found that segregation in public education has a detrimental effect upon Negro children, but denied relief on the ground that the Negro and white schools were substantially equal with respect to buildings, transportation, curricula, and educational qualifications of teachers. 98 F Supp 797. The case is here on direct appeal under 28 USC Sec. 1253.

In the South Carolina case, Briggs v. Elliott, the plaintiffs are Negro children of both elementary and high school age residing in Clarendon County. They brought this action in the United States District Court for the Eastern District of South Carolina to enjoin enforcement of provisions in the state constitution and statutory code which require the segregation of Negroes and whites in public schools. SC Const, Art 11, Sec. 7; SC Code Sec. 5377 (1942). The three-judge District Court, convened under 28 USC Secs. 2281 and 2284, denied the requested relief. The court found that the Negro schools were inferior to the white schools and ordered the defendants to begin immediately to equalize the facilities. But the court sustained the validity of the contested provisions and denied the plaintiffs admission to the white schools during the equalization program. 98 F Supp 529. This Court vacated the District Court's judgment and remanded the case for the purpose of obtaining the court's views on a report filed by the defendants concerning the progress made in the equalization program. 342 US 350, 96 L ed 392, 72 S Ct 327. On remand, the District Court found that substantial equality has been achieved except for buildings and that the defendants were proceeding to rectify this inequality as well. 103 F Supp 920. The case is again here on direct appeal under 28 USC Sec. 1253.

In the Virginia case, Davis v. County School Board, the plaintiffs are Negro children of high school age residing in Prince Edward County. They brought this action in the United States District Court for the Eastern District of Virginia to enjoin enforcement of provisions in the state constitution and statutory code which require the segregation of Negroes and whites in public schools. Va Const, Sec. 140; Va Code Sec. 22–221 (1950). The three-judge District Court, convened under 28 USC Secs. 2281 and 2284, denied the requested relief. The court found the Negro school inferior in physical plant, curricula, and transportation, and ordered the defendants forthwith to provide substantially equal curricula and transportation and to "proceed with all reasonable diligence and dispatch to remove" the inequality in physical plant. But, as in the South Carolina case, the court sustained the validity of the contested provisions and denied the plaintiffs admission to the white schools during the equalization program. 103 F Supp 337. The case is here on direct appeal under 28 USC Sec. 1253.

In the Delaware case, Gebhart v. Belton, the plaintiffs are Negro children of both elementary and high school age residing in New Castle County. They brought this action in the *Delaware Court of Chancery* to enjoin enforcement of provisions in the state constitution and statutory code which require the segregation of Negroes and whites in public schools. Del Const, Art 10, Sec. 2; Del Rev Code Sec. 2631 (1935). The Chancellor gave judgment for the plaintiffs and ordered their immediate admission to schools previously attended only by white children, on the ground that the Negro schools were inferior with respect to teacher training, pupil-teacher ratio, extracurricular activities, physical plant, and time and distance involved in travel. — Del ch —, 87 A2d 862. The Chancellor also found that segregation itself results in an inferior education for Negro children (see note 10, infra), but did not rest his decision on that ground. Id. 87 A2d at 865. The Chancellor's decree was affirmed by the Supreme Court of Delaware, which intimated, however, that the defendants might be able to obtain a modification of the decree after equalization of the Negro and white schools had been accomplished. — Del —, 91 A2d 137, 152. The defendants, contending only that the Delaware courts had erred in ordering the immediate admission of the Negro plaintiffs to the white schools, applied to this Court for certiorari. The writ was granted, 344 US 891, 97 L ed 689, 73 S Ct 213. The plaintiffs, who were successful below, did not submit a cross-petition.

2. 344 US 1, 141, 891, 97 L ed 3, 152, 689, 73 S Ct 1, 124, 213.

3. 345 US 972, 97 L ed 1388, 73 S Ct 1114. The Attorney General of the United States participated both Terms as amicus curiae.

4. For a general study of the development of public education prior to the Amendment, see Butts and Cremin, A History of Education in American Culture (1953), Pts. I, II; Cubberley, Public Education in the United States (1934 ed), chs II–XII. School practices current at the time of the adoption of the Fourteenth Amendment are described in Butts and Cremin, supra, at 269–275; Cubberley, supra, at 288–339, 408–431; Knight, Public Education in the South (1922), chs VIII, IX. See also H Ex Doc No. 315, 41st Cong, 2d Sess (1871). Although the demand for free public schools followed substantially the same pattern in both the North and the South, the development in the South did not begin to gain momentum until about 1850, some twenty years after that in the North. The reasons for the somewhat slower development in the South (e.g., the rural character of the South and the different regional attitudes toward state assistance) are well explained in Cubberley, supra, at 408–423. In the country as a whole, but particularly in the South, the War virtually stopped all progress in public education. Id., at 427–428. The low status of Negro education in all sections of the country, both before and immediately after the War, is described in Beale, A History of Freedom of Teaching in American Schools (1941), 112–132, 175–195. Compulsory school attendance laws were not generally adopted until after the ratification of the Fourteenth Amendment, and it was not until 1918 that such laws were in force in all the states. Cubberley, supra, at 563–565.

5. Slaughter-House Cases (US) 16 Wall 36, 67–72, 21 L ed 394, 405–407 (1873); Strauder v. West Virginia, 100 US 303, 307, 308, 25 L ed 664–666 (1880):

"It ordains that no State shall deprive any person of life, liberty, or property, without due process of law, or deny to any person within its jurisdiction the equal protection of the laws. What is this but declaring that the law in the States shall be the same for the black as for the white; that all persons, whether colored or white, shall stand equal before the laws of the States, and, in regard to the colored race, for whose protection the amendment was primarily designed, that no discrimination shall be made against them by law because of their color? The words of the amendment, it is true, are prohibitory, but they contain a necessary implication of a positive immunity, or right, most valuable to the colored race,—the right to exemption from unfriendly legislation against them distinctively as colored,—exemption from legal discriminations, implying inferiority in civil society, lessening the security of their enjoyment of the rights which others enjoy, and discriminations which are steps towards reducing them to the condition of a subject race.''

See also Virginia v. Rives, 100 US 313, 318, 25 L ed 667, 669 (1880); Ex parte Virginia, 100 US 339, 344, 345, 25 L ed 676, 678, 679 (1880).

6. The doctrine apparently originated in Roberts v. Boston, 5 Cush 198, 206 (1850, Mass), upholding school segregation against attack as being violative of a state constitutional guarantee of equality. Segregation in Boston public schools was eliminated in 1855. Mass Acts 1855, ch 256. But elsewhere in the North segregation in public education has persisted in some communities until recent years. It is apparent that such segregation has long been a nationwide problem not merely one of sectional concern.

7. See also Berea College v. Kentucky, 211 US 45, 53 L ed 81, 29 S Ct 33 (1908).

8. In the Cumming Case, Negro taxpayers sought an injunction requiring the defendant school board to discontinue the operation of a high school for white children until the board resumed operation of a high school for Negro children. Similarly, in the Gong Lum Case, the plaintiff, a child of Chinese descent, contended only that state authorities had misapplied the doctrine by classifying him with Negro children and requiring him to attend a Negro school.

9. In the Kansas case, the court below found substantial equality as to all such factors. 98 F Supp 797, 798. In the South Carolina case, the court below found that the defendants were proceeding "promptly and in good faith to comply with the court's decree." 103 F Supp 920, 921. In the Virginia case, the court below noted that the equalization program was already "afoot and progressing" (103 F Supp 337, 341); since then, we have been advised, in the Virginia Attorney General's brief on reargument, that the program has now been completed. In the Delaware case, the court below similarly noted that the state's equalization program was well under way. — Del —, 91 A2d 137, 149.

10. A similar finding was made in the Delaware case: "I conclude from the testimony that in our Delaware society, State-imposed segregation in education itself results in the negro children, as a class, receiving educational opportunities which are substantially inferior to those available to white children otherwise similarly situated." — Del Ch —, 87 A2d 862, 865.

11. K. B. Clark, Effect of Prejudice and Discrimination on Personality Development (Midcentury White House Conference on Children and Youth, 1950); Witmer and Kotinsky, Personality in the Making (1952), ch VI; Deutscher and Chein, The Psychological Effects of Enforced Segregation: A Survey of Social Science Opinion, 26 J Psychol 259 (1948); Chein, What are the Psychological Effects of Segregation Under Conditions of Equal Facilities?, 3 Int J Opinion and Attitude Res 229 (1949); Brameld, Educational Costs, in Discrimination and National Welfare (MacIver, ed, 1949), 44–48; Frazier, The Negro in the United States (1949), 674–681. And see generally Myrdal, An American Dilemma (1944).

12. See Bolling v. Sharpe, 347 US 497, 98 L ed 884, 74 S Ct 693, post, p 884, concerning the Due Process Clause of the Fifth Amendment.

13. ''4. Assuming it is decided that segregation in public schools violates the Fourteenth Amendment

''(*a*) would a decree necessarily follow providing that, within the limits set by normal geographic school districting, Negro children should forthwith be admitted to schools of their choice, or

''(*b*) may this Court, in the exercise of its equity powers, permit an effective gradual adjustment to be brought about from existing segregated systems to a system not based on color distinctions?

''5. On the assumption on which questions 4 (*a*) and (*b*) are based, and assuming further that this Court will exercise its equity powers to the end described in question 4 (*b*),

''(*a*) should this Court formulate detailed decrees in these cases;

''(*b*) if so, what specific issues should the decrees reach;

''(*c*) should this Court appoint a special master to hear evidence with a view to recommending specific terms for such decrees;

''(*d*) should this Court remand to the courts of first instance with directions to frame decrees in these cases, and if so what general directions should the decrees of this Court include and what procedures should the courts of first instance follow in arriving at the specific terms of more detailed decrees?''

14. See Rule 42, Revised Rules of this Court (effective July 1, 1954).

APPENDIX B

Regulation Sec. 121a.5: Definition of "Handicapped Children"

Sec. 121a.5 Handicapped children.

(a) As used in this part, the term "handicapped children" means those children evaluated in accordance with Secs. 121a.530–121a.534 as being mentally retarded, hard of hearing, deaf, speech impaired, visually handicapped, seriously emotionally disturbed, orthopedically impaired, other health impaired, deaf-blind, multi-handicapped, or as having specific learning disabilities, who because of those impairments need special education and related services.

(b) The terms used in this definition are defined as follows:

(1) "Deaf" means a hearing impairment which is so severe that the child is impaired in processing linguistic information through hearing, with or without amplification, which adversely affects educational performance.

(2) "Deaf-blind" means concomitant hearing and visual impairments, the combination of which causes such severe communication and other developmental and educational problems that they cannot be accommodated in special education programs solely for deaf or blind children.

(3) "Hard of hearing" means a hearing impairment, whether permanent or fluctuating, which adversely affects a child's educational performance but which is not included under the definition of "deaf" in this section.

(4) "Mentally retarded" means significantly subaverage general intellectual

functioning existing concurrently with deficits in adaptive behavior and manifested during the developmental period, which adversely affects a child's educational performance.

(5) "Multihandicapped" means concomitant impairments (such as mentally retarded-blind, mentally retarded-orthopedically impaired, etc.), the combination of which causes such severe educational problems that they cannot be accommodated in special education programs solely for one of the impairments. The term does not include deaf-blind children.

(6) "Orthopedically impaired" means a severe orthopedic impairment which adversely affects a child's educational performance. The term includes impairments caused by congenital anomaly (e.g., clubfoot, absence of some member, etc.), impairments caused by disease (e.g., poliomyelitis, bone tuberculosis, etc.), and impairments from other causes (e.g., cerebral palsy, amputations, and fractures or burns which cause contractures).

(7) "Other health impaired" means limited strength, vitality or alertness, due to chronic or acute health problems such as a heart condition, tuberculosis, rheumatic fever, nephritis, asthma, sickle cell anemia, hemophilia, epilepsy, lead poisoning, leukemia, or diabetes, which adversely affects a child's educational performance.

(8) "Seriously emotionally disturbed" is defined as follows:

(i) The term means a condition exhibiting one or more of the following characteristics over a long period of time and to a marked degree, which adversely affects educational performance:

(A) An inability to learn which cannot be explained by intellectual sensory, or health factors;

(B) An inability to build or maintain satisfactory interpersonal relationships with peers and teachers;

(C) Inappropriate types of behavior or feelings under normal circumstances;

(D) A general pervasive mood of unhappiness or depression; or

(E) A tendency to develop physical symptoms or fears associated with personal or school problems.

(ii) The term includes children who are schizophrenic or autistic. The term does not include children who are socially maladjusted, unless it is determined that they are seriously emotionally disturbed.

(9) "Specific learning disability" means a disorder in one or more of the basic psychological processes involved in understanding or in using language, spoken or written, which may manifest itself in an imperfect ability to listen, think, speak, read, write, spell, or to do mathematical calculations. The term includes such conditions as perceptual handicaps, brain injury, minimal brain disfunction, dyslexia, and developmental aphasia. The term does not include children who have learning problems which are primarily the result of visual, hearing, or motor handicaps, of mental retardation, or of environmental, cultural, or economic disadvantage.

(10) ''Speech impaired'' means a communication disorder, such as stuttering, impaired articulation, a language impairment, or a voice impairment, which adversely affects a child's educational performance.

(11) ''Visually handicapped'' means a visual impairment which, even with correction, adversely affects a child's educational performance. The term includes both partially seeing and blind children.

APPENDIX C: The Idaho Child-Find Model

AWARENESS

**INITIAL IDENTIFICATION
AND LOCATION**

**DIAGNOSIS/
EVALUATION**

SERVICE

REASSESSMENT

Informing Referring Recording Monitoring

Time ——————————————————>

THE CHILD IDENTIFICATION PROCESS

Reprinted by permission of Judy A. Schrag, Idaho State Department of Education, Idaho. Copyright © 1976.

AWARENESS

1. Proclamation of October as Idaho Child Find Month by Governor Andrus; Dr. Truby, State Superintendent of Public Instruction.

2. Release of information through television, radio, and newspaper media by State Department of Education, regional Child Development Centers, United Cerebral Palsy, Idaho Epilepsy League, Idaho Association for Learning Disabilities, Idaho Association for Retarded Citizens, etc.

3. Dissemination of information packets and multimedia presentations by United Cerebral Palsy of Idaho, Inc. and Idaho Epilepsy League.

4. Establishment of local task force groups—7 regions.

5. Distribution of posters, information sheets, bank statement stuffers, information booklets; as well as specific child find activities by:

   State Department of Education State and Regional Staff
   Local School Districts
   Local Task Force Groups
   Regional Child Development Centers
   Head Start Programs
   North Idaho Panhandle Child Development Association
   Idaho State School and Hospital for Retarded
   Idaho State School for the Deaf and the Blind
   Idaho Association for Learning Disabilities
   Idaho Torch
   Idaho Association for Retarded Citizens
   Local Ministers, Priests, etc.
   Local Physicians
   Lions, Jaycees and Other Local Civic and Business Groups
   Easter Seal
   Elks Rehabilitation Center
   Developmental Disabilities Council

6. Dissemination of booklet "How to Obtain Special Education Services for your Child" by League of Women Voters and the Mental Health Association to parents of handicapped children and professionals working with handicapped children.

INITIAL IDENTIFICATION AND LOCATION

1. First grade screening within local school districts.

2. School district preschool screening clinics.

3. Early Periodic Screening Programs carried out by District Health Departments and regional Child Development Centers.

4. Well-Child Clinics conducted by District Health Departments through maternal and Child Health Services.

5. Screening for vision and hearing problems conducted by Child Health Services and Idaho State School for the Deaf and the Blind.

6. Dissemination of "Growing Up in Idaho" pamphlets to assist parents in screening of their child's development and in observation of developmental lags and possible handicaps.

7. Letters to parents sent home by local school district personnel with a screening developmental scale to assist parents in screening young children as well as older out-of-school children for possible handicaps and/or developmental lags.

8. Dissemination of a screening instrument within local newspapers to assist parents in observing possible handicaps of their child, as well as to provide information as to procedures for gaining access to appropriate educational programs.

9. Other specific initial identification and screening activities by local school districts, regional Child Development Centers, and other agencies and organizations (PTA, Lions, etc.).

DIAGNOSIS/EVALUATION

Idaho state rules and regulations require that no child shall be enrolled in a special education program unless he has received a comprehensive evaluation.
Although the extent of such a comprehensive evaluation shall depend on the nature and the severity of the handicapping condition, it is a multifactored, multidisciplined assessment which takes into account the physical health and condition of the child; the psychological assets and liabilities; the assessed input, process and output communication skills of the child; the social adjustment and adaptivity; educational achievement; and the assessed intellectual level of each child.
Idaho state rules and regulations also specify that diagnosis/evaluation must utilize a multidisciplinary team approach in the evaluation of handicapped children.

1. Assistance to local school districts in diagnosis/evaluation of handicapped children by state and regional special education consultant services.
2. Assistance to local school districts in diagnosis/evaluation of handi-

capped children by Regional Child Development Centers and the North Idaho Panhandle Child Development Association.
3. Assistance and support to local school districts and other agencies for comprehensive evaluation of handicapped children through the Northwest Regional Resource Center Title VI-B, and state funds.
4. Special study on comprehensive evaluation utilizing Northwest Regional Resource Center and state resources by Idaho school psychologists and directors of special education in order to appropriately modify state rules and regulations and to develop best practices.

EDUCATIONAL SERVICE DELIVERY

Preschool Handicapped Children:

1. Intervention of young handicapped children within existing state delivery system—Child Development Centers, Head Start programs, Idaho State School for the Deaf and the Blind, Idaho State School and Hospital for the Retarded, Elks Rehabilitation Center, etc.(Classroom and home-based programs.)
2. Technical assistance by the North Idaho Panhandle Child Development Association in order to train teachers and parents working with identified preschool handicapped children; as well as to establish standard pupil assessment procedures.
3. Technical assistance and support by the Portage Project, Northwest Area Learning Resource Center, Northwest Regional Resource Center, etc.

School-Age Handicapped Children:

1. Special Education Programs (classroom and home-based) within local school districts, contractual agencies and organizations, Idaho State School for the Retarded, Idaho State School for the Deaf and the Blind, etc., utilizing state, regional, NWALRC/RRC and federal Title VI-B resources.
2. Technical assistance and support by State Department of Education state and regional consultant services.
3. Support from Title VI-D and the North Idaho Panhandle Child Development Association for inservice training of special education personnel serving identified handicapped children.
4. Special Title VI-G project to develop best practices in programming for unserved learning disabled children.

REASSESSMENT

1. Idaho state rules and regulations require that local school districts and contractual agencies provide an annual review of all handicapped children.

Index

1978 Supplement to Chapter 3 (continued from page 84)

Apparently, *Mattie T.* is the first decision under a Sec. 504 class action suit (Hairston v. Drosick was not a class action). The decision makes it clear that Sec. 504 grants immediately enforceable rights.

Other federal courts, however, have issued contrary opinions on the rights of handicapped people to sue before exhausting their administrative remedies, i.e., opinions contrary to the *Mattie T.* result. It is probable that the Supreme Court will resolve the conflict when it decides *Davis.*

n. 50. Affirmed, 556 F. 2d 184 (3d Cir. 1977).

n. 51. The plaintiffs refiled their case in state court and won, the court finding that the student had not been validly classified as handicapped under either state or federal law (P.L. 94–142) and, until so classified, could not be prevented from participating in contact sports, Kampmeier v. Harris, No. 76-7383, Sup. Ct., Monroe Cty., N.Y., Feb. 17, 1978). The state court decision, however, avoids the Sec. 504 issue and is of limited value for future cases where the plaintiff has been classified as handicapped. See OCR Policy Interpretation, 5, *Federal Register*, August 14, 1978, Part II, pp. 36034-6 (school may not exclude handicapped student from contact sports but must obtain prior parental and physician approval of student participation).

Add to text at p. 54, before "Service Priorities." See Stephan L. v. Indiana State Board of Special Education Appeals, No. F 78-6 (N.D. Ind., filed July 7, 1978), in which the plaintiff alleges that inadequate child-count procedures violate P.L. 94–142 and Sec. 504 and his rights thereunder.

A technical amendment to P.L. 94–142 (enacted in P.L. 95–561) now requires an annual child census, to be taken as of December 1, rather than a semiannual one, to be taken as of October 1 and February 1.

1978 Supplement to Chapter 9 (continued from page 218)

upheld an award of $500,000 in damages to an adult whom the school incorrectly diagnosed and educated as mentally retarded. An Illinois court has held that a student may sue a school board for damages (emotional injury) because it fails to make a proper educational placement of a learning disabled student (one outside of the "mainstream" where he was always a failure and accordingly suffered emotional damage); Pierce v. Board of Education of City of Chicago, 358 N.E. 2d 67 (Ill. Ct. App. 1976) and 370 N.E. 2d 535 (Ill. 1977), holding for the school board on the actual damages claim, not on the original issue of whether the board may be sued. Whether a school board may be sued is at issue in Whitney v. City of Worcester, 366 N.E. 2d 1210 (Mass., 1977), the state's highest court deferring a decision until the state legislature has a chance to decide whether there will be governmental immunity or governmental liability. Courts in New York, Donohue v. Copiague Union Free Schools, 407 N.Y.S. 2d 874, 1977), and California, Doe v. San Francisco School Board, 313 Cal. Rptr. 854, 60 Cal. App. 3d 814 (1976) have ruled that no "malpractice" suits can be successfully brought in those states, but the Hoffman case contradicts the earlier Donohue case in New York. Meanwhile, another malpractice case has been brought in Indiana, Doe v. Griles (No. F77-108, N.D. Ind., 1978).

n. 19. See Chapter 3 at n. 18.

n. 22. Consent order entered, see Chapter 3, n. 16.

n. 25. Case decided on merits, see Chapter 3, n. 48.